Negotiated Power in Late Imperial China

Negotiated Power in Late Imperial China

The Zongli Yamen and the Politics of Reform

JENNIFER M. RUDOLPH

East Asia Program
Cornell University
Ithaca, New York 14853

The Cornell East Asia Series is published by the Cornell University East Asia Program (distinct from Cornell University Press). We publish affordably priced books on a variety of scholarly topics relating to East Asia as a service to the academic community and the general public. Standing orders, which provide for automatic notification and invoicing of each title in the series upon publication, are accepted.

If after review by internal and external readers a manuscript is accepted for publication, it is published on the basis of camera-ready copy provided by the volume author. Each author is thus responsible for any necessary copy-editing and for manuscript formatting. Address submission inquiries to CEAS Editorial Board, East Asia Program, Cornell University, Ithaca, New York 14853-7601.

Number 137 in the Cornell East Asia Series
Copyright © 2008 by Jennifer Rudolph. All rights reserved
ISSN 1050-2955
ISBN: 978-1-933947-07-5 hc
ISBN: 978-1-933947-37-2 pb
Library of Congress Control Number: 2007941191

24 23 22 21 20 19 18 17 16 15 14 13 12 11 10 09 08   9 8 7 6 5 4 3 2 1

Cover image obtained from http://en.wikipedia.org/wiki/Image:Zongli_Yamen.jpg.

⊗ The paper in this book meets the requirements for permanence of ISO 9706:1994.

To the memory of my parents
Rome and Kathleen Rudolph

CONTENTS

ABBREVIATIONS USED IN NOTES

Archives:

ZYQD *Zongli Geguo Shiwu Yamen Qing Dang* 總理各國事務衙門清檔 (The Qing dynasty Archives of the Office for Managing Foreign Affairs). Institute of Modern History, Academia Sinica, Taipei, Taiwan.

ZYJLJB Jinling jibu 禁令缉捕 (Documents concerning the prohibitions and seizures).

ZYDFJS Difang jiaoshe 地方交涉 (Documents concerning conduct of foreign relations on a local level).

Published Collections of Documents:

DQHD *Qing hui dian* 清會典 (Collected Statutes of the Qing Dynasty). Guangxu edition. Reprint, Beijing: Zhonghua Shuju, 1991.

DQLS *Da Qing lichao shilu Dezong chao* 大清歷朝實錄德宗朝 (Veritable records of the successive reigns of the Qing dynasty, Dezong [Guangxu]) reign). Compiled by Da Manzhou diguo guowuyuan. Tokyo: Okura Shuppan Kabushiki Kaisha, 1937–1938.

DYZZ   *Dierci yapian zhanzheng* 第二次鴉片戰爭 (Collected documents of the Second Opium War), edited by Qi Sihe 齐思和, et al. Shanghai: Shanghai renmin chubanshe, 1978–1979.

GCDX   *Guangxu chao donghua xulu* 光緒朝東華續錄 (The Donghua Records, continued: Guangxu period), compiled by Zhu Shoupeng 朱壽朋. Shanghai: 1909.

GZD   *Gongzhong dang: Guangxu chao zouzhe* 宮中檔光緒朝奏摺 (Secret Palace Memorials of the Guangxu period), edited by the National Palace Museum. Taibei: National Palace Museum, 1973–1975.

ZWZJ   *Jindai Zhongguo waijiaoshi ziliao jiyao* 近代中國外交史資料輯要 (A sourcebook of imperial documents relating to the modern diplomatic history of China). Compiled by Jiang Tingfu (Tsiang T'ing-fu) 蔣廷黻. 1931–1934, Reprint, Taibei: Taiwan Commercial Press, 1958–1959.

QGF   *Qingting zhi gaige yu fandong* 清廷之改革與反動, parts 1, 2 (Qing Court reform and reactionism). Vol. 7 of *Geming yuanliu yu geming yundong* 革命源流與革命運動 (Revolutionary origins and the revolutionary movement). Zhonghua Minguo kaiguo wushi nian wenxian bian wei yuanhui 中華民國開國五十年文獻編案員會 comp. Taibei: Zhengzhong Shuju, 1963–1965.

QSG   *Qing Shi Gao* 清史稿 (Draft history of the Qing dynasty). Beijing: Zhonghua shuju, 1994.

QSL	*Da Qing lichao shilu* 大清歷朝實錄 (Veritable Records of the Qing Dynasty). 60 vols. Beijing: Zhonghua shuju, 1985–1987.
QSLZ	*Qing shi lie zhuan* 清史列傳. Beijing: Zhonghua shuju, 1987.
QXWT	*Qingchao xu wenxian tongkao* 清朝續文獻通考 (A supplement of the Qing Classified Historical Documents). Compiled by Liu Jinzao 劉錦藻. 1935. Reprint, Taibei: Xinxing shuju, 1963.
QWS	*Qingji waijiao shiliao* 清季外交史料 (Historical materials concerning foreign relations of the late Qing). 218 *juan*. Compiled by Wang Yanwei 王彥威. Beijing: Waijiao shiliao bian zuan chu, 1932–1935.
YWSM	*Chou ban yiwu shimo* 籌辦夷務始末 (The complete management of foreign affairs) 1929–1931. Reprint, Taibei: Wenhai chubanshe, 1970–1971.
YWSM-DG	80 *juan* for the Daoguang reign
YWSM-TZ	100 *juan* for the Tongzhi reign
YWSM-XF	80 *juan* for the Xianfeng reign
YWYD	*Yangwu Yundong* 洋務運動 (The Westernization movement). Edited by the Chinese Historical Society. Shanghai: Renmin chubanshe, 1961.

REIGN TITLES OF THE QING EMPERORS (1644–1911)

Abbreviations used in text and notes

SZ   Shunzi   1644–1661

KX   Kangxi   1622–1722

YZ   Yongzheng   1723–1735

QL   Qianlong   1736–1795
      The Qianglong Emperor also ruled from 1796–1799, after abdicating the throne.

JQ   Jiaqing   1796–1820

DG   Daoguang   1821–1850

XF   Xianfeng   1851–1861

TZ   Tongzhi   1862–1874

GX   Guangxu   1875–1908

XT   Xuantong   1909–1912

ACKNOWLEDGMENTS

It is with great pleasure that I acknowledge the generous and kind support from family, friends, colleagues, and institutions that I have received over the many years behind the writing of this book.

My focus on the Zongli Yamen started during my graduate school days under the steady and inspiring guidance of R. Kent Guy. Over the years, he has provided much wisdom and many insights, all of which I truly appreciate. Many others also provided encouragement while I worked on this project. The feedback I received from participants in Columbia University's Modern China Seminar and Traditional China Seminar proved invaluable. I am also grateful for the advice, comments, and assistance I have received from Robert Antony, James Anderson, Morris Bian, Samuel Ch'u, Christian de Pee, Max Huang, Robert Irick, Li Yi, Lu Hanchao, Lu Xiaobo, Steven Miles, Mary Rankin, Helen Schneider, Mark Selden, Patricia Thornton, Stephen Udry, R. Bin Wong, Madeleine Zelin, Zhang Cong, and Zhang Pengyuan. I owe a special debt to Beatrice Bartlett for her inspiring work on the Grand Council. The anonymous reviewers for the Cornell East Asia Series provided invaluable comments and insights, strengthening significantly the resulting book.

I would like to thank the editors at *The Chinese Historical Review* for allowing me to include here Chapter Four, which was first published in that journal. The comments I received from evaluators there were of great help.

This research would not have been possible without generous funding for research and travel from the Center for Chinese Studies in Taipei, the Fulbright-Hays program, the Pacific Cultural Foundation, the Office for Research at the University at Albany, and the Urban China Research Network. The early years of this project were aided by U.S. Foreign Language Area Studies fellowships, as well as generous support from the Jackson School of International Studies at the University of Washington. The support of the Institute of History and Philology and the Institute of Modern History at the Academia Sinica in Taipei allowed me to conduct my research with the Zongli Yamen materials located in the archives at the Institute for Modern History. I'd especially like to thank Zhang Pengyuan and Max Huang for their mentoring and Chen Xiyuan and Qiu Pengsheng for their willingness to share their insights and language expertise with me. The staff in charge of the archives displayed utmost patience and generosity in helping me use the archives. To all of them, I express heartfelt thanks. The staff and holdings at the National Palace Museum in Taipei were also extremely helpful. I am also indebted to the staff at the Number One Historical Archives in Beijing for helping me navigate the holdings and, in my first foray there, especially Zhu Shuyuan for patiently tutoring me in reading grass script. Li Jianhong's friendship and assistance in Beijing was invaluable. Alan Yen eased my transitions to conducting work in Taipei, Beijing, and Hong Kong by sharing his wonderful family and friends, as well as his boundless understanding of Chinese cuisine.

Jennifer Haight and Douglas Merwin read the manuscript closely and provided valuable editing advice. Amy Lelyveld designed the book cover, and Samuel Gilbert contributed his editor's eye; both have helped inspire a life-long appreciation of Chinese culture. Mai Shaikhanuar-Cota, my editor at the Cornell East Asia Center, has been unflagging in her support, and I am much indebted to her for keeping the book and me on track. The help I have received on all fronts has been impressive. Any remaining imperfection or errors are solely my own.

Finally, I would like to thank my family. My siblings and their spouses, my aunts and uncles, and my parents helped me maintain a sense of perspective and humor about this particular type of historical endeavor in today's world. Their encouragement, bets, and prodding aided me in bringing this endeavor to a close. I acknowledge their sense of humor and their support: Jeannine Rudolph and Marc Chandler, Michele Rudolph and Marc Vandenhoeck, Richard Rudolph, the late Rome and Kathleen Rudolph, Jacqueline and Geoffrey Smathers, Joan Strueber, Joseph and Nancy Strueber, and Michael and Margaret Strueber. And most heartfelt, I thank the people who have lived within the confines of the Zongli Yamen with me as I wrote this book: my husband Brandon Boyle for his confidence in me and my sons Keelan and Sullivan for happily bouncing off the walls of any Chinese compound put in their paths.

1

THE ZONGLI YAMEN
IN TIME AND PLACE

IN LATE 1850S CHINA, AFTER TWO HUNDRED YEARS of relatively peaceful rule, the Qing dynasty (1644–1911) and its leaders found themselves in the midst of a hailstorm of challenges. Internal uprisings raged in the north, south and west, with the most notable—the Taiping—extending over one-third of the empire's heartland and lasting nearly fifteen years (1850–1864). Suppression of the Nian Rebellion, which destabilized the area between Beijing and the Taiping capital of Nanjing from 1851 to 1868, occupied imperial forces as well.[1] The scope of the rebellions reflected the dynastic crises that had been building within China since the late eighteenth century. Weakening and dividing China, the internal conflicts opened the way for Euro-American imperialist inroads into the Qing Empire. Western countries assaulted the dynasty along the coast with demands for market access and higher-level diplomatic relations. Starting in the mid-nineteenth century, much to the Qing Court's dismay, Great Britain took the lead in backing its demands on China with formidable military might, culminating in the Opium Wars of 1839 to 1842 and 1858 to 1860. The constant threat of military action behind Western demands for treaties and their enforcement established gunboat diplomacy as the primary means to compel Chinese acceptance of expansive Euro-American economic interests. The breadth and frequency of the internal and external threats motivated the Qing

Court to experiment with new and old tactics alike in its search for methods and strategies to reestablish peace and maintain rule. The founding of the Zongli geguo shiwu yamen (hereafter referred to as the Zongli Yamen), China's first Foreign Office, in 1861 proved to be a pivotal moment in this quest for survival, as it marked the adoption of a new policy toward the West and, perhaps more importantly, marshaled the flexibility and dynamism of the Qing system to steer the dynasty through another fifty years of challenges.

Spanning the turbulent years from 1861 to 1901 and heading the Qing efforts to regain control of its empire through the Self-Strengthening Movement, the Zongli Yamen played a seminal role in the direction and survival of the Qing regime.[2] By virtue of its position in the government hierarchy and the timing of its creation, the Zongli Yamen's existence and actions had a significant impact on questions of central government strength vis-à-vis local activism and the government's ability to cope with internal and external problems. Consequently, analysis of the Zongli Yamen provides a window for viewing two of the most important questions of the day: the shifting balance of local, regional, and central power in the aftermath of the Taiping Rebellion, and the nature of reform during the Self-Strengthening period.[3] In other words, a close study of the Yamen's development and functioning within the Qing system contributes to the debates revolving around the nature and capacity of the late Qing state.

The Zongli Yamen also helps illuminate the possibilities for viable and effective institutional change in the late Qing. Scholars now recognize that major institutional change occurred during the dynasty, especially in its early years; the second half of the dynasty, however, is still commonly perceived as geared toward protecting existing structures, rather than as engineering innovative solutions to the complex of problems that faced society and the government. Despite the bias against the late Qing, the Zongli Yamen represents a major example of institutional reform, if the only one during that period. Scholars can no longer ignore the key that the Zongli Yamen, through its formative process and functioning, holds to our understanding of the capacity for reform in nineteenth-century China.

Delving into the Zongli Yamen as a positive case study for meaningful change allows for a clear and improved picture of how the Chinese state viewed reform and under what circumstances it was accommodated.

The scholarly literature has frequently portrayed the nature and extent of change in imperial China, whether intellectual or institutional, as constricted by the confines of Confucianism. Full examination of the Zongli Yamen shows, however, that change, if examined in context, was not only possible within the Chinese bureaucracy, but significant mechanisms existed by which to generate it. In the late Qing, the goal of the Zongli Yamen was to strengthen China's system in the face of threats, revealing the vitality of a mature bureaucracy in restructuring itself. The various stages in the Zongli Yamen's founding and development suggest transformation rather than continuity and exhibit the dynamism that allowed the Qing regime to last nearly three hundred years. In the complicated world of the late nineteenth century, as in the complex world of the new millennium, exploring the process of reform is well worth our attention. Through this study of the Zongli Yamen, I provide an example of institutional reform that speaks to how the mature Qing bureaucracy restructured itself to meet the exigencies of the day.

Views of the Past

Because the Zongli Yamen played an important role in navigating the problematic relationship with Western countries, early accounts of it view the very act of establishing the institution as a move toward adopting Western methods of diplomacy; consequently, they focus primarily on its state-to-state interactions, excluding its domestic functioning and internal meaning. The diplomatic emphasis is partly due to past scholarly expectations that the creation of the institution itself and the subsequent Self-Strengthening period resulted solely from Western diplomatic and commercial actions in China and that the efforts, believed to be aimed at achieving Western-style modernization, were wrought from the Chinese government by the impact of Western actions. This approach is predicated on the assumption that the inherent nature of the Chinese governmental system was static and required exogenous stimuli in order to progress substantially toward modernization and that all efforts to achieve modernization were in response to Western actions. The first assessments of the Zongli Yamen, written in the 1950s and earlier, contain the above assumptions and fall under the "impact-response" rubric of analysis. Most notable are the accounts of the Zongli Yamen in treatments of coastal treaty ports and diplomatic history, with Ssu-yü Teng and John King Fairbank's influential *China's Response to the West* (1954) as a prime example.[4]

A corollary to the "impact-response" treatment of the Zongli Yamen is an approach that stresses the steadfastness of Chinese tradition at the expense of modernity. In these accounts, conservative Confucianism obstructs the Chinese road to progress, as defined by the Western path to modernity. In studies of nineteenth-century Chinese governance, this modernization approach regularly highlights China's qualitative deficiencies in its response to Western stimuli. Scholars, with one eye on the Euro-American bar, aim to discern what went wrong with China and to ascertain why China did not manage to meet that standard by modernizing like the Euro-American nations or even Asia's own Meiji Japan. With their concentration on deficiencies in Chinese society that prevented China's effective response to the West, the works either dismiss Chinese reform efforts as inherently inadequate and "traditional" or they sacrifice Chinese actors' agency in those efforts by over-emphasizing that of Western actors. The underlying question in both approaches of why China did not make a stronger, more sustained and more significant effort to meet the challenge of the West shapes the historical narratives that result.[5]

Stressing linear development consistent with Western experience and expectations, modernization literature portrays a China dominated by a static Confucian state incapable of generating meaningful reform. Within this framework, the Zongli Yamen is judged by Western expectations for change and action leading to modernization.[6] The seeming ineptitude of the Qing to meet the challenges of the day ultimately led to the 1911 Revolution. Responsibility for the failure of the Qing dynasty, according to this school of thought, lay with the persistence of traditional approaches, with the Zongli Yamen as a collaborator protecting tradition at the expense of change.[7] To further this line of reasoning, the Zongli Yamen, because it emerged from Chinese tradition, simply could not represent a significant change in institutional form and was incapable of either generating or leading real constitutional reform. The Western-centric orientation of the basic assumptions behind the modernization framework has prevented a more balanced examination of the process and possibilities of change within the traditional Chinese system.[8]

Many scholars of political change in late Qing China have focused on the reign of the Tongzhi emperor, known as the Tongzhi Restoration (*Tongzhi zhongxing*, 1862–1875), and the Self-Strengthening period as critical times of lost opportunity in imperial China's history, times when China could have chosen the path of modernization and did not.[9] The decade-long Tongzhi Restoration was a respite of sorts for China from Western aggression. The Qing Court and government had already been forced to accept diplomatic relations with Western countries by means of the unequal treaties. The new Tongzhi emperor seemingly changed the orientation of the court toward a cooperative relationship with the treaty powers, allowing the signatory powers to enjoy political and economic privileges and status, in the hope that additional warfare could be avoided. During the Restoration, the Qing Court restored internal order following the Nian and Taiping rebellions, as well as the military assaults from the West. The former left the court struggling to reassert central control over areas torn by the effects of the rebellions and dependent on local elite for stability. The latter posed the problem of asserting sovereignty in the face of foreign aggression and intimidation and devising strategies for retaining legitimacy while addressing the complexities of the foreign encroachments. Through the upheaval of the Second Opium War that immediately preceded the Tongzhi emperor's reign, three leaders emerged who steered China in its new policy direction, changing key aspects of the political machinery of the Qing bureaucracy in the process. Under their guidance, the Qing Court created the Zongli Yamen and adopted the new policy of adherence to treaty obligations. To its Euro-American counterparts, China seemed to be joining the Western system of international relations and the "family of nations."[10]

Despite Western hopes, Qing government and society did not Westernize according to Western expectations; nor did the atmosphere of Sino-Western cooperation last through the events of the early-1870s. Because of the unmet expectations, modernization scholars have argued that the Tongzhi Restoration adopted the superficial approach of placing new policies on old institutions to manage the West. Accordingly, as portrayed, the policies of the period had no roots in the Confucian system and therefore could not flourish, or alternatively, the Confucian system was too inflexible to generate or absorb innovative policies. In either case, the resulting assessment is the same: Tongzhi policies were doomed to failure. Modernization scholars determined that Tongzhi Restoration reformers were not interested in reform or modernization in the Western sense; rather they aimed to restore the glory of the Confucian system, as the name given the period implies.

The contribution and influence of Mary Wright's *The Last Stand of Chinese Conservatism*, one of the main works exploring the Zongli Yamen, continue today; however, the limitations of her modernization approach diminishes that book's analytical power in explaining the value of change in Chinese terms. Wright presents Confucianism as posing the biggest obstacle to Chinese modernization. Meaningful institutional reform could not occur until Confucianism was overcome. Thus, the Zongli Yamen, in Wright's account, ultimately becomes less significant than it is, because it emerged from within the Confucian framework.

Although modernization paradigm scholarship associates the Zongli Yamen with the Tongzhi Restoration, its origins are actually in the Xianfeng reign (1850–1861). Because the tones and concerns of the two reigns differed in many respects, the association with one or the other is noteworthy. Scholars who have utilized a modernization approach have portrayed the Xianfeng emperor as dismissive of the West and not open to modernization. Instead of the study of international law and treaty fulfillment, he and his reign are marked by war advocacy and hostility toward the West. Nonetheless, the Xianfeng emperor and his advisors approved the creation of the new Qing Zongli Yamen, which strove to reestablish and maintain peace through diplomacy. Therefore, despite Western depictions of the reign as stagnant or inflexible, sufficient momentum for action and reform existed, if out of necessity, by the end of the Xianfeng reign. The Tongzhi reign, on the other hand, has long been associated with the restoration of a more peaceful and stable Confucian rule. By often designating the Zongli Yamen as a Tongzhi creation, scholars construct it as "Confucian," meaning it was structurally and socially nonchallenging. This ideological identification defines the capacity for institutional change as equally limited and does not allow for serious consideration of the potential for institutional change within the existing system. At issue are the interpretation of change, the identification of innovation, and the assessment of the equivalency of the concept of reform in the nineteenth-century Chinese and nineteenth-century Euro-American contexts.[11]

For other Zongli Yamen scholars, the issue of personality has the greatest explicative value for understanding the organization. In these renditions, Prince Gong, one of the Yamen founders, and his relationship to the Court determined the fate of the Zongli Yamen's efforts.[12] Like Wright, Fairbank and Hsu, personality scholars seek to identify dysfunction and explain the failure to achieve modernity at the expense of examining the processes that indicated substantial institutional change was underway. By focusing on personality rather than the questions with which the personalities concerned themselves, the resulting works do not recognize that powerful Qing officials not only viewed institutional change as possible, but also were actually attempting to implement it.[13] More importantly, owing to their concentration on personality as the critical component behind the evolution of the Zongli Yamen, they discount institutional factors.

Forty to fifty years ago, Masataka Banno, Tseng-tsai Wang, and S.M. Meng each took an institutional approach to the Zongli Yamen and thus laid the basis for this work's neo-institutionalist approach. Their scholarly accounts provide solid narratives of the Zongli Yamen's development; their works, however, like that of their predecessors, contain underlying assumptions that shape their analyses and preclude a positive assessment of change: why did the Qing not succeed at change, and why were the innovations of the Zongli Yamen insufficient? In other words, they stop short of examining the Zongli Yamen as an important instance of meaningful institutional change that emerged from a dynamic system, although Meng does maintain that the Zongli Yamen should be taken seriously as an innovation within the limits of the Confucian system.[14] While these authors rightfully emphasize the role of the state, they fail to question the assumption of conceptual equivalency of reform in the Qing and Euro-American contexts.

Likewise, scholarship on the Zongli Yamen that has been published by Chinese scholars in the Chinese language has focused mainly on foreign policy implementation or organizational aspects of the institution, with a few scholars examining the role of personality in the success and ultimate failure of the Yamen. Although the older Chinese-language works provide much information on the structure and main personages of the office, like their Western counterparts, they do not treat the Yamen as a means for understanding the process of institutionalization and questions of provincial versus central power during the late Qing. Wu Fuhuan's book-length study of the Zongli Yamen is the most recently published in Chinese and is an excellent source for descriptions of various Yamen positions and the responsibilities of those who held those positions. However, he does not address the evolution of the Zongli Yamen as an analytical tool for examining the process of reform.[15]

The Shift to China-centered Scholarship

The majority of the literature on the Zongli Yamen and the late Qing period stands in contrast to recent works focusing on the early Qing central government, which have not been burdened with the question of modernization and the prognosis of Qing failure. Interestingly, scholarship on the earlier Qing period emerged, at least in part, as a reaction to the influence of modernization theory and its pre-dominantly negative assessments of the late Qing. A new generation of historians in the 1970s and 1980s asked questions different from those of their predecessors; instead of infusing their approach with Western-centric interpretations of modernization, they focused on examining Chinese problems in a Chinese context—what Paul Cohen termed "China-centered" questions.[16] In contrast to modernization framework results, the new scholarship of the "China-centered" approach reveals evidence of what enabled the dynasty to survive for nearly three hundred years.[17]

Utilizing empirical evidence, "China-centered" scholars document the important and dynamic changes that took place during the Ming-Qing transition and beyond. In his *The Internal Organization of the Ch'ing Bureaucracy*, Thomas Metzger analyzes the nature of early Qing bureaucracy. Most striking for this study of the Zongli Yamen is Metzger's discussion of the shaping of Qing governmental power through an appellate process of decision making, resulting in institutional flexibility.[18] In this vein, Silas Wu and Beatrice Bartlett each analyze the origins and development of the Grand Council.[19] As the last major institutional development during the Qing before the Zongli Yamen, the evolution of the Grand Council holds potential keys to understanding the process that led to the creation and development of the Zongli Yamen. Bartlett and Wu view the Grand Council and the Qing Court in far more positive terms than previous generations have viewed the Zongli Yamen. Their research results demonstrate the flexibility of the Qing system, as opposed to its morbidity, and their state orientation resonates squarely with the topic of reform.

Most pertinent is Bartlett's work; she shows how the Grand Council originated in a temporary committee consisting of high Inner Court officials. An ad hoc, extra-bureaucratic group of officials charged with a specific project eventually, through a process of institutionalization, became the emperor's closest advisory body and the most powerful governmental body in the Qing structure. The use of concurrent titles granted the ministers access to personnel and resources and added to their authority and responsibilities. The slow institutionalization of a committee of three changed the entire hierarchical structure of the Qing government. The Qianlong emperor's utilization of Chinese and Manchus and the dominant role of Manchu officials in the evolution of the Grand Council help identify the contribution of Manchu practices and institutions in the evolving Qing bureaucracy.[20] Bartlett's account of Grand Council development as a process of flux and growth over a fifteen-year period has important implications for a more positive assessment of the development of the late Qing Zongli Yamen.

The contrast between the positive portrayals of the China-centered works on the Grand Council and the negative Western-centric modernization characterizations contained within much of the literature on the Zongli Yamen is needlessly stark. The differing views of the Zongli Yamen and the Grand Council have discouraged the comparison of the two organizations, though such a comparison, I argue, sheds light on the founding and evolutionary processes of the Zongli Yamen. In light of the shift in scholarship from forty years ago, when most of the works on the Zongli Yamen were written, it is time to reexamine the Zongli Yamen. In this study of the Zongli Yamen, I move to question the assumption of the basic conceptual equivalency of reform by asking how the institutions of the Qing bureaucracy shaped the definitions of and possibilities for reform and demonstrating how those options presented real opportunities for substantial change.

Toward Revising Our View of the Zongli Yamen

The divide in earlier scholarship between the successes of European industrialization and the modernization that accompanied it and the seeming Qing stagnation that occurred under the rule of the Manchus started to disappear with the emergence of the China-centered framework and now continues with other approaches that seek to reassess the Qing's place in Asia and the world. Moreover, the great economic successes of the People's Republic of China (PRC) have also contributed to a reassessment, as the fast-paced growth of the PRC's commercial economy cannot be comprehended without understanding the legacy of native commercial systems that helped China flourish throughout most of its imperial age. In addition, the capacity of the current Chinese regime to sponsor major state-led infrastructural projects, such as the Three Gorges Dam, that facilitate the extraction of resources and national development bring to mind the dynamism of the state during the early Qing period. The weight of the newer literature suggests that the late Qing state did not lose its capability to rule and innovate, but its efforts in these areas have been interpreted through the Western analysis of the Qing's failure in its diplomatic and military encounters with Euro-American nations, as well as its late nineteenth-century economic problems, leading ultimately to its fall in the 1911 Revolution. Breaking with past assessments of conceptual equivalencies between the West and the late Qing and turning our lens back to the nineteenth century to reexamine the Qing's state capacities and revisit its state-led efforts yield a narrative of positive continuities between the late Qing and later regimes.

"China-centered" research exploring the nineteenth century has produced many excellent studies that have contributed to our understanding of China as a multifaceted and diverse place that cannot be neatly packaged within a single narrative. Details and nuance have emerged that have helped fill and texture the broad strokes of the histories that previously focused almost solely on the state and a more general Chinese experience. However, most studies of nineteenth-century China adhering to the China-centered approach have been local studies of society or economy that examine discrete events or processes; the approach has less often been applied to questions of central governance. The cumulative knowledge of late Qing society, as well as the positive assessment of the early Qing state, has encouraged historians of Qing governance and politics to return to the nineteenth century to critique and revise the negative stereotypes embedded in earlier accounts.

One challenge that presents itself immediately is how to place central governance within the diverse context and multitude of locales that constituted the multiethnic Qing Empire. Only by recognizing the Qing state's ability to accommodate the diversity of regional and local circumstances can we recognize that the Qing government, even in its last decades, used a variety of government strategies that incorporated flexibility and accommodation to adapt to challenges and obstacles effectively.[21] The Qing state certainly encountered the West; that interaction, however, must be viewed not only in terms of the world of interstate interactions but also in terms of Qing norms and domestic functioning. The reality of the warfare that accompanied the Opium Wars and the treaties that concluded them reveals a tangible impact of the West on China; yet we cannot equate Chinese reforms of the Self-Strengthening period with an effort geared solely to smoothing Sino-Western altercations and achieving international parity through Western-defined modernization. China's problems in the nineteenth century were manifold, and although difficulties with the Euro-American powers dominated the attention of the Court at times, so too did domestic issues. Endogenous, long-term trends and indigenous practices, as well as exogenous imperialism, contributed to the transformative nature of the challenges faced by China in the nineteenth century and contributed to shaping the questions and answers Chinese posed about their society and government.[22] The question remains how best to understand this matrix of practices, events, and places.

A recent trend in scholarship has started to pull back the lens from a focus on the local and China-centered, in order to achieve a broader determination of how the Qing experience fits into the bigger picture of the Euro-American world and Greater Asia. By removing the West's unique status derived from its modernization-related economic miracle and by discussing the Chinese economy in terms of broad factors, instead of identifying China's development by its particularity, the trend places China in a greater world context.

R. Bin Wong in *China Transformed* argues that scholars must dislodge the privileged position of Eurocentric theories and models in the study of Chinese history. He warns, however, that scholars cannot revise historical studies of the Chinese past by totally eliminating European models, but rather, they should engage the European experience in a process of bidirectional comparisons in order to make the practice of historical inquiry symmetrical, so that similarities and differences are assessed together and contribute to our understanding of both sides of the comparison. Wong asserts that historians must examine broad sweeps of time, rather than discrete events, in order first to identify historical trends and, second, to place them within their socioeconomic, institutional, and cultural contexts; only then can historians achieve the scope necessary to allow for meaningful bidirectional comparison. In his study of the state and economy, Wong does not attribute European industrialization and Chinese lack thereof to an inherent strength in the society of the former and a native weakness in the nature of the societal structure of the latter. Rather, Wong stresses the capacity of the late nineteenth-century Qing state to maintain and reproduce social order, especially in its ability to raise revenues and mobilize men to put down rebellions. In stressing Qing state capacity, Wong reminds us of the anomalous nature of the European state-making experience as described by Charles Tilly.

Andre Gunder Frank in *ReOrient* likewise stresses that nineteenth-century European successes and strengths cannot be understood in terms of Eurocentrism, which equates the rise of the West with European superiority. Rather, Frank argues that global trends and economic cycles best explain nineteenth-century power fluctuations. In *The Great Divergence*, Kenneth Pomeranz shows that as late as the eighteenth century, northwest Europe and China were roughly on a par in vital areas that are recognized as contributing to modernization. However, by the nineteenth century, a "great divergence" occurred; a divergence that resulted in northwest Europe and China taking very different paths. Pomeranz argues that the success of Europe was due not to the nature or inherent superiority of the

British social system itself, but rather to a matrix of specific and contingent geographical and economic advantages, most notably the proximity of coal supplies in England to water routes, the markets of its colonies, especially India, and the resources of the New World. Simply put, Great Britain had new frontiers with felicitously spaced resources, which the British Empire aptly pursued to its advantage. China, on the other hand, did not share this level of serendipitous ecological convergence. By focusing on factors outside of societal systems, Pomeranz contends that the Industrial Revolution did not grow out of a particular European model or experience, but rather, in essence, from geographical and geological contingencies. Thus, the Euro-American trajectory to power in the nineteenth century was historically conditional; likewise, the nineteenth-century Chinese trajectory in which China experienced defeat at the hands of the Euro-American powers must be considered in light of its contingencies.[23]

More recently, Takeshi Hamashita has argued for the incorporation of China into a broader Asian regional system. His study of maritime Asia and treaty port networks demonstrates the need to direct scholarly questions asked of China to Greater Asia, even for the topic of treaty ports, perhaps the area that has been most clearly associated with Western imperialism. In contrast to the image of a nineteenth-century China being dragged against its will away from the tribute system into the family of nations and international law that still lingers from modernization school literature, Hamashita believes that the nineteenth century in China is best understood from a perspective that concentrates on internal changes in East Asia. The treaty ports indeed played an important role, not only because they display the strength and vibrancy of Euro-American imperialism, but also, and more importantly, because they demonstrate the increased dynamism of relations within the region and within the Qing sphere.[24]

The above authors caution effectively against using the Western experience in industrialization and modernization to generate sweeping theories or frameworks by which to analyze the diversity of global experiences. Just as importantly, they have contributed to a reconceptualization of the understanding of China in the sixteenth to nineteenth centuries. By utilizing regional or global perspectives, they present China as an integral part of world history, rather than as unique and confined by its physical boundaries.

The second trend in literature on the Qing has been the questioning of the very nature of the rulership of the Qing dynasty. Earlier scholarship portrays the Manchu rulers, who established and governed the Qing dynasty, as quickly assimilating to the Chinese Confucian and institutional environment, adopting Chinese customs, practices, and rulership, resulting in the Qing governmental system being defined and bound by Confucian practices and precedents handed down through the dynasties. In this view, the Qing dynasty and the Manchu ethnicity assimilated to Han culture and became Sinicized.[25] The newer works of Evelyn Rawski, Pamela Crossley, Edward Rhoads, Mark Elliott, and Peter Perdue put more emphasis on the steppe heritage of the Qing Empire, arguing, individually, for the distinctiveness of the Manchus in terms of imperial ideology, emperorship, or as a social group. As with earlier works, these authors recognize the importance of identifying the Manchus as a conquest dynasty, but they do so to stress that the Manchu Qing dynasty managed to rule a vast and diverse empire for nearly three hundred years; thus, for them, what makes the Qing rulers impressive is not their ability to assimilate, but rather just the opposite: their ability to incorporate Manchu customs, as well as the customs of the various groups whom they ruled, into a system that allowed for disparate needs over time and space.[26] Rawski argues that during the Qing, bureaucratization "took place over a wide range of social institutions" and was a "hallmark of Qing administration."[27] She identifies this trend as a particular characteristic of Manchu rule, rather than as a general effect of Chinese institutions. Pamela Crossley points out that Nurhaci, the founder of the Qing, utilized the elasticity of Jurchen lineages and practices to accomplish his goals, and through small innovations, they eventually became the basis of the Qing dynasty's banners, a cornerstone of Qing rule.[28] In *The Manchu Way*, Mark Elliott explores the complex evolution of the banner system, linking its development to the reality of achieving political goals and to the usefulness of creating a common identity and destiny. Through his study, we see the emergence of a complex Manchu system that became bureaucratized to meet the needs of Qing rulership.[29] In another work, Elliott demonstrates the conscious transition from Nurhaci to his son and successor, Hong Taiji, in the interpretation of the Manchu heritage and the subsequent expansion of vision for the Qing from a northern dominant force based on inheriting the Jurchen Jin legacy to include that of an East Asian power with legitimate claims to the Mandate of Heaven. In this way, Elliott argues, the Qing managed to maintain "a dual basis for their imperial enterprise," keeping "one foot in the central plain and the other in the steppe."[30] Edward Rhoads shows that even in the last decades of the dynasty, when many scholars have assumed very little Manchu identity remained, awareness of Han–Manchu differences contributed to tensions and the alienation of the Chinese elite. In particular, he notes the survival of the Eight Banner System into the 1920s and connects the banner system closely to Manchu identity. Rhoads also demonstrates that in the last years of the dynasty, the Manchu regent Zaifeng (the father of the young Puyi, who had become emperor on the death of the childless Guangxu emperor in 1908) exacerbated Han–Manchu tensions by attempting to concentrate power in the hands of Manchu princes at Court, thereby illustrating the active role of imperial princes in governing, even at the end of the dynasty.[31] Finally, Peter Perdue's study of the Qing frontier, *China Marches West*, stresses the innovation involved in steppe empire-building and integrates the Manchu regime with the greater Eurasian world.[32] The shift toward the recognition of the persistence of Manchu identity throughout the Qing dynasty, along with Bartlett's work emphasizing the contribution of Manchu practice to Qing institutions, point toward the need for a reconsideration of the Zongli Yamen as an institution that emerged from both the Chinese and Manchu traditions.

The Zongli Yamen Today

Despite the dramatic evolution of the state of the field since the days of John King Fairbank, our understanding of the Zongli Yamen has remained largely the same, with one significant exception. Richard Horowitz has heeded the call of China-centered literature to apply theories and approaches of the social sciences to our understanding of China. Horowitz presents the Zongli Yamen as the central Chinese organization spearheading a state-building effort in the late Qing dynasty in ways that parallel the European experience. According to Charles Tilly, in early modern Europe, state-building occurred in response to warfare between emerging, competitive states and was closely linked to the emergence of capitalism and nationalism. In order to compete successfully, states improved military capabilities, rationalized their bureaucracies, developed efficient taxation procedures, and created police forces to maintain stability and order.[33] Through his exploration of the applicability of Tilly's state-building model to the first twenty years of the Zongli Yamen's history, Horowitz helps return the State to late Qing studies. In addition, he provides a comparative basis for relating happenings in China to similar phenomena in Europe. By concluding that the Zongli Yamen ultimately failed not because of ideological weakness, but because of structural weaknesses in the Qing governmental system, Horowitz helps frame the debate for this work.[34] In a more recent work, Horowitz places Chinese efforts and experiences in a broader international context by demonstrating that the unequal treaties were part of a broad system of expansion employed by the British Empire not only in China, but also in Siam and the Ottoman Empire, highlighting the role of interstate relations. He argues that the unequal treaties put pressure on the unequal states to transform themselves. Horowitz makes a convincing case for global patterns and policies of Euro-American colonialism and expansion broadly affecting reform efforts in China, Siam, and the Ottoman Empire.[35]

While the work of Horowitz certainly advances the literature on both the Zongli Yamen and the applicability of social science theory to China, his framework is limited by the European models and experiences behind the development of that theory.[36] The bureaucratic rationalization seen by Horowitz places the Chinese experience in a greater context and allows us to situate China within the world history of the development of nation-states. However, I believe our understanding of the Zongli Yamen and its development is incomplete without further exploration of its Chinese administrative environment and the Manchu traditions behind its creation.

Approach and Organization

In this study, I explore the evolution of the Zongli Yamen as a process with Manchu institutional precedent and emphasize the parameters provided by the Qing State and its institutions for the establishment and subsequent functional operation of the Yamen. Moreover, I examine how the Zongli Yamen, in turn, regenerated and affected the structure of the State. The interplay between the two reveals an inner dynamism inherent in the Qing that is comparable to but separate from that of the Western experience. With greater internal under-standing of the late Qing state, we can move forward in efforts to incorporate more fully the Qing state into the greater world and regional contexts.

Specifically, the Zongli Yamen provides an opportunity to examine the extent of a positive, internal process of change through institution building, a progression that involved power brokering and power accrual in the immediate case and that shifted meanings of existing institutions in lasting and significant ways. While the cumulative contributions of the above China literature provides context for this study, the literature of historical institutionalism also informs my approach.[37] With its focus on institutional dynamism and the interaction of institutional and ideational variables, historical institutionalism departs from monocausal and determinist theories to allow for explanations of change that are not constrained by an overlay of the limitations of continuity. Rather, a historical institutionalist approach explains change by demonstrating that political struggles and developments are mediated by their institutional settings, and that institutions, while not the sole factor in determining outcomes, structure the debate and influence outcomes. Here I show how Qing institutions and established and new expectations shaped the Zongli Yamen's development and how the new Zongli Yamen, in turn, reshaped Qing institutions. By emphasizing the active role of institutions in shaping policy, this approach helps avoid institutional determinism and the pitfall of politics shaping institutions.[38]

While bolstering the Qing dynasty, the Zongli Yamen engendered meaningful change in the way the Qing administrative hierarchies functioned. The founders of the Zongli Yamen, by negotiating its accrual of power, navigated a course through the complexities of the Qing bureaucracy that left a legacy for a more ministerial form of government, as indicated by the formal change of the Zongli Yamen in 1901 to the Ministry of Foreign Affairs. By focusing on four sources of institutional dynamism, as outlined by Kathleen Thelin and Sven Steinmo, I analyze the process that created the Zongli Yamen and made it functional, thereby presenting a new view of the functioning and internal power relationships of the Qing government that illuminates the nature of change in and the internal dynamic of the Chinese governing system.[39]

Chapter Two examines the first of these sources by tracing Qing mechanisms for the handling of foreigners in the nineteenth century. The centerpiece of the analysis is how the use of the extra-bureaucratic office of imperial commissioners gave the Qing Court the flexibility to maneuver in a period when contact with Westerners took on new meanings. As gunboat diplomacy became more threatening, the Qing Court sidestepped regular bureaucratic channels and brought foreign affairs closer to the throne, not in literal terms, but in the appointment of imperial commissioners who had increasingly close ties to the emperor. This process culminated in the appointment of three men who represented the three highest levels of Qing governance and who then worked to institutionalize the process of foreign affairs through the establishment of the Zongli Yamen. By starting with the use of imperial commissioners as the origins of the Zongli Yamen, I demonstrate that the founding period of the Zongli Yamen preceded its formal establishment in 1861. Qing mechanisms for change, in the form of the institution of imperial commissioners, were activated with Lin Zexu's appointment in 1839 and became increasingly salient over the next two decades. This trajectory of change reflects first Manchu practice and then Chinese bureaucratic functioning, with the example of the Grand Council's founding one hundred years earlier providing clear precedent. In both cases, institutional dynamism was manifested in the slow rise to prominence of an informal group of ministers backed by the emperor that then transformed into a new and powerful regular part of the bureaucratic hierarchy.

In Chapter Three, institutional dynamism takes a different form: the adoption of new strategies and goals in the face of challenge. The exogenous force of the unequal treaty system, which played a persuasive role in galvanizing leading Qing advisors toward making peace with the West, is first examined. A discussion of treaty terms highlights the structural obstacles facing Qing high ministers and informed the attitudes of Qing officials handling foreign affairs. With the proposal to establish a highly placed new Qing institution, the Zongli Yamen, to handle foreign affairs, debate ensued. The second half of Chapter Three analyzes the deliberations by examining how the Zongli Yamen as proposed differed from the Zongli Yamen as initially established.

Chapter Four demonstrates how once the Zongli Yamen was established, its ministers worked to adjust the existing provincial administrative apparatus to bring offices that had frequent contact with and responsibilities toward Westerners under Yamen control. By reorganizing the office of *daotai*, or circuit intendant, to bring it within the Yamen's domain and by working with the newly established Superintendents of Trade, the Zongli Yamen created overlap between the territorial and foreign affairs hierarchies, enabling it to use the manpower in both to fulfill its duties as head of foreign affairs and the various Self-Strengthening projects.

Chapter Five argues through an analysis of cases involving local negotiations with foreigners that the Zongli Yamen successfully penetrated lower levels of government to fulfill its goals of establishing and maintaining the direction of foreign affairs. Through its continual strategic maneuvering within institutional constraints, Zongli Yamen ministers managed a process of gradual change that achieved the goal of altering the Qing administrative structure to create an operational foreign affairs administration with the Zongli Yamen functioning in an integrative capacity. From the act of requiring quarterly reports from local officials in the provinces and from the resolutions of individual cases within the reports, we see how the Zongli Yamen became both the overseer and participant of the local process of on-site negotiations with foreigners. Just as important, we see how the Zongli Yamen was able to systematize the handling of affairs within its jurisdiction and implement central government directives. Chapter Six continues case analysis to demonstrate that the Zongli Yamen succeeded in imposing a coherence encompassing national goals and policy aims on the local conduct of foreign affairs. Through cases that involve foreign involvement in activities prohibited by treaty, we see that the communication networks established by the Zongli Yamen to disseminate information bear fruit, as officials reference other provinces' cases in their analysis of their own cases and a unified approach to the local treatment of foreign affairs emerges.

Through Chapters Five and Six, we see that the Zongli Yamen's field administration functioned on two levels. On one level, it managed to keep the Zongli Yamen abreast of circumstances far from the capital. More importantly, it provided a means for the Yamen to involve itself in provincial matters, when necessary. On a second level, we see that foreign relations were not limited to the capital. In fact, the formation of foreign policy extended beyond the capital and into the localities where contact with foreigners occurred. Thus, foreign policy formation was a bidirectional process. Local and provincial officials contributed to its formation through their reports, investigations, and suggestions. And Yamen ministers participated through their guidance and their setting of policy aims and directives. In effect, the evolution of the Zongli Yamen into the head of a foreign affairs administration that penetrated the provinces changed the nature of decision making and policy making in the Qing, leaving it more complicated and multilayered.

Scope and Sources

Because the Qing dynasty extended over a vast empire and the Zongli Yamen archival holdings reflect its magnitude, I have delineated the scope of this study to include two important areas of the Zongli Yamen archives, namely, "Local Negotiations" and "Prohibitions and Seizures." Documents concerning three provinces, Fujian, Hubei, and Zhili, each with a distinctive relationship to the center, form the basis of the case studies. Cases from Fujian, with foreign trade predating the establishment of the Zongli Yamen, shed light on efforts to centralize foreign contact in areas distant from the capital. Hubei, on the other hand, had not had significant contact with foreigners prior to the treaty system. Even after the Treaties of Tianjin of 1860, foreign travel to Hubei was hindered by the ongoing Taiping Rebellion; thus Hubei cases demonstrate how the Zongli Yamen extended control of foreign affairs to areas with no previous foreign affairs experience. Zhili, as the metropolitan province, was extremely important to the security of the Qing Court. The emergence of the powerful post of the Northern Superintendent of Trade in Tianjin gave Zhili provincial officials a close tie to the Zongli Yamen.

Not surprisingly, among the Zongli Yamen's first efforts was a restructuring of the administration of on-site foreign negotiations in the provinces. This was necessary in order for the new organization to penetrate the Qing bureaucracy. The restructuring extended to provinces with long histories of foreign contact, like Fujian, and those that only started to have frequent interactions with foreigners after the Treaties of Tianjin and the Conventions of Beijing in 1860, like Hubei and Zhili. The centralizing reforms resulted in the resolution of most commercial and ordinary disputes at the local or provincial level. However, lines of decision making and command were established that allowed for, and at times demanded, the involvement of the central government in matters of state security or with national implications. Analysis of cases from the three provinces demonstrates that the Zongli Yamen retained overall central control of foreign relations.

From this perspective, the Zongli Yamen, both in origin and operation, was an innovative Qing institution that emerged from a flexible Qing tradition in the face of serious challenges. Analysis of the Yamen vis-à-vis the Qing institutional hierarchy reveals that the Zongli Yamen succeed in inserting itself into the heart of the Chinese bureaucratic machinery. From its origins as a progression of imperial commissioners to its institutionalization through administrative reorganization, the case of the Zongli Yamen illustrates the capabilities of the Qing to generate meaningful change within the Chinese context. In addition, the Yamen's effectiveness in developing and maintaining an operating foreign affairs administration reveals how institutional change occurred in Qing China. By examining the Zongli Yamen anew, the nature of institutional change in Qing China emerges as a process based on the negotiation of Manchu and Chinese institutions and power. Understanding that process grants us considerable new insights into the ability of the late Qing government to adjust to emerging demands domestically and internationally, as well as its capability of restructuring accordingly the standing of its administrative hierarchies. And from this, we acquire a more sophisticated appreciation of the meaning of change and reform in the complex and diverse Chinese world.

NOTES

1. In addition to the Nian and Taiping rebellions, the Miao rebellions engulfed parts of southwest China from 1854 to 1873, while Muslim ethnic and religious movements and rebellions required government attention and resources for most of the 1860s and 1870s in western China. The Panthay Muslim Rebellion disrupted Yunnan from 1856 to 1873.

2. The Self-Strengthening Movement (*Ziqiang yundong*) lasted, in a broad sense, from 1861 to China's defeat in the 1895 Sino-Japanese War. Self-strengthening (*ziqiang*) referred to official efforts to bolster the Qing government vis-à-vis the Western imperialist powers and to Qing policies aimed at restoring sound government in the aftermath of the Taiping Rebellion. The term *ziqiang* itself has deep roots in Chinese history, but Zhao Shuji, a Hanlin Academy compiler, was the first to use the term in the context of the nineteenth-century threats, followed by Feng Guifen. In 1901, the Zongli Yamen became the Ministry of Foreign Affairs (*Waiwu bu*). For details on the guiding principles of the Self-Strengthening Movement and on the history of the term, see David Pong, "The Vocabulary of Change: Reformist Ideas of the 1860s and 1870s," in David Pong and Edmund S.K. Fung, eds., *Ideal and Reality: Social and Political Change in Modern China, 1860–1949* (Lanham, MD: University Press of America, 1985), 25–61.

3. Paul Cohen has written very useful historiographical discussions of the Self-Strengthening period and late Qing China, as well as an article touching on the historical legacy of the reforms. I have drawn on his work as well as several other authors' useful discussions. See Paul A. Cohen, "Self-Strengthening in China-Centered Perspective: The Evolution of American Historiography," *Qingji ziqiang yundong tao hui lun wen ji* (Taipei: Zhongyang yanjiu yuan jindai shi yanjiu suo, 1988), 5–35; and "The Post-Mao Reforms in Historical Perspective," *The Journal of Asian Studies* 47, no. 3 (August 1988): 519–41. Thomas Kennedy discusses writings from both the United States and Taiwan in his "Self-Strengthening: An Analysis Based on Some Recent Writings," *Ch'ing-shih wen-t'i* 3, no. 1 (November 1974): 3–35. For a survey of writings from Taiwan, Hong Kong, and China, as well as the United States, see Li Zhigang, "Ziqiang yundong," in *Liushi nian lai de Zhongguo jindai shi yanjiu*, vol. 2 (Taipei: Zhongyang yanjiu yuan jindai shi yanjiu suo, 1989), 691–718. Chen Jiang discusses scholarship from Mainland China on the period in "Recent Historiography of the Western Affairs Movement," in *Late Imperial China*, 7, no. 1 (1986): 112–27. K.H. Kim covers Japanese scholarship in *Japanese Perspectives of China's Early Modernization: A Bibliographic Survey* (Ann Arbor: University of Michigan Center for Chinese Studies, 1974). Judith Farquhar and James Hevia offer an interesting discussion of American scholarship, including that focusing on the late Qing, centering on concepts of culture in "Culture and Postwar American Historiography of China," *positions* 1, no. 2 (Fall 1993): 486–517. For an overall analysis of the general paradigms and approaches of American scholarship on China, see

Paul Cohen's *Discovering History in China: American Historical Writing on the Recent Chinese Past* (New York: Columbia University Press, 1984).

4. Ssu-yű Teng and John K. Fairbank, *China's Response to the West: A Documentary Survey, 1839–1923* (Cambridge, MA: Harvard University Press, 1954).

5. John King Fairbank is also the best-known figure associated with this approach. His work and that of his students is sometimes referred to as the "Harvard School." Fairbank's early works relied mainly on documents concerning treaty ports, which quite predictably focused on the West and encouraged a Western-centric view of China. In his later years (1980s), Fairbank moved away somewhat from a modernization framework. See Fairbank, *Trade and Diplomacy on the China Coast: The Opening of the Treaty Ports, 1842– 1854* (Cambridge, MA: Harvard University Press, 1953); Fairbank, *The United States and China* (Cambridge, MA: Harvard University Press, 1979); "The Creation of the Treaty System," in *The Cambridge History of China*, vol. 10, pt. 1 (New York: Cambridge University Press, 1978). For a later work of Fairbank, see *The Great Chinese Revolution: 1800–1985* (New York: Harper and Row, 1986).

6. Fairbank's predecessors S. Wells Williams and Hosea Morse also focused on the West as the main force in nineteenth-century China. Many sinologists of the 1940s and 1950s, including Immanuel Hsu, contributed to the modernization analysis of China. In the 1960s, Mary Wright started to search for a more satisfying analysis of China; nonetheless, the influence of the modernization paradigm permeates her work on the Tongzhi Restoration. See S. Wells Williams, *The Middle Kingdom: A Survey of the Geography, Government, Literature, Social Life, Arts, and History*, revised 1883 edition (Taipei: Ch'eng-wen Publishing, reprint, 1965); Hosea Ballou Morse, *The International Relations of the Chinese Empire*, 3 vols. (originally published by Kelly and Walsh, Ltd., in Shanghai in 1918; reprinted by Ch'eng-wen in Taipei, 1978); Immanuel C.Y. Hsu, *China's Entrance into the Family of Nations: The Diplomatic Phase, 1858–1860* (Cambridge, MA: Harvard University Press, 1960); Mary Clabaugh Wright, *The Last Stand of Chinese Conservatism: The T'ung-Chih Restoration, 1862–1874* (Stanford: Stanford University Press, 1957).

7. The influence of the tradition-modernity approach is waning but still felt. A recent work by Fei-ling Wang incorporates elements of this approach in the name of modernization theory. Wang examines labor allocation patterns in China to explain the persistence of tradition in China and the resultant difficulty of achieving Chinese modernity. See Fei-ling Wang,

Institutions and Institutional Change in China: Premodernity and Modernization (New York: St. Martin's Press, 1998).

8. Tani Barlow has argued that the Cold War political agenda of China scholars in promoting the Western-impact/modernization approach to understanding China skewed studies of China by removing the trope of colonialism and making China, in universal terms, the exception (in the case of Fairbank) that would eventually follow the path of the United States. The agenda of Western social sciences precluded a China-oriented understanding of events and patterns. See Tani Barlow, "Colonialism's Career in Postwar China Studies," *positions*, 1, no. 1 (Spring 1993): 224–68.

9. See Mary Wright's *Last Stand of Chinese Conservatism* on the Tongzhi Restoration, and Joseph Levenson's *Confucian China and Its Modern Fate* (Berkeley: University of California Press, 1968), vol. 1, 59–78, on the implications of Confucianism for the Self-Strengthening period. Levenson argues that the Self-Strengthening *tiyong* (essence-utility) formulation of promoting the use of Western techniques to gird the essence of China contained a basic contradiction that doomed any modernization effort to failure. For an extension of this outlook, see Valerie Cromwell and Zara Steiner, "The Foreign Office Before 1914: A Study in Resistance," in *Studies in the Growth of Nineteenth Century Government*, Gillian Sutherland, ed. (Totowa, NJ: Rowman and Littlefield, 1972), 167–94.

10. The title of one of Immanuel Hsu's works reflects how this expectation extended well past Western contemporaries and into the twentieth century. See Hsu, *China's Entrance into the Family of Nations*. For another example of a work that focuses on diplomacy and how China was to interact within the international framework, see Reuben Tse-min Ting, "The Establishment of the Tsungli Yamen and the Dispatch of the First Chinese Mission to Foreign Powers," unpublished Masters thesis, University of Washington, 1949.

11. In her thought-provoking study of the battle over words and translation and the powerful role of language in the creation of expectations and roles in interstate relations, Lydia Liu raises the problem of equivalencies in translation between different languages and different cultures. Focusing on the nineteenth-century contemporary translation of treaties and Henry Wheaton's *Elements of International Law* (1864), she explores the struggle of "making hypothetical equivalences between the semiotic horizons of different languages" and the increasing acceptance of those initially makeshift arrangements over time. Her treatment of the issue contributes to this study not only in terms of subject matter but also in terms

of raising the concept of equivalencies in the context of reform both for Qing contemporaries and for scholars who have come after them. Lydia H. Liu, *The Clash of Empires: The Invention of China in Modern World Making* (Cambridge, MA: Harvard University Press, 2004), 5–30, 108–13.

12. See Earl Swisher's *Early Sino-American Relations, 1841–1912: The Collected Articles of Earl Swisher,* Kenneth Rea, ed. (Boulder, CO: Westview Press, 1977); Jason Parker's *The Rise and Decline of I-Hsin, Prince Kung, 1858– 1865: A Study of the Interaction of Politics and Ideology in Late Imperial China* (Princeton, NJ: Princeton University Press, 1979); and Tony Yung-Yuan Teng's "Prince Kung and the Survival of the Ch'ing Rule (1858–1898)," Ph.D. dissertation, University of Wisconsin, 1972.

13. Scholars of Japan's late nineteenth-century Meiji political history have not remained bound by the assumption that change and reform could be only in response to the Western threat. Najita Tetsuo illustrates how a "conceptual consciousness," or intellectual framework, evolved over the course of Confucian Tokugawa Japan that allowed the Meiji reformers to transform Japanese society. Meiji leaders shared a framework for debate that had been forming over the previous 100 years. Long before the arrival of the West, intellectuals and leaders had realized the incongruities of the ideals of Confucianism and the realities of government and society. Thus, Najita stresses cultural and intellectual changes as contributing to the flow of politics and the economy of Japan. By doing so, he brings to the fore the desire of intellectuals for change and the flexibility within the overarching Confucian framework to accommodate new developments. In Japan, the basic "conceptual consciousness" became corrosive to the existing order and aristocratic rule; hence, the Meiji leaders were able to overhaul government and society. See Najita Tetsuo, "Conceptual Consciousness in the Meiji Ishin," in Nagai Michio and Miguel Urrutia, eds., *Meiji Ishin: Restoration and Revolution* (Tokyo: United Nations University, 1985). Although Japan and China have taken very different courses since the mid-nineteenth century, the idea of a complex intellectual framework within a Confucian society that allows for many different paths should be seriously considered in China as well. Sinologists must recognize diversity within tradition and internal imperatives for flexibility. Such an approach is developed on the China side in *Reform in Nineteenth Century China,* Paul A. Cohen and John E. Schrecker, eds. (Cambridge, MA: East Asian Research Center, Harvard University, 1976). For instance, Marianne Bastid shows through her discussion of *qingyi* or "pure counsel" that the views of those labeled as "pure counsel" conservatives were not necessarily opposed to reform. See Bastid, "Ch'ing-I

清 議 and the Self-Strengthening Movement," in *Proceedings of the Conference on the Self-Strengthening Movement in Late Ch'ing China, 1860–1894*, 2 vols., sponsored by the Institute of Modern History, Academia Sinica (Taipei: Institute of Modern History, Academia Sinica, 1987).

14. See Masataka Banno, *China and the West 1858–1861: The Origins of the Tsungli Yamen* (Cambridge, MA: Harvard University Press, 1964); Tseng-tsai Wang, *Tradition and Change in China's Management of Foreign Affairs: Sino-British Relations 1793–1877* (Taipei: China Committee for Publication and Prize Awards under the auspices of Soochow University, 1972); S.M. Meng, *The Tsungli Yamen: Its Organization and Functions* (Cambridge, MA: East Asia Research Center, Harvard University, 1962).

15. See Wu Fuhuan, *Qingji Zongli Yamen yanjiu* (A study of the Qing Zongli Yamen) (Taipei: Wen Jin Press, 1995); Liu Guanghua, "Wan Qing Zongli Yamen zuzhi ji diwei zhi yanjiu" (A study of the Late Qing Zongli Yamen's organization and position), Masters thesis, Zhengzhi University, Taiwan, 1973; see also his "Zhong-Fa zhanzheng yiqian Zongli Yamen dui wai zhengce zhi yanjiu" (A study of the Zongli Yamen and foreign policy before the Sino-French War), Ph.D. dissertation, Zhengzhi University, Taiwan, 1981. See also Chen Siqi, "Zongli Yamen sheli beijing ji qi jiaose zhi yanjiu" (A study of the background of the establishment of the Zongli Yamen and its role), Masters thesis, Zhengzhi University, Taiwan, 1985; Luo Bingmian, "Zongli Yamen yu Manzu benwei zhengce" (The Zongli Yamen and basic Manchu policy) in *Qingji Ziqiang Yundong Yantanhui lunwen ji* (Proceedings of the Conference on the Self-Strengthening Movement in Late Ch'ing China, 1860–1894) (Taipei: Institute of Modern History, Academia Sinica, 1987), 161–83; Zhang Zhongfu, "Yapian zhan qian qingting banli waijiao zhi jiguan yu shouxu" (The Pre-Opium War Qing foreign policy organizations and methods) in *Waijiao yuebao*, 2, no. 2 (February 1933); Zhang's "Zi yapian zhanzheng zhi yingfa lianjun qi zhong qingting banli waijiao zhi jiguan yu shouxu" (The Qing dynasty's foreign policy organizations and methods in the period from the Opium War to the British and French Allied Occupation), *Waijiao yuebao* 2, no. 5 (May 1933); his "Zongli geguo shiwu yamen zhi yuanqi" (The origins of the Zongli Yamen), *Waijiao yuebao* 3, no. 7 (July 1933); and his "Qingting banli waijiao zhi jiguan yu shouxu" (The Qing Court's organizations and procedures for handling foreign affairs), in Bao Daopeng, Li Dingyi, and Wu Xiangxiang, eds., *Zhongguo jindaishi luncong*, vol. 3 (Taibei: Zhengzhong Shuju, 1956). For works focusing on personality, see Duan Changguo, "Gong qin wang Yixin yu Xian Tong zhi waijiao yu zhengzhi jiufen" (Prince Gong and disputes of

foreign policy and government during the Xianfeng and Tongzhi reigns, 1858–1864), Masters thesis, National Taiwan University, 1973; and Wang Mingcan's "Yixin dui xifang de renshi" (Yixin's Knowledge of the West), Masters thesis, Dong Hai University, Taiwan, 1993. Some older works focus on diplomatic capacity formation: see Liu Zhicheng, "Qingchao zongli geguo shiwu yamen" (The Qing dynasty Zongli Yamen), *Qinghua zhoukan*, 41, nos. 11, 12 (1934); Liu Xinxian, "Zhongguo waijiao zhidu de yange" (The evolution of the Chinese foreign relations system), in *Zhongguo jindaishi luncong*, Bao Daopeng, Li Dingyi, and Wu Xiangxiang, eds. Series I, vol. 5 (Taibei: Zhengzhong Shuju, 1956); Chen Wenjin's "Qingdai zhi zongli yamen ji qi jingfei" (The Qing Zongli Yamen and its expenses), *Zhongguo jindai jingjishi yanjiu jikan*, 1, no. 1 (November 1932); and Qiu Zuming, "Zhongguo waijiao jiguan zhi yange (The evolution of China's foreign policy organizations)," *Waijiao pinglun*, vol. 4, 5 (May 1935).

16. See Cohen, *Discovering History in China*, 149–98, especially 153–54. The first challenge to the modernization approach came in the late 1960s as a political response by scholars who viewed the response to the West and modernization approaches as an apology for imperialism and the U.S. involvement in Vietnam. The *Bulletin of Concerned Asian Scholars* (1968–2000, now published as *Critical Asian Studies*) was established specifically to challenge the dominant influence of modernization and the Harvard School. James Peck is most closely associated with the imperialist approach and its challenge to modernization literature. See James Peck, "The Roots of Rhetoric: The Professional Ideology of America's China Watchers," *Bulletin of Concerned Asian Scholars* 2, no. 1 (October 1969): 59–69. For an influential debate between Peck and Fairbank on their respective approaches, see Fairbank and Peck, "An Exchange," *Bulletin of Concerned Asian Scholars* 2, no. 3 (April–July 1970): 51–70. Cohen discusses the imperialism approach and challenge in chapter 3 of *Discovering History*.

17. For example, see Madeleine Zelin, *The Magistrate's Tael: Rationalizing Fiscal Reform in Eighteenth Century Ch'ing China* (Berkeley: University of California Press, 1985); R. Kent Guy, *The Emperor's Four Treasuries: Scholars and the State in the Ch'ien-lung Era* (Cambridge, MA: Harvard University Press, 1987); Philip Kuhn, *Soulstealers: The Chinese Sorcery Scare of 1768* (Cambridge, MA: Harvard University Press, 1990).

18. See Thomas Metzger, *The Internal Organization of the Ch'ing Bureaucracy: Legal, Normative, and Communication Aspects* (Cambridge, MA: Harvard University Press, 1973).

19. See Silas H.L. Wu, *Communication and Imperial Control in China: Evolution of the Palace Memorial System, 1693–1970* (Cambridge, MA: Harvard University Press, 1970). Bartlett's work has become the definitive work on the Grand Council. See Beatrice Bartlett, *Monarchs and Ministers: The Grand Council in Mid-Ch'ing China, 1723–1820* (Berkeley: University of California Press, 1991).

20. Bartlett, *Monarchs and Ministers*, 139–48.

21. Excellent examples of studies that achieve this can be found in Robert J. Antony and Jane Kate Leonard, eds., *Dragons, Tigers, and Dogs: Qing Crisis Management and the Boundaries of State Power in Late Imperial China* (Ithaca, NY: Cornell East Asia Program, 2002).

22. See Mary Backus Rankin, "Social and Political Change in Nineteenth-Century China," in Merle Goldman and Andrew Gordon, eds., *Historical Perspectives on Contemporary Asia*, (Cambridge, MA: Harvard University Press, 2000), 42–84.

23. R. Bin Wong, *China Transformed: Historical Change and the Limits of the European Experience* (Ithaca, NY: Cornell University Press, 1997); Charles Tilly, "Reflections on the History of European State-making," in *The Formation of Nation States in Western Europe*, Charles Tilly, ed. (Princeton, NJ: Princeton University Press, 1975); Andre Gunder Frank, *ReOrient: Global Economy in the Asian Age* (Berkeley: University of California Press, 1998); Kenneth Pomeranz, "Beyond the East-West Binary: Resituating Development Paths in the Eighteenth-Century World," *Journal of Asian Studies* 61, no. 2 (2002): 539–90; and *The Great Divergence: China, Europe, and the Making of the Modern World Economy* (Princeton, NJ: Princeton University Press, 2000).

24. Takeshi Hamashita, "Tribute and Treaties: Maritime Asia and Treaty Port Networks in the Era of Negotiation, 1800–1900," in *The Resurgence of East Asia: 500, 150, and 50 Year Perspectives*, Giovanni Arrighi, et al., eds. (London and New York: Routledge, 2003), 17–50.

25. See Franz Michael, *The Origin of Manchu Rule in China: Frontier and Bureaucracy as Interacting Forces in the Chinese Empire*, (Baltimore: John Hopkins University Press, 1942; reissued by Octagon Books in 1965). There have been at least partial exceptions; John Watt distances local Qing government from the moral bindings of *ren* or benevolence in Confucian government, but not the structural bindings. See John R. Watt, *The District Magistrate in Late Imperial China* (New York: Columbia University Press, 1972).

26. Pamela Crossley provides a very good discussion of the merits and demerits of identifying the Liao, Jin, Yuan, and Qing dynasties as conquest

dynasties and other dynasties as Chinese. She argues that all dynasties, whether they are of Han origin or not, are, in essence, conquest dynasties. See Pamela Crossley, *A Translucent Mirror: History and Identity in Qing Imperial Ideology* (Berkeley: University of California Press, 1999, 29–30.

27. Evelyn Rawski, *The Last Emperors: A Social History of the Qing Imperial Institutions* (Berkeley: University of California Press, 1998), 296.

28. Crossley, *A Translucent Mirror,* 150–53. In an earlier work, Crossley discusses the history of Manchu identity and its relationship to Chinese nationalism. See Crossley, *Orphan Warriors: Three Manchu Generations and the End of the Qing World* (Princeton, NJ: Princeton University Press, 1990). Nurhaci is also written Nurgaci.

29. Mark C. Elliott, *The Manchu Way: The Eight Banners and Ethnic Identity in Late Imperial China* (Stanford, CA: Stanford University Press, 2001).

30. Mark C. Elliott, "Whose Empire Shall It Be? Manchu Figurations of Historical Process in the Early Seventeenth Century," in Lynn A. Struve, ed., *Time, Temporality, and Imperial Transition: East Asia from Ming to Qing,* (Honolulu: Association for Asian Studies and University of Hawaii Press, 2005), 32–44, quotation on 34.

31. He also attributes the creation of the Manchus as an ethnic group, as opposed to an occupational caste, to the dismantling of the Eight Banner System in the mid-1920s. See Edward Rhoads, *Manchus and Han: Ethnic Relations and Political Power in Late Qing and Early Republican China, 1861–1928* (Seattle: University of Washington Press, 2000), 121–72, 287–89.

32. Peter C. Perdue, *China Marches West: The Qing Conquest of Central Eurasia* (Cambridge, MA: The Belknap Press of Harvard University Press, 2005).

33. Charles Tilly, "Reflections on the History of European State-making," 6, 50–80.

34. See Richard Horowitz, "Central Power and State Making: The Zongli Yamen and Self-Strengthening in China, 1860–1880," Ph.D. dissertation, Harvard University, 1998. For a positive discussion of the applicability of Tilly's theory of state building to China, see Horowitz, "State Making Theory and the Study of Modern Chinese History," *Newsletter of Modern Chinese History,* Institute of Modern History, Academia Sinica, No. 19, (1995): 84–98.

35. Richard Horowitz, "International Law and State Transformation in China, Siam, and the Ottoman Empire during the Nineteenth Century," *Journal of World History* 15: 4 (December 2004): 446–55.

36. For a cautionary word about the application of European concepts to the Chinese context, see R. Bin Wong, "Great Expectations: The 'Public

Sphere' and the Search for Modern Times in Chinese History," *Studies in Chinese History* 3 (October 1993): 7–49.

37. For an overview of neo-institutionalism, of which historical institutionalism is one branch, see Ellen M. Immergut, "The Theoretical Core of the New Institutionalism," *Politics and Society* 26:1 (March 1998): 5–34. For a discussion of historical institutionalism, see Kathleen Thelen and Sven Steinmo, "Historical Institutionalism in Comparative Politics," in Sven Steinmo, Kathleen Thelen, and Frank Longstreth, eds., *Structuring Politics: Historical Institutionalism in Comparative Analysis,* (New York: Cambridge University Press, 1992).

38. The theory of punctuated equilibrium put forth by Stephen Krasner at first reading seems to help explain the establishment of the Zongli Yamen. The Qing's long stable environment was punctuated by both external and internal crises in the mid-nineteenth century, causing governmental debate and conflict over the best approach and seemingly abrupt institutional change followed by stasis once the emergency passed. Mary Wright's work, written twenty years earlier than Krasner's, appears to foreshadow his argument. The problem, however, is politics—in Wright's case Confucianism—becomes the overriding agent and other institutional factors unduly diminished. See Stephen D. Krasner, "Approaches to the State: Alternative Conceptions and Historical Dynamics," *Comparative Politics* 16:2 (January 1984): 223–46.

39. Thelen and Steinmo, 16–17.

2

BUILDING CHANGE,
ONE MAN AT A TIME

IN 1839, IMPERIAL COMMISSIONER LIN ZEXU charged onto the world stage by confronting the British Empire over its participation in the trafficking of opium. Lin's actions precipitated the First Opium War (1839–1842) and ushered in the era of unequal treaties defined by Western imperialism. The narrative of Lin's actions and Western gunboat diplomacy are well known; the sequel to it, however, is not. Over the course of the next twenty years, the practice of appointing imperial commissioners to conduct foreign affairs that started with Lin accelerated and finally culminated in the establishment of a formal Foreign Office. The Zongli Yamen's establishment did not represent a foregone conclusion, but rather a process of consensus building predicated on the Qing practice of appointing imperial commissioners and the important precedent of the Grand Council's formation.

The crisis environment in the mid-1800s required the Qing Court and bureaucracy to search for means to solve the many problems challenging China. For the first time, Western nations had brought military power to bear on China's coast and used it to change the balance of power in East Asia. Internal rebellions, such as the Taiping and the Nian, also ravaged the Chinese landscape. The dual predicaments contributed to an atmosphere that required new government approaches and brought to the forefront the inherent flexibility of Qing institutions and practices. Among these, the appointment of imperial commissioners (*qinchai dachen*) to handle negotiations with foreigners prior to 1861 and the subsequent creation of the Zongli Yamen in 1861 suggest the ability of the traditional Qing bureaucracy to evolve and adapt to the changing environment.

The creation and formalization of the Zongli Yamen was a remarkable process of negotiation and adaptation to evolving situations. Because the process actually started decades before its establishment, historians of the late Qing, who most often look to the Second Opium War for the Yamen's origins, have long misunderstood it. A focus on the use of imperial commissioners, from the appointment of Lin Zexu to the appointment of Prince Gong (Gong Qinwang Yixin), Wenxiang, and Guiliang, during the chaos that accompanied the allied expeditionary forces' occupation of Beijing, allows for a clearer picture of the Zongli Yamen's institutional development to emerge. The years immediately preceding 1861 created an environment that permitted departures from the status quo—a status quo that was predicated on flexibility within the Qing system. With the proposal written by Prince Gong, Wenxiang, and Guiliang during the aftermath of the Second Opium War, which put forth a new type of office to handle affairs with the Western countries, the possibilities for meaningful change within Qing China emerged.[1]

Imperial Commissioners: A Step Toward the Throne

Appointed by the throne on an ad hoc basis, imperial commissioners handled specific tasks and missions that no regularly established bureaucratic office was equipped to manage.[2] In keeping with the temporary nature of the assignment, the title carried no official rank of its own, but usually the rank of governor-general was bestowed on the appointee, demonstrating the importance of the task at hand. However, the Board of Rites did not issue a seal to an imperial commissioner, highlighting the temporary nature of the position.[3] Because of their extra-bureaucratic status, imperial commissioners could have narrow or broad responsibilities, depending on the needs of the Qing Court. In the case of mid–nineteenth-century relations with foreigners, the imperial commissioners were charged with handling increasingly complex problems. During the Opium Wars and negotiations with Western powers, the throne appointed a series of imperial commissioners to manage related responsibilities and crises, placing the commissioners in key roles in foreign affairs.

Throughout this period, officials appointed as imperial commissioners and charged with handling negotiations with Westerners grew closer to the Court in terms of blood and power, signifying both an increasing importance of the role and of Western relations to the Court. Intimacy with the emperor brought greater power of negotiation and authority to the imperial commissioners; moreover, the increased power reflected the adaptability of the Qing Court in novel circumstances. As the Court appointed men with progressively higher rank and ever closer blood ties to the throne, imperial commissioners were able to assume new responsibilities and greater discretion in negotiations, providing the Court with necessary flexibility. Eventually, the increased reliance on imperial commissioner appointments culminated in a more permanent, institutionalized solution to foreign affairs—the establishment of the Zongli Yamen in 1861.

Chinese World Order and the West

The traditional understanding of a Sino-centric world order placed Chinese foreign relations into what has come to be known in the West as the tribute system. According to the accepted wisdom, the tribute system served China well in its dealings with neighboring and distant peoples until the arrival of Western military might in the middle of the nineteenth century. In this view, the tribute system, a manifestation of the traditional Chinese world order and power structure, formed the backbone of Chinese relations with non-Chinese states for centuries.[4] The Chinese emperor served as the one universal ruler, the Son of Heaven, responsible for all people, Chinese and non-Chinese alike. In this role, he assumed nominal leadership for all peoples. As a result, states had to first recognize the Chinese emperor's exalted position before friendly relations with China could be forged and systematized. Surrounding states, desiring or requiring commercial interactions with the Chinese people, accepted the tributary framework as necessary for official relations, resulting in the de facto regulation of foreign trade by the tribute system. Once a state submitted to the Chinese Court as a tributary, it could send envoys at set, predetermined intervals with tribute gifts to Beijing; the emperor, in turn, would bestow gifts on the envoys, resulting in a form of trade. Moreover, envoys could engage in trade for a short time (specified by the Court) while in the capital and sometimes at other places as well. Thus, the tribute system acted as a way of binding neighboring states to the Chinese order while providing a venue for commerce. Consequently, commercial relations became bound to the Chinese conception of world order; trade was the prerogative of the emperor and granted by his imperial grace. In turn the emperor and, by extension, the Chinese state received prestige from the tribute states, and thus, legitimization.

More recent scholarship has started to question the traditional understanding of the tribute system as a comprehensive whole. That is to say, not all contact with foreigners necessarily came under the rubric of the tribute system, and there were different applications of the system to achieve different purposes. The accumulation of empirical knowledge of different periods of Chinese history has undermined the monolithic view of the tribute system and yielded a richer view of the nature of foreign contact.[5] Moreover, case-by-case examinations of encounters with foreign powers during the Qing reveals the flexibility of Qing traditions. Within the statecraft tradition of China, for instance, foreign relations were viewed as a matter of defense, not tribute. For example, treaties, which rested on the assumption of equality, were forged with imperial Russia in the seventeenth and eighteenth centuries to solve the border and trade problems between the neighbors.[6] Trade relations with Inner Asian neighbors, including Russia until 1858, fell under the jurisdiction of the *Lifan yuan* or Board of Colonial Affairs. James Hevia in *Cherishing Men From Afar* demonstrates that the Manchu Qing Court worked to practice its influence over the "multitude of lords" that existed in

Inner Asia not through the traditionally conceived tribute system, but through a highly ritualistic, ceremonious form of influence negotiation. By focusing on foreign relations as a solution to pragmatic problems, rather than as part of a comprehensive cosmological whole, we can avoid the analytical landmines embedded in the traditional tribute system that Hevia's work so powerfully explodes.[7]

Tribute-bearing embassies and tribute-centered relations did exist during the Qing with such states as Korea, Siam, Vietnam, and Ryukyu. Relations between tributary states and the Qing government ordinarily fell under the jurisdiction of the Common Residence for Tributary Envoys (*huitong siyi guan*) supervised by the Board of Rites. The regulations governing the tribute missions of, and hence relations with, neighboring states were stipulated and recorded in the *Collected Statutes of the Qing Dynasty (Da Qing huidian)*.[8]

As troubles with non-Chinese peoples shifted from the northwestern frontier to the eastern maritime frontier with the arrival of Western merchants and military power, the flexibility the Qing had demonstrated in dealing with border issues in the northwest extended to the southeast. The Common Residence for Tributary Envoys section in the 1818 revision of the *Collected Statutes* recorded a distinction between tributary states and Western countries, whose relations with China were recognized as purely commercial and not ritualistic.[9] Fixed periods for tribute missions were not set for Western nations, because of the great distances involved. The tribute system, in other words, was not the sole means for conducting foreign affairs with the West. In fact, after the disputes over the kotow in the 1793 Macartney and 1816 Amherst missions, the Court tried to avoid the tribute system in its contact with Western officials in order to keep Western trade far from Beijing and thereby limit its impact on the heartland of China and avoid the embarrassments and questions raised by the upset of the ritualistic balance of relations.[10]

Scholars have portrayed the nineteenth-century Canton cohong (*gonghang*) system, which controlled trade between Chinese and foreign merchants from the mid-1700s to the First Opium War, as a variation of the traditionally conceived tribute system and an unchanging Chinese political order or *tizhi*, despite the revisions in the 1818 edition of the *Collected Statutes* that reflected implicit acknowledgment of new circumstances.[11] The most critical element of the cohong system, as far as official relations with the West were concerned, was that no Westerner, including representatives of European governments, had direct access to the Chinese provincial government, let alone the central government in Beijing. Instead, trade was conducted in and limited to Canton. On the Chinese side of the cohong system were thirteen monopolistic "hong" or guild merchants licensed by the throne for a set period of time in return for their guaranteeing good behavior of foreign crews and merchants and their payment of generous contributions and presents to Beijing. On the Western side, were thirteen "factories" or trading posts on an island in the Pearl River, at which foreigners could conduct trade under strict guidelines. Not only did trade go through the hong merchants, but complaints in other areas did as well. A communication or grievance from a foreigner had to first be conveyed in the form of a petition to a hong merchant; then, that merchant would forward it to the Hoppo, the Court-appointed superintendent of maritime customs. The inherent problems of this restrictive arrangement were manifold from the Westerners' point of view, but no Western government pushed hard for change until the dissolution of the East India Company monopoly of trade in 1834. At that time, the responsibility for the management of Chinese affairs shifted from the Company to the British government. Conflict with the Qing regime began as the British tried to make the shift from solely commercial to political relations, and the Chinese tried to maintain only commercial relations with Western countries at China's borders.

The Emperor's Men

Even though the Qing Court did not embrace Western-style diplomatic contact in response to new British demands, the Court did recognize the urgency and uniqueness of the times. In 1839, a development occurred in China's handling of the Western states: the Daoguang emperor (r. 1821–1850) appointed Lin Zexu as imperial commissioner to investigate the affairs in Canton and the problems arising from Western contact, namely the opium trade.[12] Lin, while governor-general of Hubei and Hunan, had imposed severe measures to effectively suppress the use of opium in his provinces. Worried by Lin's warnings of the danger of opium to the empire and inspired by his success in clearing Hubei and Hunan of the drug, the Court summoned Lin to Beijing in 1838. After several imperial audiences, Lin was appointed to examine and solve the opium problem in the Canton area, where he arrived in March of 1839.[13] British subjects and then their government interpreted his confiscation and destruction of British opium as an affront to British sovereignty. The Opium War that resulted not only abolished the Canton cohong system, but also changed the international order in Asia with its concluding Treaty of Nanjing (1842).

The appointments of Lin and later imperial commissioners were remarkable for a number of reasons. Because imperial commissioners were directly responsible to the throne and not part of the regular bureaucratic institutions and because they served as the emperor's link to foreign affairs on site, they controlled the relay of foreign affairs information to the Court. Through this role, they participated in the decision-making process at the center. Direct access to the emperor meant that imperial commissioners did not have to maneuver through regular bureaucratic channels, as did most officials. This advantage became increasingly significant as later commissioners grew closer to the throne; with this closeness came enhanced influence in policy making.[14]

The combination of imperial commissioners and unequal treaties formed the backdrop for relations and negotiations between the Qing Court and the West for the next twenty years. By ratifying the Treaty of Nanjing, China and Great Britain technically recognized each other's equality and, thus, ended, if it had ever existed in relation to the West, the tribute system.[15] At this point, the Chinese government had made no institutional or constitutional alteration in operations that reflected an enduring institutional change to address the new situation and the newly imposed framework; the use of an imperial commissioner thus revealed a flexibility in approach and an increased sense of urgency on the part of the Qing Court. The appointment of an imperial commissioner as an extra-bureaucratic official whose tenure ended with his particular mission did not in itself constitute or indicate a desire for permanent institutional change. But, Lin's appointment should be viewed as the beginning of a process of adjustment and adaptation that eventually resulted in what we can term constitutional change or a shift in the ordering of the state.[16]

After the debacle resulting from Lin Zexu's provocation of the Opium War, the Daoguang emperor continued this process in May 1842 by appointing Qiying as imperial commissioner to negotiate peace with the British.[17] Qiying, a Manchu vice president of the Board of War and military lieutenant-governor of Rehe (Jehol), possessed power by title and rank and by his status as an imperial clansman. Qiying's appointment reflected the Court's association of Lin's failure not with the office he had filled, but with shortcomings of Lin's policy and person. Qiying, it was hoped, could serve as a remedy with his greater prestige and different, conciliatory policy. His appointment revealed the Court's personalistic view of the post of imperial commissioner: by choosing an imperial commissioner closer to the throne, the Court made the post itself more powerful. In addition to versatility, the appointment of Qiying also demonstrated the Court's openness to a change in policy; Qiying tried a new tactic of developing a conciliatory orientation toward the Western powers that involved direct Chinese contact with them.

Unlike Lin, Qiying had direct contact with the foreigners; thus, he had a better understanding of Western strength and Western differences than had Lin or officials at Court. For engaging Western officials directly, however, Qiying had to apologize to the emperor and explain its necessity: "If we restrained them by the ceremonial forms used for dependent tribes, they would certainly not consent to retire and remain in the status of Annam and Liuqiu since they do not accept our calendar nor receive an imperial patent of investiture."[18] With his use of some of the phrasing and framework of the tribute system to explain his stance, Qiying conveyed his belief that the underlying conception of the Chinese world order was not universal. In the above memorial, Qiying was certainly not advocating a change in the Chinese order, but he recognized the need to handle Westerners differently from tributary states. His appointment reveals a willingness on the part of the Qing Court to accept this view.

Qiying acknowledged that the West did not subscribe to the Chinese worldview. And although Qiying and his cohorts may have considered the behavior of Western gunboats and merchants to be barbaric, they could not ignore the effects of Western aggression and military might. By personally addressing Western officials, Qiying implicitly expressed awareness that direct communications with the foreigners would aid the management of foreign affairs. He hoped that through his actions Westerners could be individually "soothed," friction avoided, and problems with the West solved on a large scale.

However, direct contact with foreign officials by Qing high officials ran counter to the accepted Chinese practice. The *Book of Rites* states "The minister of a prince had no intercourse outside his own state, thereby showing how he did not dare to serve two rulers."[19] In other words, a Chinese official who invited direct contact with representatives of a Western sovereign, especially one who did not accept subservient status to the Chinese emperor, would be acknowledging that foreign leader's legitimacy. Only those officials specially designated by the emperor to handle affairs with non-Sinicized peoples could do so without challenging existing practice. Even in the case of the imperial commissioner in Canton, intermediaries were to relay contact between the Western officials and the imperial commissioner in order to avoid the potential contradiction. Thus, high officials appointed by the Court were to have only indirect contact with Western representatives. By ordering one official in Canton to be solely responsible for Western trade affairs, the Court effectively insulated most Qing officials and all Western officials from the central Qing governmental structure. Western businessmen and government officials alike found the arrangement problematic; for matters involving policy or political relations, they were confined to dealing exclusively with the specially assigned imperial commissioner in Canton (but could not consult him in person) and were not allowed direct access to the throne in distant Beijing, despite the equality granted in the Treaties. Thus, even with Lin's military failure and Qiying's relatively high position within the power structure, Qiying received criticism from both sides for his conciliatory approach.[20]

In 1844, the office of governor-general of Guangdong and Guangxi (based in Canton) assumed responsibility for foreign relations when the emperor bestowed on the position the concurrent title of imperial commissioner with the responsibility of handling Western trade affairs. With the order, the Canton commissioner became the official channel of diplomacy between the Qing Court and the West until the 1858 reappointment of Qiying to the post of imperial commissioner. From the perspective of the Court, Canton's distance from the capital functioned as an advantage in that it assured foreigners would be handled far away from the seat of central power. The distance also had the inadvertent effect of stationing those officials who had the most contact and knowledge of foreigners far from the opportunity to exert personal influence at imperial audiences in Beijing. With the barrier of distance and prevalence of prowar attitudes toward the West at Court, selective reporting on the part of the imperial commissioner to the throne was certainly possible and even probable at times. Aware of the fact that the throne depended on the imperial commissioner for information on which to base decisions and concerned about selective reporting, Westerners disparaged the Canton commissioner system as unworkable.[21]

This distance to Court for an imperial commissioner, however great physically, was not as great as it appeared to be to contemporary Westerners. True, an imperial commissioner in Canton did not have the regular opportunity to convey opinions personally at Court, but he did have direct access to the emperor through his appointment as imperial commissioner and frequent submission of memorials. The emperor thereby directly received information regarding foreigners, eliminating the need to rely on information filtered up through regular bureaucratic channels. This practice, combined with the high rank of the imperial commissioners, arguably meant that the emperor received more, not less, direct and reliable information on dealings with the West.[22] In fact, once negotiations moved to North China and the imperial commissioners consistently belonged to truly influential categories (hereditary and imperial princes) in the decision-making scheme, one can convincingly argue that imperial commissioners brought foreign relations closer to the Court. And as most imperial commissioners belonged to the imperial clan, they were direct representatives of the interests of the Manchu Court.

The linked issues of the actual standing of the imperial commissioners vis-à-vis the emperor and Western access to the imperial commissioners are key to understanding foreign relations between the West and China, both at this time and during that of the later Zongli Yamen. Since the pre–Zongli Yamen Qing Court only communicated with Western consuls through the medium of the imperial commissioners, those who held this title, with their powers as Commissioners and their positions within the bureaucracy, became extremely important in diplomatic relations. Because in the estimation of Westerners (and this was true) the imperial commissioners did not have final decision-making powers in negotiations, they did not represent the person of the sovereign, like their Western counterparts who were invested with the title of plenipotentiary.[23] The imbalance resulted in indirect negotiations, with the imperial commissioner repeatedly communicating with the emperor before decisions were made. In contrast, Western plenipotentiaries could negotiate and settle matters in the name of the sovereign.[24]

In Western eyes, the two types of officials did not have equal standing. Despite the many edicts from 1842 on instructing commissioners to "act as the circumstances require,"[25] the commissioners for the most part relayed information to the emperor, who retained decision-making powers. This was partly due to the tenuous nature of the appointment of an imperial commissioner and partly due to the general power structure of the Qing system. As for the former, the emperor granted the title on a temporary basis and withdrew it upon completion of the specified mission. Bearers of the title were imperial appointees and therefore subject to dismissal should the emperor not be pleased.[26] In addition, the bearer's lack of an official seal only highlighted the temporary nature of the position and put the bearer at a disadvantage in relation to his Western counterparts. Since the seal would have been the Qing imperial commissioner's equivalent of the Western plenipotentiary's signature, its absence proved conspicuous; without it, no treaty could be signed by the imperial commissioner and be considered final and binding—pending the approval of the sovereign as a formality rather than out of necessity. Moreover, no decisions could be made at the negotiation site and then be presented to the sovereign for acceptance as in the British system.[27] Furthermore, the imperial commissioner had complete responsibility for the outcome of the specified project, but no real instructions from the emperor as to how to proceed. In negotiations, he had only the power to exercise the will of the emperor within the limits of his commission; this entailed a constant flow of memorials to and from the emperor for verification.[28] In effect, the imperial commissioner possessed full power to negotiate any result that the emperor would eye as advantageous.

It was over the issue of direct access to the seat of Qing power that the British turned the Arrow Incident of 1856 into a pretext for treaty revisions.[29] Lord Elgin, the British plenipotentiary, believed that Britain could not maintain peaceful relations with China if foreign relations were delegated to the provincial governments.[30] And it was over the issue of the limited powers of Imperial Commissioners Guiliang and Hengfu, the governor-general of Zhili, appointed to negotiate at Tianjin in August 1860, that those negotiations broke down, and the British and French armies marched on Beijing.[31]

The Qing system placed limits on the imperial commissioners largely because, in theory, all legitimate power resided in the person of the emperor. Thus, only the emperor could approve negotiation results. Nonetheless, hampered by an environment of military weakness, the commissioners might accept treaty terms that the emperor would ultimately reject. The repetition of this scenario frustrated

Western diplomats and contributed to their demand for either the appointment of a plenipotentiary in the Western sense or direct access to the Qing Court and the emperor. Although it is true that the restrictions placed on the functioning of the imperial commissioners hampered their functioning to a degree, overall, those assigned to the post of imperial commissioner enjoyed significant leeway in negotiations. The limitations, though real and recognized by imperial commissioners themselves, did not negate the potential for flexibility inherent in the position.

Despite the broadening of the responsibilities of imperial commissioners and despite Chinese assertions that their powers were equivalent to those of foreign plentipotentiaries, the extent to which these officials differed from their Western counterparts became even more evident when the Chinese themselves asserted it. In 1858, Lord Elgin refused to accept the appointment of Tan Tingxiang, the governor-general of Zhili,[32] as imperial commissioner to negotiate in Tianjin because he lacked full powers like those given to Qiying in 1842. Tan wrote to Elgin insisting that China did not have the equivalent title of plenipotentiary now or in 1842. Rather, Qiying and Yilibu, the two imperial commissioners negotiating in 1842, had submitted their work to the throne as they deemed necessary and the occasion required, without independent authority.[33] Tan quite clearly recognized the difference between the two types of officials. He also knew that within the Chinese context, the imperial commissioner was the closest equivalent of the Western plenipotentiary.

Sixteen years after Qiying's first appointment to the post, however, the imperial commissioners were granted, with qualifications, the negotiating power that allowed them to enter meaningful negotiations with their Western counterparts. In a June 1858 edict, the Xianfeng emperor granted "full powers" to Guiliang and Huashana[34] after the Western forces were so bold as to occupy Dagu near Tianjin and threaten Beijing:

> ... As affairs have not been managed well, I have specially despatched Guiliang and Huashana to proceed to Tianjin for discussions and negotiations. From the communications of the various countries, we see that [the various countries] still regard Guiliang and Huashana's power to make decisions independently as doubtful. Let Guiliang and Huashana clearly enlighten and guide them in this. If the matter is reasonable and if [the West] truly desires a cessation of hostilities, then they can grant all that is not injurious to China and it will be approved; you need not worry further regarding this. As Guiliang [and Huashana] were chosen by Me, they must carefully act in accordance with national institutions. They must silently examine the true intent of others. Except for those articles, which are not in accord with propriety, they ought to act suitably according to the situation. Let them follow their judgment in managing. Be diligent about this![35]

With the emperor's inclusion of so many caveats for the commissioners' complete power, Guiliang and Huashana had little real chance of meeting the demands of the militarily superior and aggressive Western powers and/or of conceding "nothing injurious to China." Even without such limitations on the commissioners' authority, subsequent Chinese attempts to nullify certain clauses accepted by Guiliang and Huashana—followed by complete abrogation of the treaty—demonstrated to Britain's Lord Elgin the limited power of the two commissioners. Thus, in 1860 Lord Elgin again felt the need to raise the issue of full powers. He received a response from the Xianfeng emperor that stated the two offices of plenipotentiary and imperial commissioner were equivalent in fact, differing only in name. The emperor admonished Elgin to remember that negotiations were to explore mutually acceptable solutions, not one-way compliance with Great Britain's demands. By distinguishing clearly between what was possible and what was impossible, imperial commissioners exercised full powers in the name of the emperor.[36] Again the ambiguity of the definition belied a basic disparity between the two types of officials. In the Chinese case, the emperor as monarch passed final judgment on what exactly could be yielded and retained. Nonetheless, the powers of the imperial commissioners had increased over the course of the negotiations with the West.

Perhaps the closest the Xianfeng emperor came to issuing full powers in the Western sense was two years earlier in June 1858. At that time he recalled Qiying to negotiate once again with the West. In appointing him imperial commissioner, the Xianfeng emperor granted him relatively broad powers:

> Once Qiying has arrived in Tianjin, he can decide himself when to meet with the foreigners. As Qiying knows the officials who negotiated the original Treaty [of Nanjing], he will be imperial commissioner together with Guiliang and Huashana. They are all to use the seal that has been issued. In acting as the situation demands, Qiying does not need to consult with Guiliang and his colleague. Rather he can at once personally guide the foreigners. He may add new concessions to those already granted if necessary, but he should think of a way to prevent the demands concerning the opening of the Yangzi to trade and travel in the interior. He must avoid a rupture in the negotiations ... The situation is dangerous; we cannot but conduct our negotiations as the situation demands, but if the previously mentioned demands [e.g., trade on the Yangzi and travel in the interior] are decided on, it will be difficult to approve [the treaty] ... Qiying should know what matters can be granted and what matters can not be granted. He necessarily will have control of the situation; I for my part will not control him from afar.[37]

The edict represents the investiture of far more extensive powers than those granted Guiliang and Huashana earlier the same month. The emperor obviously had great faith in Qiying, as demonstrated by the liberty he permitted Qiying to grant further concessions and in issuing him a seal. Notably, the emperor retained the right of ultimate approval as indicated by his stipulations regarding travel in the interior and trade on the Yangzi. Even so, the above edict was the closest the Xianfeng emperor had come to granting full powers to one of his imperial commissioners. Only once when the situation became even more urgent and the imperial princes took over negotiations did the emperor extend his powers further. Unfortunately for the emperor and Qiying, in 1857 the British had captured the person and archives of Governor Ye Mingchen during their occupation of Canton and recovered files containing memorials in which Qiying explained his conciliatory policy of "soothing the barbarians." The British found the policy and the wording offensive. Consequently, the British refused to work with Qiying. Qiying was recalled in disgrace, and his newly acquired powers as imperial commissioner were for naught.[38]

Nonetheless, the power of imperial commissioners had been extended, and Guiliang and Huashana managed to negotiate the Treaty of Tianjin. Despite the powers granted to the imperial commissioners, the emperor and the Court were displeased with the treaty terms. Consequently, before the treaty ratification scheduled to occur in Beijing the following year, the Court hoped to eliminate the articles that gave Westerners rights to legations in the capital as well as three other articles it found particularly damaging: foreign travel in China's interior, the opening of the Yangzi River to trade, and an indemnity for military expenses and the occupation of Canton until it was paid in full.[39] Ideally, the disapproved articles would be excised and the treaty would be ratified without Western travel to Beijing.

In an effort to eliminate the necessity of Western forces returning north in 1859 for treaty ratification, the Court adopted a plan in December 1858 to make Shanghai, already the center of foreign interests, the center of foreign relations and, thus, the place for the upcoming treaty ratification.[40] In order to prepare, the Xianfeng emperor appointed He Guiqing as imperial commissioner in charge of "Managing the Affairs for the Various Nations" (*banli geguo shiwu*) and transferred the responsibilities of the Canton imperial commissioner from Canton to Shanghai, thereby establishing Shanghai as the official site for diplomacy.

He Guiqing, already serving as the governor-general of Jiangnan and Jiangxi, was to be imperial commissioner concurrently. However, He's double duties made it difficult for operations to proceed smoothly. Sir Frederick Bruce of England commented to his compatriot Lord John Russell that He's duties as governor-general were centered in Nanjing, while his residence for his Shanghai duties was in Changzhou, 130 miles from Shanghai. Not only was the physical distance problematic for speedy resolution of diplomatic issues, but He's duties as governor-general could always be used as an excuse not to meet with foreign ministers whenever he wanted to avoid an issue.[41] Bruce was not alone in his concern over the double responsibilities. Commissioner He himself believed the governor-general should not serve as the imperial commissioner; rather, he thought, a high official from Beijing should be appointed to the position full-time.[42] Thus both sides viewed the arrangement as inadequate, owing to the importance of the responsibilities.

The inadequacy of the situation led to a quick escalation in the development of the post of imperial commissioner.[43] In 1860, following their defeat the previous year at Dagu, the Allied French and British forces went north to ratify the Treaty of Tianjin in Beijing. At first Guiliang and Hengfu were sent to Tianjin to negotiate. Lord Elgin, however, detected "control from afar" and moved on to Tongzhou. Before learning of the break in Tianjin, the emperor appointed Prince Yi (Yi Qinwang, Zaiyuan)[44] and Grand Councilor Muyin[45] on September 10, 1860, to intercept the British minister Harry Parkes in Tongzhou. Parkes was reportedly on his way to the capital to make sure all was in order for Elgin's subsequent arrival. Prince Yi and Muyin were to prevent Parkes from going to the capital and were to send him back to Tianjin.[46] When it became clear that Elgin would be arriving in Tongzhou as well, Prince Yi's role changed: he became the first imperial prince to become involved directly in negotiations with the West. Prince Yi's rank as an imperial prince of the first degree granted him a more secure position vis-à-vis the Court than previous negotiators, and his personal closeness to the emperor allowed him more leeway in making decisions. On September 14 and 17, Prince Yi and Muyin reached agreements with the British and French, respectively. While they acceded to most of the Allies' demands, including the exchange of ratification in Beijing, and brought nego-tiations to the verge of peace, the imperial commissioners remained adamant on one point: the emperor would grant no audiences to Western officials. British insistence on delivering a letter from the Queen in person finally led to a stalemate, the arrest of Parkes, and yet another rupture in negotiations. Elgin proceeded to advance with his troops—this time to Beijing itself. Imperial acceptance of all but the audience concession was noteworthy. While the negotiations ultimately resulted in crisis, the princely status of the main negotia-tor had lent legitimacy to the need for further concessions and gar-nered the necessary support from the emperor.

Beijing Negotiations: Closer to the Throne

In June of 1858, the Xianfeng emperor had assembled a group of three imperial princes and two grand councilors to form an informal and ad hoc Bureau of Defense (*xunfang ju*). This was a temporary grouping to advise the emperor during the first Allied advance on Tianjin. According to Banno Masataka, even after the immediate crisis had passed, the three appointed princes—Hui (Hui Qinwang, Mianyu), Yi, and Zheng (Zheng Qinwang, Duanhua)—continued to serve in a special advisory capacity to the emperor. This group of close advisors expanded to include the Princes Gong and Dun (Dun Qinwang, Yizong). Consistent with the deliberative aspect of the Manchu Qing government, they could be summoned *in toto* or in subgroups. Their personal status as imperial princes assured them of proximity to the throne. Their role as extra-bureaucratic advisors in addition to their princely status extended to them even greater power in the form of access to the emperor. This group was ad hoc and informal in nature but comprised what is referred to as the Council of Princes, since the emperor regularly consulted them as a group.[47] The involvement of high-level princes in consultations on foreign affairs is decidedly significant, for it was through such a process that high-level consensus could be created. Princely consultation, however, was not new; the practice had roots in Manchu tradition. In fact, the Yongzheng emperor (r. 1723–1735) had earlier in the dynasty tried to escape the preponderance of influence of such deliberative bodies when he searched for mechanisms for administering imperial requirements. Eventually, the Grand Council was created after a series of experiments with techniques for consolidating the emperor's rule and the emperor's subsequent decision to rely on a team of favorite close advisors for the ministerial administration of military and other important and urgent affairs.[48]

With the joint forces of the British and French (unofficially accompanied by the Americans) moving on the capital and the resultant flight of the Xianfeng emperor to the imperial Summer Palace at Rehe, a perceptible change in orientation occurred in the Court—peace became an urgent necessity and appropriate officials were needed to arrange it. But who could meet the challenge? On September 21, 1860, the Xianfeng emperor appealed to his younger half-brother Prince Gong to take over negotiations; the emperor acknowledged that "peace is now difficult to make" and told his half-brother "to communicate with the foreigners in your own name" but to try to avoid face-to-face encounters with them, and instead send subordinates Heng Qi and Lan Weiwen, if necessary. Simultaneously, Prince Yi and Muyin were relieved of their diplomatic duties.[49] According to the phrasing of the edict, Prince Gong's powers were comparable to those granted previous negotiators; likewise, his power to act in his own name was circumscribed by the temporary nature of his authority; nonetheless, the edict reflects increased standing and powers for the title of imperial commissioner by virtue of the prince's close relationship to the emperor and recognition of the urgency of the negotiations.

The extremity of the circumstances and the emperor and Court's sojourn in Rehe, distant from the capital, necessitated increased discretionary powers for the imperial commissioners; only a negotiator with close blood ties to the emperor carried the authority and legitimacy to make palatable the decisions resulting from the increased discretionary powers. For this reason as well as the extent of the emergency, the emperor accepted Prince Gong's October 24, 1860, report in which he informed the emperor that he had met personally with British officials following the Chinese surrender of Anding Gate (*Anding men*) and the British burning of the Summer Palace. More significantly, Prince Gong acquired the power, a first for an imperial commissioner, to appoint lower officials (*weishu zhushi*), albeit temporarily, with Prince Gong initially making the appointments and the emperor later giving imperial sanction to the selections. Subsequent memorials made clear that the emperor also appointed two high ranking Manchu Bannermen, Guiliang, a leading peace advocate and a grand councilor, and Wenxiang, a grand secretary, probably sympathetic to war advocates, as imperial commissioners to assist Prince Gong.[50]

Who was Prince Gong, and why was he chosen for this formidable task? Like Prince Yi, he was an imperial prince of the first rank and an advisor to the emperor. The two princes shared equally high imperial rank and access to the Xianfeng emperor; clearly, neither of these two factors gave Prince Gong the advantage over Prince Yi; nor could they account for the replacement of Prince Yi by Prince Gong. Moreover, Prince Yi had nearly succeeded in achieving peace; he did not lack negotiation skills. However, Prince Gong possessed a distinguishing characteristic that made him more appropriate than Prince Yi: his relative position within the Council of Princes.

Two different approaches toward the West had emerged within the Council of Princes, the supporters of each vying for influence over the Emperor. Since the first defeat of Qing forces in Canton in 1842, a struggle had been occurring within the Court between advocates of peace and advocates of war, forming what is loosely termed here as the war and peace parties. War partisans promoted a conservative root and branch extermination policy of the British problem, as exemplified by Lin Zexu; peace advocates believed in managing the British through negotiations, as demonstrated by the pragmatic flexible approach of Qiying.[51] Both sides focused on the same dilemma, namely, deterrence of the increasing threats from the provocative Westerners. According to Banno, of the five princes of the Council, Yi and Zheng were vehemently antiforeign and anxious to expel the barbarians. Prince Dun's views were difficult to ascertain. Prince Hui seemed to have originally acted as a mediator between the two groups and adopted a conciliatory approach when circumstances so dictated.[52] As late as June 6, 1858, when Guiliang, Huashana, and Qiying had already been dispatched to Tianjin for negotiations, Prince Gong presented a memorial to the throne urging resolution through war. Only in late 1858, once the reality of Western aggression arrived in the north, did Prince Gong adopt a stance advocating peace through negotiation.[53] His selection reflected the relative influence of the two groups and the emperor's own change in orientation toward a peaceful settlement.

When Western forces occupied Beijing and then burned the Summer Palace on October 18, 1860, a quick peace settlement, regardless of policy orientation, became the top priority. Prince Gong, Guiliang, and Wenxiang, by decree of the emperor, shouldered the responsibility of saving the Qing Empire from destruction at the hands of the joint Western forces. War advocates, although cognizant of the extremity of the situation, still harbored hope for future victory through war. Prince Gong, for his part, had become a firm proponent of establishing and maintaining peaceful relations. Even in such dire circumstances with peace clearly necessary for survival, the two leading peace advocates among the three negotiators took care not to appear too conciliatory. In fact, the tone of the memorials sent to the emperor at Rehe vacillated between being hawkish and dovish. Although obvious that peace could not wait if the dynasty were to survive the occupation of the capital, the commissioners waited for a consensus on the necessity of accepting Western terms to emerge before they agreed to them. Once they had the backing of the Court,

Prince Gong signed the Conventions of Beijing, which confirmed and broadened the Treaty of Tianjin, on October 24 and 25, 1860.[54]

After the Conventions of Beijing were signed, the emperor remained in Rehe, and the three imperial commissioners remained in charge of foreign affairs in their extra-bureaucratic capacity. Although some scholars have referred to the existence of an "office for the management of peacekeeping" (*fuju*) or the "office for soothing the barbarians" (*fu yi ju*), for this period between the signing of the Conventions of Beijing and the establishment of the Zongli Yamen, no such office existed. According to Wu Fuhuan, the term *fuju* was used to describe the function of the three commissioners rather than a specific office.[55]

The maintenance of the position of the three imperial commissioners, in other words, remained tenuous and solely at the emperor's discretion. However, the increased reliance on the discretion of Prince Gong and a small group of highly placed ministers for handling affairs, especially those related to military campaigns, had the potential for much more, as demonstrated by the precedent of the development of the Grand Council. Beatrice Bartlett's account of the Grand Council's period of origin—for she convincingly shows that it emerged slowly and was not simply created at one stroke—powerfully illustrates the inherent flexibility in Qing practices. The Yongzheng emperor's reliance on a small group of highly placed and highly trusted ministers slowly became institutionalized into the most powerful integrative body of the Qing dynasty.[56] In all likelihood, the existence and importance of this precedent was not lost on the Xianfeng emperor and his Court.

Changing the Constitution: The January Memorial and Its Aftermath

With the signing of the Conventions of Beijing in 1860, peace had been restored, but the war advocates had not been placated, and Prince Gong and his colleagues found themselves in a difficult position. Maintaining the peace required a strategy to consolidate it as official policy. The three imperial commissioners, having witnessed the strength and destructive capabilities of the Western Powers, recognized the need for a new central institution to promote and maintain a policy advocating peaceful relations with the West. The organization would have to be highly placed within the Qing institutional hierarchy to ensure its standing vis-à-vis the Court and the bureaucracy. Formalizing and expanding the temporary committee that had conducted the negotiations could create such a body. In the Qing system high provincial officials and advisors had the prerogative to make proposals to the emperor and thereby to share in the formation of policies and power.[57] To this end, the Xianfeng emperor received a memorial and memorandum on January 13, 1861, from the three imperial commissioners advocating a sharp departure in the conduct of foreign relations.[58]

To begin with, Prince Gong, Guiliang, and Wenxiang proposed a new foreign policy direction, which China would follow for the next decade. They proposed that the Court "operate according to the treaties and not allow the foreigners to infringe upon them or exceed them even slightly. If on the outside we are trustworthy and friendly while secretly employing the 'loose rein,' then in a few years, although there may occasionally be foreign demands, the foreigners will not be able to do us sudden harm."[59] This brief policy statement seemingly incorporated old and new stages of Chinese foreign relations. The "soothe and control" method practiced by Qiying, whereby the foreigners were to be unwittingly guided by hidden Chinese motives, can certainly be detected. But for the first time, the old concept appeared in conjunction with fulfillment of treaty obligations. In fact, the latter now took precedence over the former. The emperor's previous practice of disregarding signed treaties was to end. Instead, the Qing government would strictly and meticulously enforce treaties in order to regain some control over the empire's fate and manage the Westerners by Western standards. In this way, the Qing Court could alter the orientation of the treaties to express the limitation of, not the minimum of, foreign rights in China.[60]

As is implied in the term "unequal treaties," the Western demand for equal treatment in the Chinese order had not been reciprocated by the Western countries in the terms imposed on China. Instead, the treaties served as a tool for gaining commercial rights in an age of Western commercial expansion. The infringements on China's sovereignty written into the treaties relegated China to an inferior status within the community of nations that the West insisted China join. With limited choices, Prince Gong hoped that strict adherence to the treaties would lead to a positive working relationship with the West. By "demonstrating trustworthiness" he hoped China could "gain their confidence" and "then, even in matters not included in the treaties, they will not act treacherously."[61] Thus despite the fact that China's traditional concept of "control" had not been officially replaced by the Western concept of equal sovereign states, the Western framework gained primacy and became operative. We can even hypothesize that Prince Gong's inclusion of tributary rhetoric was meant to placate the war advocates by making the inevitable more palatable—part of the consensus-building process crucial to major policy changes in the Qing.

The acceptance of the Conventions of Beijing brought with it the reality of foreign legations in Beijing the following spring. The opposition to foreign ministers residing in Beijing had been stiff because of the perceived threat to dynastic prestige and the Chinese world order.[62] Prince Gong managed to delay the most injurious part of the problem by acquiring written assurance from the British and French ministers that they would not insist on an audience until the Xianfeng emperor was well enough to return to Beijing. The emperor never returned, dying in Rehe on August 17, 1861. With the ascension of the child Tongzhi emperor, Prince Gong again received assurances from the foreign envoy that requests for imperial audiences would wait until the boy reached the age of majority. Upn the death of the Xianfeng emperor, the split between the war and peace parties reemerged. The Tongzhi emperor's regents, named by his father, favored a hard line toward the West, leading Prince Gong and the Empress Dowagers to stage a successful coup d'état against them.

Two of the regents, Princes Yi and Zheng, who were also members of the Council of Princes, were ordered to commit suicide. Prince Gong and the peace party prevailed. Among the charges against the collaborators was obstruction of foreign affairs and negotiations—a clear indication that the new foreign policy direction had been firmly adopted.[63]

Accommodating official interactions that would accompany legations required a new arrangement. The appointment of another imperial commissioner in Shanghai or any provincial official as liaison for foreign diplomats did not meet treaty requirements. Article V of the Treaty of Tianjin with the British required that a grand secretary or president of a Board be appointed as the official to handle foreign affairs; the Russian Treaty stipulated that a senior member of the Grand Council or a senior grand secretary handle Russian affairs. Both treaties stipulated high-level *central* government management of foreign relations. Significantly, however, neither required the establishment of a separate foreign office.

The prompt withdrawal of troops from Beijing and Tianjin (except those foreign troops remaining in Tianjin as stipulated by the treaty as a guarantee against indemnity payment) encouraged some Chinese officials to conclude that the foreigners had no territorial designs on the Chinese land or people. In addition, the withdrawal encouraged the nascent belief that because the Western Powers stressed reason and reliance on international law, they could be trusted and treated with sincerity and respect; or at the very least, China need not wage war against them.[64] Some scholars, like Feng Guifen, believed that in an atmosphere of peace and respect China could learn the strengths of Western science.[65] Only then could the Court entertain the possibility of working with the West in purging the land of the currently raging Nian and Taiping rebellions.

Prince Gong and his colleagues reflected the growing perception for a need to institutionalize the new foreign affairs policy when they drafted a six-article memorandum and attached it to the January 13 memorial; as the next chapter shows the articles would alter the structure of the bureaucracy by creating a foreign office to manage the new demands of the late nineteenth century.[66] Taken together, the articles aimed to provide the mechanism to implement the new policy direction, solidify the powers of the imperial commissioners, and establish an institution that would redistribute power at the highest institutional levels in order to accommodate the conduct of foreign relations at the central government level. Because of the importance and implications of the matter, the emperor submitted the articles to a deliberative council, including the Council of Princes, for comments and a demonstration of support before proceeding.

Of the imperial princes, only Prince Gong had been ordered to remain in Beijing and not flee to Rehe with the emperor. Likewise, Wenxiang was the sole grand councilor left in the capital and Guiliang the only grand secretary. A few other lesser, though still high-ranking officials, mainly Manchus, remained to assist them. The situation presented Prince Gong with both obstacles and opportunities; he was the emperor's representative in relations with the Western countries, but because he was in Beijing, he did not have immediate and physical access to the Emperor through audiences—thereby potentially diminishing his influence over the emperor.[67]

To overcome the problems of physical distance and opposing views, Prince Gong employed a number of methods to retain and garner further influence at Court. First, his status of imperial commissioner gave him substantial leverage, as he was charged with the duty of saving the Qing Empire from destruction. Second, he maneuvered to gather imperial support by sending the emperor a memorial requesting honors for those officials under Prince Gong's charge who had been involved in the peace process. On December 17 and 24, in two edicts, the Xianfeng emperor acceded and bestowed honors on fifty-five people.[68] The Prince had managed to acquire imperial sanction and honors for his controversial negotiations; by doing so, he simultaneously bolstered and legitimated his position vis-à-vis the Court.

Prince Gong also relied on the continued presence of the remaining Allied troops in Tianjin to further pressure the war advocates and the emperor into accepting his arrangements for peace. He further manipulated the emperor's fear of the Allied troops by linking troop removal with the establishment of the Zongli Yamen, and in a supplementary memorial to his original Yamen proposal, he reported that he had determined from Thomas Wade that British expenses in Tianjin were burdensome and that British troops would, therefore, like to withdraw.[69] He continued:

> They suspect that after they [the Western troops] are removed, China will have other preparations [for war], and consequently they do not dare withdraw. He [Wade] had come to Beijing to glean information. When we saw him he had not yet clearly elucidated this ... In order to dispense with his doubts, I divulged to him that we planned to establish a general office for foreign affairs that would be solely responsible for managing foreign affairs. When Wade heard this, he was extremely pleased. He had considered the previous Canton system ineffective. He found handling foreign affairs in Shanghai ineffective as well. Thus the Westerners believed they had had no alternative but to come to Beijing. By establishing an office for foreign affairs, we would be fulfilling a long unmet demand.[70]

By divulging plans to establish the Zongli Yamen, Prince Gong increased the pressure to approve it—especially since Wade had responded so favorably. The emperor's desire for foreign troops to withdraw from Beijing sooner rather than later provided further impetus to formalize the machinery of the peace policy. The prestige from the honors and pressure from foreign troops aided the cause of the peacemakers by fostering consensus and an environment conducive to new approaches, but they did not in themselves create mechanisms for the continuance of the policy of peace. That awaited the emperor's decision on if and how the new Foreign Office would be established.

Views of Change

Qing efforts to handle the situations created by the early treaties demonstrated an effort on the part of the Qing Court to meet the contingencies of the time. Because the Qing Court and bureaucracy did not consider it imperative to enter the system of international relations as defined by Westerners of the nineteenth century, Westerners viewed the Qing as lacking sincerity and lagging in effort. The fact that issues that concerned Sir Henry Pottinger during negotiations with Qiying continued to head many Western diplomats' agendas for the next twenty years, through the time of Prince Gong and beyond, contributed to the belief that the Qing Court did not share interest in solving diplomatic problems and, consequentially, the lasting Western view that Qing actions were not fundamentally oriented toward change. When Western forces occupied Beijing, Prince Gong and his colleagues built on the imperial commissioner tradition already in use to strengthen the Chinese position by establishing the Zongli Yamen, representing a major institutional departure.

Imperial commissioners, then, who had long held an extra-bureaucratic place within the Qing system, played a critical, yet previously unrecognized, role in the creation of the Zongli Yamen. First, the nature of an imperial commissioner's appointment allowed for direct access to the emperor and the right to bypass the regular administrative hierarchy. As time passed, the increasing closeness to the emperor of the men appointed to the role in terms of their blood, rank, and counsel allowed for the increased influence of the imperial commissioners over the emperor. Second, the nature of the successive appointments of the imperial commissioners to handle foreign affairs indicated a growing concern with foreign affairs and ultimately a growing recognition among the commissioners for a substantive change in the handling of foreign affairs. Third, the use of imperial commissioners mirrored in significant ways the process used during the last previous major institutional overhaul of the Qing dynasty—that of the Grand Council.

The dispatching of imperial commissioners and the increasing discretion granted them by the throne reflected the Qing Court's growing apprehension over the deteriorating situation with the West. In fact, the assignment of imperial princes to handle negotiations and the ultimate creation of an organ devoted to foreign affairs headed by an imperial prince clearly demonstrated the concern of the Qing Court. Moreover, the process reflected the evolution of a consciousness on the part of the Qing government for significant measures and reform. Just as important, the evolution in the appointments of the imperial commissioners and the establishment of the Zongli Yamen were manifestations of the ability to reform the Qing administrative structure. The successive crises of Western military threats and an occupied capital rallied the inherent flexibility of the Qing system. The serious efforts on the part of the high ministers who worked to alter the Qing bureaucratic structure to accommodate new demands and needs reflected an atmosphere conducive to substantive change that built up to and surrounded the creation of the Zongli Yamen. With the discussion of the establishment of the office, new possibilities opened for Qing administration. The resolution of debates on the structure of the Yamen reveals divisions within the Court and the strength of those who opposed the Yamen as anything more than a temporary answer. However, the development of the Zongli Yamen over time reflects a path of institutional development that had only been seen before in the growth of the Grand Council. Just as the Grand Council, over the course of its evolution, acquired power through its supervision of communication flow and the various concerns of the Court, so too did the Zongli Yamen, over the course of the decade following its establishment, cement its position as an integrative governmental body by forging links throughout the bureaucracy in order to channel matters concerning foreign affairs its way.

NOTES

1. Prince Gong Yixin was the sixth son of the Daoguang emperor and the brother of the Xianfeng emperor (the Daoguang emperor's fourth son). By the time he began negotiating with Western officials, Prince Gong had already served as a grand councilor and lieutenant-general of a Banner. Prince Gong was married to Guiliang's daughter. For Prince Gong's biography, see Arthur W. Hummel, ed., *Eminent Chinese of the Ch'ing Period, 1644–1911*, 2 vols. (Washington, DC: U.S. Government Printing Office, 1943–1944), vol. 1, 380–84, and *QSG* [Draft history of the Qing dynasty—hereafter cited as *QSG*], 9105–57. Wenxiang's family belonged to the Manchu Plain Red Banner. In 1845, be became a *jinshi* degree holder. After a series of posts in both the provinces and the capital, Wenxiang was appointed in 1858 junior vice-president of the Board of Rites and concurrently a grand councilor. For more on Wenxiang, see Hummel, vol. 2, 853–55, and *QSG*, *juan* 386, *liezhuan* 173, pp. 11, 687–88. Guiliang, also a Manchu, was a member of the Plain Red Banner. Among his provincial posts were terms as governor-general of Hubei and Hunan (Hu Guang) and governor-general of Fujian and Zhejiang (Min Zhe), and then of Yunnan and Guizhou. He also served as governor-general of Zhili from 1853 until 1857. In 1857, he was promoted to be a grand secretary. For more on Guiliang, see Hummel, vol. 1, 428–30, and *QSG*, *juan* 388, *liezhuan* 175, pp. 11, 707–78.

2. Metzger discusses the use of specially appointed commissioners as a means of accommodating reform in imperial China. He views substitution of personnel as one indication of the normative flexibility of the imperial order. See Metzger, *The Internal Organization*, 53–59.

3. See H.S. Brunnert and V.V. Hagelstrom. *Present Day Political Organization of China*, A. Beltchenko and E.E. Moran, trans. (Shanghai: Kelly and Walsh, 1912; reprinted by Ch'eng Wen, Taipei, 1978), nos. 330 and 984.

4. Exactly how long is debatable. John King Fairbank, in his many works that mention the tribute system, dates the system to the Zhou dynasty. Fairbank wrote frequently of the tribute system and its influence and continuity from the Zhou to the Qing. For some examples, see Fairbank, "China's World Order: The Tradition of Chinese Foreign Relations," *Encounter* (December 1966): 14–20; and Fairbank and Teng's, "On the Qing Tributary System," *Harvard Journal of Asiatic Studies* 6 (1941): 135–246; and Fairbank's *Trade and Diplomacy on the China Coast* or *The United States and China*. Fairbank's many works display what has been, until recently, the

accepted wisdom on the tribute system, with some scholars adding modification to the dating and implementation. Morris Rossabi dates the origins of the tribute system to the Han, but shows that China was one "among equals" during the Song period (960–1279) in its dealings with its neighbors. See Morris Rossabi, *China and Inner Asia: From 1368 to the Present Day* (New York: Pica Books, 1975). John Wills places the tribute system's actual implementation in the Ming—and confined to the Ming. See John Wills, "Tribute, Defensiveness, and Dependency: Uses and Limits of Some Basic Ideas about Mid-Ch'ing Foreign Relations," *American Neptune* 48, no. 4 (Fall 1988): 225–29. These works acknowledge the existence of a tribute system worldview, but differ on when it actually dominated the Chinese court.

5. For examples, see John Wills, *Embassies and Illusions: Dutch and Portuguese Envoys to K'ang-hsi, 1666–1687* (Cambridge, MA: Council on East Asian Studies, Harvard University, 1984); and Wills, "Tribute, Defensiveness, and Dependency." During the Song dynasty, despite a tributary framework, the Chinese Court employed language that reflected equal standing in relations with the Jurchen Liao and Khitan Xixia states. See Morris Rossabi, ed., *China Among Equals: The Middle Kingdom and Its Neighbors, 10th to 14th Centuries* (Berkeley: University of California Press, 1983). James A. Anderson has recently taken a look at the uses of the tribute system in an earlier period between the Song Court and the rulers of the Viet peoples, in order to show how tribute was used for multiple purposes, including trade and legitimacy, on both sides of the border. See Anderson, *The Rebel Den of Nùng Trí Cao: Loyalty and Identity along the Sino-Vietnamese Frontier* (Seattle: University of Washington Press, in association with NUS Press, Singapore, 2007).

6. The Manchu Court had two treaties with Russia, the Treaty of Nerchinsk (1689) and the Treaty of Kiakhta (1727); both used language reflecting the two parties were equal sovereign states.

7. See James Hevia, *Cherishing Men From Afar: Qing Guest Ritual and the Macartney Embassy of 1793* (Durham: Duke University Press, 1995), especially 1–20.

8. *Da Qing hui dian, Guangxu* (Collected statutes of the Qing Dynasty, Guangxu edition), hereafter cited as *DQHD*, lists tributary states as Korea, Liuqiu, Annam, Cambodia, Siam, Sulu, and Burma. *Da Qing hui dian, Guangxu huidian* (Taipei: Wen Hai Publishing Co., 1967), Reprint of *Guangxu ji hai* (1899), 39. 1–2. *DQHD, juan* 64–68 covers the Lifan Yuan's responsibilities and regulations for relations with Mongols and other central Asian peoples.

9. Thomas Metzger in *The Internal Organization of the Ch'ing Bureaucracy* maintains that the distinction between Western countries and tribute states

in the 1818 (Jiaqing reign) *Collected Statutes* entry in and of itself gave commercial relations full legal recognition and can be seen as a change in the "unchanging" political order or *tizhi*. See Metzger, *Internal Organization*, 206. Immanuel Hsu, on the other hand, sees the distinction between tributary states and Western countries in the *Collected Statutes* as a way to extend the fiction of the tribute system while avoiding another embarrassing Macartney mission. See Hsu, *China's Entrance*, 10.

10. In 1793 George Lord Macartney, ambassador of Great Britain, traveled to Beijing for an audience with the Qing dynasty's Qianlong emperor at which Macartney famously refused to kotow (*koutou*) to the emperor. Macartney associated performance of the kotow with acknowledgment of the submission of the British monarch to the Qing emperor. Previous to Macartney, seventeen Western missions had taken place, all performing the kotow. Lord Amherst followed the precedent of Lord Macartney in deciding ultimately not to perform the kotow. For the traditional view of the Macartney mission, see Hsu, *China's Entrance*, 1–18. For an account of the Amherst mission, see William Rockhill's "Diplomatic Missions to the Court of China: The Kotow Question II," *The American Historical Review* 2, no. 4 (July 1897): 627–43. For a recent and convincing revisionist view of the Macartney mission that focuses more on the guest ritual aspect of Chinese foreign relations, see James Hevia's *Cherishing Men From Afar*. See also Hevia's "Sovereignty and Subject: Constituting Relations of Power in Qing Guest Ritual," in *Body, Subject and Power in China*, Angela Zito and Tani E. Barlow, eds. (University of Chicago Press, 1994).

11. According to Immanuel Hsu, established practice toward nonsinicized peoples pending their adoption of Chinese ways justified the Canton cohong system. See Hsu, *China's Entrance*, 9–11.

12. *Chou ban yi wu shi mo* [The complete management of foreign affairs] (Taipei: Wen hai chu ban she, 1970–1971), reprint of the 1929–1931 edition published by Beiping gugong bowuyuan (hereafter cited as YWSM-DG for Daoguang reign, YWSM-XF for Xianfeng reign, and YWSM-TZ for Tongzhi reign); YWSM-DG 5.16–17.

13. For more on Lin, see Arthur W. Hummel, *Eminent Chinese of the Ch'ing Period, 1644–1911* (Washington, DC: U.S. Government Printing Office, 1943–1944), vol. 1, 511–14. See also, *QSG, liezhuan* 156, p. 11,489. Frederic Wakeman portrays the experiences of various classes of Cantonese society in terms of relations with Western merchants in the years building up to the Opium War, including Lin's relationship with the cohong merchants, which were not smooth; see Frederic Wakeman, Jr., *Strangers at the Gate: Social*

Disorder in South China, 1839–1861 (Berkeley: University of California Press, 1966), 11–51.

14. As will be demonstrated later in this chapter, this trend reached its apex with the appointment of the emperor's brother (Prince Gong), a grand councilor (Wenxiang), and a grand secretary (Guiliang) to negotiate with the Western states after the British and French armies had invaded Beijing in 1860. These three ministers, representing the highest levels of Qing governmental power, founded the Zongli Yamen.

15. Article II of the Treaty of Nanjing guaranteed the right to establish consuls in the open ports of Canton, Amoy, Fuzhou, Ningbo, and Shanghai. Article V granted the right of free trade in the ports and abolished the Hong merchant monopoly; "Treaty of Nanjing" as reprinted in Tseng-tsai Wang *Tradition and Change*, 220–26. For the Chinese version and each Article's subsequent updates, see *HCCTLC* 467.2.

16. Here, I am using the term "constitutional" as Philip Kuhn has used it to discuss nineteenth-century China in terms of the modern Chinese state; that is to say, as "a set of questions about the legitimate ordering of public life." See Kuhn, "Ideas behind China's Modern State," *Harvard Journal of Asiatic Studies* 55, no. 2 (December 1995): 295–96.

17. Qiying was a member of the Manchu Plain Blue Banner. He was probably a descendant of Murhaci, a brother of Nurhaci, the founder of the Qing dynasty. See Qiying's entry in Hummel, *Eminent Chinese*, vol. 1, 130–32, for a synopsis of his background and career. See also, *QSG, liezhuan* 157, 11,505–6.

18. Quoted from an 1844 memorial from Qiying to the emperor, long after the treaty had been negotiated, as translated in Teng and Fairbank, *China's Response*, 39.

19. See *Li Chi: Book of Rites, An Encyclopedia of Ancient Ceremonial Usages, Religious Creeds, and Social Institutions*, translated by James Legge, edited with introduction and study guide by Ch'u Chai and Winberg Chai (New Hyde Park, NY: University Books, 1967), ch. IX.

20. Sixteen years after Qiying's initial negotiations, mixed feelings at Court toward his approach still haunted him. When the emperor recalled Qiying to diplomatic duty to negotiate in Tianjin in 1858 along with Guiliang and Huashana, Prince Gong among others voiced concern that Qiying would give too much to the foreigners. Chinese princes and ministers viewed Qiying as being too friendly with foreigners. Westerners, on the other hand, saw Qiying as untrustworthy, as they discovered Qiying's conciliatory language a mask for condescension and manipulation. The British negotiators at the

time (Lord Elgin, Horatio Lay, and Thomas Wade) criticized and embarrassed Qiying in the most damning way by producing documents authored by Qiying from the files seized from Ye Mingchen's Canton archives and reading the contents aloud to Qiying, Guiliang, and Huashana. The documents contained language that the British found demeaning and objectionable. Because of the way the Western officials publicly embarrassed Qiying and laid the failure of negotiations at his feet, Qiying was humiliated. Disgraced, Qiying was found guilty in June 1858 by an Imperial Tribunal on which sat Princes Gong, Hui, Yi, Zheng, and Dun (the Council of Princes, see discussion below), and ordered to commit suicide. For an account of Qiying's demise, see Hsu, *China's Entrance*, 38–45.

21. The captured files of Governor-general Ye Mingchen illustrated this point to the British and French. S. Wells Williams points out that misrepresentation on the part of the Canton commissioners was not necessarily intentional, but resulted from the inability of the commissioner to rightly judge circumstances—especially when, as in the case of Ye, the commissioner refused to have any dealings with the Western powers. See Williams, *The Middle Kingdom*, vol. 2, 653. For an account of Ye Mingchen, see J.Y. Wong, *Yeh Ming-ch'en: Viceroy of Liang Kuang 1852–8* (Cambridge: Cambridge University Press, 1976).

22. In "Imperial Powers and the Appointment of Provincial Governors," R. Kent Guy argues that special appointments of governors provided the emperor with a valuable tool to fill the special needs of a particular province, to impose policy directions, and to facilitate communication with the provinces. Special appointments bypassed the method of the emperor choosing from routine lists of qualified officials *(kai lie)* prepared by the Board of Personnel. By specially appointing a governor, the emperor placed a representative of Court interests, if not of the emperor's personal interests, in sensitive provincial posts. Guy's research raises interesting, similar issues for the selection of imperial commissioners. See Guy, "Imperial Powers and the Appointment of Provincial Governors in Ch'ing China, 1700–1900," in Frederick P. Brandauer and Chun-chieh Huang, eds., *Imperial Rulership and Cultural Change in Traditional China* (Seattle: University of Washington Press, 1994), 248–80.

23. Patricia O'Neill's discussion of Qing relations with England and the Netherlands indicates that the origins of Western plenipotentiaries and ambassadors were perhaps similar to the development of imperial commissioners. See Patricia O'Neill, "Missed Opportunities: Late Eighteenth

Century Relations with England and the Netherlands," Ph.D. dissertation, University of Washington, 1995.

24. Despite the Western complaints about the lack of Chinese plenipotentiaries, Westerners who held this title and power encountered problems with the acceptance of their handiwork by their own sovereigns as well. The most famous case of this was the dismissal of Charles Elliot in 1841 for not exacting better terms from the Chinese after the first Opium War in the Convention of Chuanbi. Lord Palmerston was angry with Elliot for accepting terms short of what he had been instructed to obtain. Palmerston refused to ratify the treaty Elliot had negotiated, fired Elliot, and appointed Sir Henry Pottinger as the new plenipotentiary. The example of Elliot demonstrates that Western plenipotentiaries' power was actually limited, at least when their work did not please their superiors.

25. See, for example, *YWSM-DG* 57.33, 58.1; *YWSM-XF* 23.7,13, 35; 24.19, 39.

26. Silas Wu, *Communication and Imperial Control,* 12.

27. Charles Elliot's negotiation of the 1841 Convention of Chuanbi and its subsequent rejection, as earlier noted, confirmed that the handiwork of a Western plenipotentiary was not, in fact, accepted on every occasion.

28. Tseng-tsai Wang, *Tradition and Change,* 6–7, 79–80, 92; see also *YWSM-XF* 21.13–15, 26, 29

29. In brief, in October 1856 Qing forces seized the lorcha *Arrow* for suspected opium running. Since the vessel had an expired registration to a British firm and was flying the British flag, the British consul Harry Parkes was able to use the incident to push for British diplomatic demands. For accounts of the Arrow War and the British demands, see Morse, *International Relations,* vol. I, 414–37; and J.Y. Wong, "The 'Arrow Incident': A Reappraisal," *Modern Asian Studies* 8, no. 3 (1974): 373–89; J.Y. Wong, "Harry Parkes and the 'Arrow' War in China," *Modern Asian Studies* 9, no. 3 (1975): 303–20; and J.Y. Wong, *Yeh Ming-ch'en.* Morse relies solely on Western sources for his account. Wong uses both Chinese and Western sources.

30. Quoted in Banno, *China and the West,* 13. At this time, the governor-general of Guangdong and Guangxi concurrently carried the title of imperial commissioner to handle foreign affairs.

31. See Banno, *China and the West,* for the narrative, especially 34.

32. Tan Tingxiang belonged to a group of high officials who advocated peaceful relations with the Western powers, rather than war.

33. Hsu, *China's Entrance,* 32. Yilibu, an imperial clansman and member of the Manchu Bordered Yellow Banner, served as governor of Shanxi and governor-general of Yunnan and Guizhou, then of the Liang Jiang region of

Jiangsu, Jiangxi, and Anhui. He participated in the warfare and negotiations of 1840–1841 surrounding the negotiation of the Treaty of Chuanbi before being called to negotiate the Treaty of Nanjing. For a biography of Yilibu, see Hummel, *Eminent Chinese*, vol. 1, 387–89, and *QSG, juan* 370, *liezhuan* 157, 11, 503–4.

34. Huashana, a Manchu, was president of the Board of Personnel.

35. *YWSM-XF* 23.35.

36. *QSL-XF* 326.13.

37. *YWSM-XF* 24.38–39.

38. For a discussion of Ye Mingchen, the governor-general of Canton, during the Arrow Incident, see Li Yi's article, "Zai ping Ye Mingchen de buzhan buhe bushou," *Guangzhou yanjiu* 1 (1987): 51–54.

39. Articles 2 and 3 outlined British rights to diplomatic residence in Beijing. Article 9 allowed travel in the interior, Article 10 opened the Yangzi River to trade, and the Separate Article dictated an indemnity and the occupation of Canton until paid in full. See Hsu, *China's Entrance*, 55–71, for a discussion of the articles.

40. This was only after the initial plan of having the treaty abrogated in return for British exemption from customs duties proved untenable.

41. Banno, 106.

42. *YWSM-XF* 35.14–17

43. For a narrative of the background and negotiations of the Tianjin Treaty, see Chen Gonglu, "Siguo Tianjin tiaoyue chengli zhi jingguo" (The process of establishing the Tianjin Treaty), in *Zhongguo jindaishi luncong*, Bao Zunpeng, Li Dingyi, and Wu Xiangxiang, eds., vol. 3 (Taipei: Zhengzhong Shuju, 1956).

44. For an account of Prince Yi (d. 1861), see Hummel, vol. 2, 924.

45. Muyin was also president of the Board of War. Both he and Prince Yi belonged to the War faction, which will be discussed shortly. For more on Muyin see *QSG, juan* 387, *liezhuan* 174, 11,699.

46. I draw from Banno's account in this paragraph. Banno, *China and the West*, 34–35.

47. During the period of the Arrow War and beyond, Prince Hui's name appears as author of many memorials. The appearance of the character *"deng"* ("etc.") placed after Prince Hui's name indicates that Prince Hui was part of a group. Banno analyzed to whom the *"deng"* referred; he found that the character suggested the five princes mentioned above either *in toto* or in subgroups. Banno, in my view, convincingly demonstrates that the emperor consulted the five princes as a group. See Banno, *China and the West*, 57–65.

Immanuel Hsu, on the other hand, believes that there is no evidence for reference to a formal council of princes. See Hsu, *China's Entrance*, 65–66. For a contemporary Western reference to the Council of Princes, see S. Wells Williams, *The Middle Kingdom*, vol. 2, 690.

48. Bartlett, 46–64, 258–59.

49. *YWSM-XF* 62.34.

50. *YWSM-XF* 70.20.

51. Tseng-tsai Wang, *Tradition and Change*, 75–76. For a discussion of war advocates among the Han Chinese literati, see James Polachek, *The Inner Opium War* (Cambridge: Council on East Asian Studies, Harvard University Press, 1992).

52. The princes' attitudes have been described and analyzed by Banno. See Banno, *China and the West*, 66–75.

53. For a comparison of Prince Gong's pre-Beijing negotiation attitudes with his post-negotiation attitude, see Ting, "Establishment of the Tsungli Yamen," 24. See also Wang Mingcan's master's thesis "Yixin dui xifangde renshi" and Jason Parker's *The Rise and Decline of I-Hsin, Prince Kung*.

54. Tseng-tsai Wang reproduces the English version on pp. 251–56 of *Tradition and Change*. The Chinese version is printed in *HCCTLC* 467.12. This collection also indicates previous and subsequent updates by topic.

55. Wu Fuhuan determines that referrals to such an office in compilations such as the Guangxu edition of the *Collected Statutes* (GXHD, 1899) has misled some authors into believing that a formal office by that name existed. His examination of documents from late 1860, however, revealed no mention of such an organization. Instead, Wu suggests, only in compilations made decades later did the term become mistakenly identified with an office. See Wu Fuhuan, *Qingji Zongli Yamen Yanjiu*, 6–10. The *Draft History of the Qing Dynasty* states that the *fuju* was the predecessor of the Zongli Yamen; see the entry for the *Waiwu bu* in *QSG* (Beijing: Zhonghua Shuju, 1977), *zhi* 94, *zhiguan* 6, 3447.

56. Bartlett, chapters 3, 4, and 5.

57. Thomas Metzger calls this "appellate decision making." See Metzger, *The Internal Organization of the Ch'ing Bureaucracy*, 176–77. Appellate decision-making power arguably became even more important in the late Qing when the emperor and the center were weaker than in the early Qing when the center was stronger.

58. The memorial had actually been drafted in Beijing on January 11; it reached the emperor in Rehe on January 13, *YWSM-XF* 71.17–26. See Appendix A for a full translation of the memorial and memorandum.

59. *YWSM-XF* 71.18–19. The memorial and Six-Article Memorandum are also printed in *JZWZJ*, II, 323–28. Although the above translations are mine, the memorial and memorandum have also been translated by J.L. Cranmer-Byng in "The Establishment of the Tsungli Yamen: A Translation of the Memorial and Edict of 1861," *Journal of the Hong Kong Branch of the Royal Asiatic Society* 12 (1972): 41–54.

60. Mary Wright discusses the new orientation. See Wright, *Last Stand*, 232.

61. *YWSM-XF* 69.8–9.

62. *YWSM-XF* 62.14–15.

63. *YWSM-XF* 70.23–27 and *YWSM-XF* 88.34. Shih-shan Tsai in "Ch'ing Diplomacy: Structure and Functioning," *Asian Profile* 4, no. 1 (February 1976): 4, discusses some of these events.

64. *YWSM-XF* 69.9.

65. See Teng and Fairbank, *China's Response*, 50–57, on Feng Guifen's views.

66. *YWSM-XF* 71.19.

67. Morse, *International Relations*, vol. 2, 53.

68. Memorial: *YWSM-XF* 70.20–21; Edicts: *YWSM-XF* 70.21–23, 36.

69. Wade had come to Beijing to investigate reports of the appointment of another imperial commissioner in Tianjin.

70. *YWSM-XF* 71.28–29.

3

FORGING CONSTITUTIONAL CHANGE?

TWO RELATED REALITIES FACED THE QING COURT IN 1861. First, the new round of treaty negotiations that ended the Second Opium War expanded the unequal treaty structure and opened China further to Western advance and exploitation. The Qing Court was reeling from the prospects of unwanted levels of foreign commerce taking place in a good swath of the empire and the foreign legations in Beijing. And second, if the new foreign policy direction were to indeed bring stability through strict adherence to treaty regulations, then serious thought had to be directed to structuring how that could happen. Although the unequal treaty system has been covered in great detail by many historians, a brief discussion of it follows, as its arrangements directly affected the proposed Zongli Yamen. The impact of the treaty terms on the resolution of the new Zongli Yamen's structure can then be more thoroughly analyzed.

The Treaty Structure

With the ratification of the Treaties of Tianjin and the Conventions of Beijing in 1860, the basic framework for the "unequal treaty system" was complete. In the period from the first Opium War to the start of the round of treaties ending the second Opium War, China signed treaties with Great Britain, the United States, and France, as well as Belgium, Sweden, and Norway.[1] As many diplomatic histories of the period attest, missing from these treaties was the principle of equality between sovereign nations; rather, the treaties were unilaterally beneficial to the Western signatories. The treaties' inclusion of the most-favored-nation clause and extra-territoriality, combined with the imposition of tariff rates, were the most damaging to China and formed the basis of the inequalities.[2] The treaties also established the right of missionaries to proselytize, as well as resulting in efforts to extend extra-territoriality to Christian converts, causing tensions pertaining to ideological differences. Although the main forces in negotiating the unequal treaties were Great Britain, the United States, and France, by the application of the most-favored-nation clause, sixteen other countries also obtained the rights and privileges won by the main treaty powers.[3] In addition, the number of treaty ports increased from the original five along the coast to include cities throughout China, making much of China subject to the effects of the treaties. All of these factors contributed to the urgency of creating a workable Foreign Office that could oversee the new terms and attempt to control the expanding opportunities for trade and conflict.[4]

The most-favored-nation clause was arguably the most insidious of all privileges wrung from China by the Western powers. Just as damaging, the clause also allowed privileges gained in future treaties to be transferred to any signatory of a treaty that included the most-favored-nation clause. In effect, with this clause China signed away the right to negotiate with individual countries, making it all the more imperative to stem the flow of the erosion of Chinese sovereignty through additional unequal treaties brought on by war.[5] The second most powerful privilege, extra-territoriality, called for foreign nationals involved in criminal offenses in China to be tried not by Chinese courts, but by courts of their native countries. In most cases, offenders were tried by the consul of the respective treaty signatory, broadening geographically the treaty signatory's sovereign authority to China. Together, these two privileges complicated the job of Chinese local officials in handling on-site disputes with foreigners. Local and provincial officials could not be certain of the effects of new treaties and revisions as they were signed in terms of their extension at the local level to the nationals of existing treaty signatory states.[6] Moreover, because of the issue of extra-territoriality, once an infringement of treaty terms was determined, local officials were wary of overstepping their bounds. If any national of a signatory power committed an offense in the closed interior of China, he was taken to an open port where a consul of his country resided.[7] Likewise, Chinese subjects involved in crimes against foreigners were subject to Chinese law, rather than foreign law. The first—foreign nationals subject to their own nations' laws—far outweighed the second—Chinese nationals subject to Chinese law—in significance, with the net effect of extra-territoriality being the involvement of foreign consuls in minor, as well as major, litigations. For local officials, this translated into increased communications and contact with foreign representatives. If confusion resulted, it triggered higher-level governmental involvement on the part of the Qing foreign affairs administration.[8]

Although extra-territoriality, a hallmark of the unequal treaty system, was demanded by Western officials to protect Western residents from the Chinese penal code, considered by Western officials to be barbaric, and is viewed in the world of nation-states as an infringement on sovereignty, the phenomenon in the Chinese context is more complicated. The Qing had precedents from the Sino-Manchu tradition for handling the Western demand for Western jurisdiction over cases involving both Chinese and Westerners in China. Pär Cassel argues that the longstanding Qing practice of "legal pluralism" allowed for differing of treatment for different ethnic groups under Chinese law; the Qing Banner system quite clearly demonstrates differentiation in treat-ment of population groups. The application of this principle to Westerners in the form of extra-territoriality did not stray from past methods; rather, Qing officials adopted familiar practice when faced with the foreign demands for extra-territoriality. Extra-territoriality evolved from the Treaties of Nanjing to the Treaties of Tianjin to mean that all concerned national parties were to be involved in adjudicating cases involving Chinese and foreigners. While in most locales, this meant the involvement of local Chinese officials and foreign consuls, for residents of Shanghai, with its international settlements, it meant the involvement of the Shanghai Mixed Court.[9]

The combined effect of most-favored-nation status and extraterritoriality became more serious with the opening of additional cities to Western presence. Western treaties divided Chinese ports into treaty ports, open ports, and ports of call, each with different allowances and limits for foreign activity. Designated treaty ports were listed in the treaties as such. In these cities, foreigners could freely trade; moreover, treaty powers held the right to open consulates. After 1870, foreigners could reside in all treaty ports. In addition to foreign consulates, treaty ports also hosted customhouses to regulate the foreign trade occurring in the city. The second category, ports open to trade, differed from treaty ports in that open ports did not house foreign consulates; nor did they have customhouses. Foreign traders could trade in these ports, but permanent residence of foreigners in open ports was prohibited. Because of the distances involved in trade and transport along the Yangzi River, a third category of ports—ports of call—existed. Foreign-owned steamers were limited to calling at these ports for both freight and passengers or passengers only.[10] With the extent of movement allowed and number of cities involved in foreign trade, opportunities for contact and conflict with the local population increased, potentially spreading the thin Qing bureaucracy even thinner in areas where China could ill afford confrontation. For proponents of a peace policy based on strict adherence to treaty terms, centralized control and monitoring of foreign activity was key.

The unequal treaty system also removed tariff determination from China's control. The French and British Treaties of Tianjin revised tariffs on foreign goods; the new rate, to be applied uniformly, was set at 5 percent of the value of the traded goods at that time. Through the most-favored-nation clause this new rate applied to all treaty powers that had included the most-favored-nation clause in their treaties. The treaties determined that tariffs were subject to revision after a ten-year interval. Although tariff rates were determined by treaty, the regularization of the tariffs collected from foreign goods benefited the Qing government as well. Revenue collected through the Imperial Maritime Customs

Bureau, informally begun during the Taiping Rebellion and formalized with the Treaties of Tianjin, became one of the Qing central government's main sources of discretionary income in the late nineteenth century.[11] Collection of customs revenue in the form of duties, then, took on significance for the Qing government in general and for the Zongli Yamen, as head of the foreign affairs and customs administration, in particular.

Besides regularizing the amount of duties collected from foreigners, the intent of the Western powers in setting tariff rates and collection was to eliminate some of the rampant graft that occurred in the process of tariff collection by Chinese officials. Before the treaty system the collection of duties on foreign goods reflected the nature of the Qing governmental style. That is, Chinese officials responsible for customs at each point of interaction with foreign businessmen extracted additional fees as duties. Not only did this style of fee paying frustrate Western merchants, but also the Qing central government did not benefit from the extra fees. With a set percentage of Imperial Maritime Customs revenue slated to be forwarded to the Zongli Yamen and the central government, it was in the interest of officials at Court to gain control of the process of revenue collection.

The treaty system tariff for foreign goods created confusion by operating alongside native trade. In essence, there were two tariff systems operating, one for native goods and one for Western goods. Transit fees or likin (*lijin*) on native goods subjected Chinese merchants to paying import and export fees on goods whenever they left and entered a port—for each and every port.[12] Foreign businessmen were exempted from these transit fees by paying the uniform tariff of 5 percent of value set by the treaties and a single transit duty, which did not exceed 2.5 percent *ad valorem*. Chinese merchants, on the other hand, paid transit fees at every native customs house (*chang guan*). Twenty-nine key ports housed native customhouses, including five seaports. With the advantage belonging to the foreign businessman in tariffs and to the Chinese merchant for markets, distinctions between the native and foreign trade tariffs became more and more difficult to maintain, especially as Chinese merchants started to trade Western goods and likewise Westerners began to handle native products. With each system offering its own benefits, both Chinese and Western businessmen tried to capture as many advantages as possible. Chinese merchants tried to avoid the native trade transit fees on goods moved between cities by shipping goods on Western vessels.[13] Western businessmen, too, manipulated the system by using Chinese ships to penetrate the interior. It was in the Qing government's interest to regulate the burgeoning trade to its greatest financial advantage, collecting foreign duties to the fullest extent. Moreover, Zongli Yamen policies to enforce treaty terms strictly in order to prevent future encroachments on Qing sovereignty demanded that Western merchants adhere to treaty terms and not trade inland. Because of extra-territoriality, Qing recourse for dealing with treaty violations was limited. The treaties, however, did allow illegally traded merchandise to be confiscated by the Chinese government.[14] As recorded in the archives, this option was exercised by Qing authorities on many occasions.

Distinctions in the treaties between goods that could be traded by Chinese merchants and goods that could be bought and sold by Western merchants caused confusion within the provinces. The treaties banned Western trade in guns, munitions, and implements of war. In addition, salt, for which the Qing government maintained a monopoly, could not be sold by foreigners. The treaties deemed all of the above goods contraband; other war-related goods, such as sulfur, brimstone, and saltpeter, could be imported by Westerners only when requisitioned by the Chinese government.[15] The Taiping Rebellion disrupted salt transport along the Yangzi through the mid-1860s. Despite the Qing ban on Western travel through government blockades into Taiping territory, some foreign boats, using the protection of their arms and foreign flag, convoyed Chinese vessels up and down the river. Although the ban on travel was officially lifted in 1860, the government still discouraged foreigners from traveling the Yangzi. However, according to one such adventurer, William Mesny, such trips proved extremely profitable, if dangerous. Salt bought for one dollar per bag along the coast would bring up to thirteen dollars per bag in Hankou.[16] The promise of high profits inspired many foreign merchants to buy and sell their goods in areas not open to trade by treaty, leading to the flouting of treaty terms. Reports of such local treaty offenses were directed to the Zongli Yamen.

Structuring Foreign Affairs

The six articles of the memorandum attached to the memorial of January 13, 1861, proposing the Zongli Yamen sketched the structure of an organization that could implement the newly proposed foreign policy of treaty fulfillment and, more significantly, institutionalize the pursuit of peace. The obligations of the treaties were broad; the Conventions of Beijing, for example, covered topics as divergent as the opening of Tianjin trade and the problem of coolie emigration. The powers and scope of the newly proposed organization had to be equally extensive if it were to be able to oversee and enforce treaty terms. Managing the broad range of duties involved while simultaneously negotiating the complex bureaucratic world of the late Qing required that any such new body be highly placed and integrative in nature.

The only existing Qing institutions possessing a standing similar to that proposed were comprehensive deliberative bodies, since only at the highest level of the hierarchy did rank, access to a wide-range of pertinent information, and active participation in the decision-making process converge. The Qing bureaucracy consisted of several parallel hierarchies—civil administration in the capital, military administration, and territorial provincial administrations—each structured vertically with the emperor at the apex. Besides the emperor, only the Grand Council occupied a position that permitted an integrative function.[17] Organs below the Grand Council were typically relegated to the administration of regulations and routine matters of their particular responsibilities. Within each hierarchy, an organization could issue orders to subordinate bodies within its jurisdiction and settle routine matters, while policy issues had to be memorialized to the throne. Because of this structure, the Six Boards[18] and provincial administrations operated as equals, with governors or governors-general heading each provincial bureaucracy.[19] Organs with equal standing in separate hierarchies could not directly instruct each other; nor could organs in two different branches of the vertical hierarchy directly issue orders to each other, regardless of their relative standings within their own branches. This lack of horizontal linkages made integrative authority within the Qing imperative. The Grand Council served the emperor in an advisory manner, meeting with the emperor daily to discuss memorials, to draft outgoing responses (edicts), and to determine imperial policy. With such overarching responsibilities and knowledge as well as daily contact with the emperor, the Grand Council was the most powerful official organization within the Qing hierarchy.[20]

For officials in the regular bureaucracy, standing within the hierarchy and their resultant place in the memorial system determined access to information. Qing officials utilized two different systems for sending memorials to the capital. The first was the routine system; routine memorials *(tiben)* traveled through regular bureaucratic channels and were routed to appropriate committees and offices by longstanding rules as to who or what office should handle certain topics. The second means was the palace or secret memorial *(zouzhe)*.[21] With the latter, select, high-ranking officials could bypass regular bureaucratic channels and send memorials directly to the emperor. Only the emperor and the grand councilors perused these secret documents. Once the emperor, with the advice of the Grand Council, composed a response or rescript, the memorial was returned to the sender. At the emperor's discretion, he could direct the sharing of a secret memorial by indicating that a certain office should be made aware of the document (*gaibu zhidao*). Or, a grand councilor who held a concurrent appointment as an official in a particular Board might share relevant memorials with his Board. For most officials, access to information was determined by their particular office, with the office's areas of responsibility defining its regular access to government documents. Consequently, advisory capacity, especially in areas not pertaining to an official's assigned domain, was weak.

The Grand Council was quite naturally the organization to be modeled. Thus the six articles on the founding of the Zongli Yamen submitted to the emperor in January 1861 aimed to establish an institution at the top level of power that would be on a par with the

Grand Council and that would re-create its integrative function. Notably, all six of the memorandum articles concerned, in one way or another, the control of communication and information—the backbone of integration and decision-making power in the Qing system.

It is significant that formally the Grand Council had never superseded the Grand Secretariat in power, at least as listed in *The Collected Statutes of the Great Qing Dynasty*. Rather, the Grand Council had gradually eased into its top position and assumed primacy over the Grand Secretariat through practice and access to the secret memorial system. Until the last *Collected Statutes* issued by the Qing in 1899, the main responsibilities of the Grand Secretariat continued to be "managing and discussing the administration of the celestial realm, promulgating the emperor's will, and regulating the statutes of the government."[22] The *Collected Statutes* records imperial military affairs, on the other hand, as the domain of the Grand Council. In fact, however, by the nineteenth century the Grand Council held sway over the Grand Secretariat as the most powerful central government organization. Thus, for the Zongli Yamen to become a powerful organization, it did not have to acquire formal powers immediately; rather, it could accrue them over time, much in the manner of the early Grand Council. Following the Grand Council's institutional path to influence, however, required access to information, the key to the Grand Council's authority and to power in the Qing.

The differences in the January 13, 1861, memorial and memorandum proposing the Zongli Yamen and the January 20 edict establishing it are well worth scrutiny. For in the differences, we can discern debates and positioning that affected Qing governance for the next forty years.[23]

The first article addressed control and hierarchy and therefore served as the keystone for the new Zongli Yamen's position and power. By far the most complex of the articles, it aimed to achieve a number of important goals. Article One defined the Yamen's scope and positioned it in the governmental structure by placing it in the communication chain-of-command and outlining its general relationship to the Grand Council:

> In Beijing, we request that a general office be established for the management of the affairs of the various foreign countries to be solely responsible for foreign affairs. We observe that, hitherto, foreign matters have been reported by memorial by the governors-general and governors of the provinces and collected by the Grand Council ... We request the establishment of an Office for the Management of the Affairs of the Various Foreign Countries (*zongli geguo shiwu yamen*), under the leadership of imperial princes and high ministers. Because the Grand Councilors draft the imperial edicts, if they do not have a hand in its affairs, we fear there will be discrepancies. Therefore, we request that they serve concurrently in the new office ... We suggest that its staff come from the secretaries serving the Grand Secretariat, the Six Boards, the Court of Colonial Affairs, and the Grand Council, with eight Manchu and eight Chinese officials being selected and serving in rotation. In ordering its responsibilities, the new office will manage all matters in the style of the Grand Council.[24]

The most striking feature here is the proposal for the central control of foreign affairs. When examined in the light of the parallel structure of Qing bureaucratic hierarchies, the centrality is all the more striking. Since its development and rise to ascendancy in the eighteenth century, only the Grand Council had formally occupied such a central position. The memorialists now directly proposed a second such coordinating body; in fact, they openly compared the new office to the Grand Council by suggesting it operate in the same manner as the Grand Council.

The very name chosen, "Office for the Management of the Affairs of the Various Foreign Countries," has significance as well, for the name excludes mention of trade. Under the tribute and Canton cohong systems, the rubric of trade had defined foreign relations. Thus, the proposed name for the new office removed it from the system set up for tributary relations, thereby broadening the scope of foreign affairs. Commercial affairs would no longer officially and solely define relations with Western countries. The article thus both implicitly and explicitly recognizes that management of foreign affairs with Western countries did not operate within the tribute framework. Just as significantly, a permanent institutional solution was to replace the ad hoc status of the imperial commissioners.

The subsequent interjection of the term "trade" (*tongshang*) in the January 20 edict that actually established the Zongli Yamen threatened to relegate the organization to the old foreign policy system of equating commercial relations with political relations.[25] In a memorial on January 26, Prince Gong and his colleagues presented their case once again, this time employing an implicit threat of the danger involved in displeasing the West while their troops were still in Tianjin:

> Now, they already know that we have established the Zongli Yamen to handle Chinese negotiations with foreign nations ... Their reputation is well known and we are thoroughly versed in their natures. If they see the term "trade" in communications and dispatches, they will inevitably suspect that we are only handling trade affairs and will not want to work with us causing their complaints to certainly increase ...[26]

To facilitate remedying the situation, Prince Gong informed the Western envoys that the word "trade" would be removed, increasing expectations that the Court would do so. The Western troops certainly posed a continued danger to the dynasty, and appeasing these armies had a certain immediate logic; however, this episode can also be viewed as part of Prince Gong's efforts to build support for the fledgling office. The emperor approved, and the Board of Rites issued a new seal without the controversial term. The memorialists had withstood an effort to limit the comprehensive standing they wished to establish for the new Yamen. Although a reading of Zongli Yamen documents reveals that both seals, with and without the word "trade," were subsequently used, the seal omitting the term was used much more frequently.[27] Some scholars have argued that the placement of "commerce" or "trade" in the Yamen seal is sufficient evidence of the Qing's inability to change its basic outlook and systems, since the term alludes to the tributary nature of the foreign relations under the Yamen. Both seals, with and without the term, were legitimate; however, the existence of the seal including the term does not by itself substantiate the charge of Qing inability to change, and the name on the seal alone cannot determine the Zongli Yamen's place in the Qing hierarchy. The controversy over the seal's wording provides a tangible example of the change that was at stake. The fact that both seals remained, indicating that at the moment of founding no clear consensus of the Zongli Yamen's status existed, only increases the significance of subsequent developments.

Choice of personnel also highlighted the Yamen's potential importance and power. Manchu princes and the highest Court officials were to comprise its leadership, with a Prince of the first rank taking general control. Prince Gong occupied this position for the Zongli Yamen's first twenty years. Thus, links to both the Manchu imperial house and the Chinese bureaucracy were to be strong.[28] The Yamen's structure reflected a Manchu form of collegial decision making and strikingly resembled the model of the Grand Council. The clause that called for the inclusion of grand councilors strove to coordinate and ensure information accessibility—recognition that the Grand Council was at that time the most powerful body in the hierarchy, responsible for foreign and domestic policy. Overlapping personnel, as demonstrated by its effective use in the early years of the Grand Council, represented a technique for power accrual for a new institution by allowing it to extend into the realms of established offices. Concurrent appointments worked to the advantage of the fledgling Grand Council in the previous century and now did the same for the fledgling Zongli Yamen.[29]

In the case of the Zongli Yamen, Russia had specified in its treaty arrangements with the Qing that communications be handled through a grand councilor or a specially appointed grand secretary; as a result, the Russians had been sending diplomatic communications solely through the Grand Council. Such existing treaty stipulations necessitated close cooperation between the Zongli Yamen and the Grand Council. Unless grand councilors served concurrently at the Yamen and had access to information sent there, misunderstandings would occur between the two organs and with foreigners as well. Also, because of the grand councilors' high position in the Qing bureaucracy, their inclusion in the new Yamen would give it immediate credibility both within China and with the foreigners. In addition to including Prince Gong, the memorialists spelled out the benefit of having at least Grand Councilor Wenxiang serve in the Zongli Yamen after the emperor refused an initial request for more general concurrent service:

> Presently your servant Wenxiang manages foreign affairs. The foreigners know he is a grand councilor and consider this extremely important. When a foreign minister has a document for the Grand Council, it can be accepted through Wenxiang at the Zongli Yamen; in addition, he can meet with them without their complaining.[30]

It was crucial for the success of the new foreign policy and young institution that the militarily strong Westerners accept the arrangements as satisfactory. Considering that the most vexing problem in the imperial commissioner system had been "full powers," the Yamen had to be structured to fit such a description, while being consistent with the general Qing institutional power structure. The four Western powers correctly considered the Grand Council to be the leading decision-making body. Therefore it was imperative to establish immediately the Zongli Yamen on an equal footing with the Grand Council in the realm of foreign affairs. Including grand councilors on the Yamen's controlling board was the simplest, most expedient way of doing this. Because concurrent service was a method of accessing power in the Qing bureaucracy, allowing for grand councilors on the Zongli Yamen board accorded with established practice.[31] The emperor consequently agreed to let Wenxiang concurrently serve in both organs. In fact, during the Yamen's first year of operation, four of the ten grand councilors were among its seven ministers. Substantial overlap in personnel with the Grand Council proved to be an asset to the new organization.[32]

In addition to the communication aspect of power, the first article also addressed institutional and influential aspects of power. Efforts to institutionalize the peacemaking group through, for example, the bestowal of honors indicated that Prince Gong and Guiliang intended to retain leadership of the Yamen, along with Grand Councilor Wenxiang, rather than simply be replaced by grand councilors. For the proposed foreign policy to work, strong advocates of peace had to be firmly in place in the leadership, even as opposition from war advocates in Rehe continued to complicate the process. The commissioners, aware of this, demonstrated their institutional interests in retaining the power they had developed during negotiations. When reminding the emperor of the risk involved in displeasing the Westerners on the issue of using the term "trade," the commissioners took the opportunity to also remind him that "The foreigners, in all cases, treat us your servants as in charge of these [foreign] affairs."[33] The commissioners' removal or sidelining would involve military risk. By serving as the core of the Zongli Yamen, the three memorialists engineered representation from the Council of Princes, the Grand Council, and the Grand Secretariat—the three strongest informal and formal branches of the Qing government, both institutionally and in of terms influence.

The first article also set out a brief structure for the secretarial staff. Stipulating that Yamen secretaries be drawn from the Grand Council, the Grand Secretariat, the Six Boards, and the Lifan yuan (Court of Dependencies), the article assured the Zongli Yamen of expert help in many areas. A later memorial explained the rationale for dividing responsibilities among the secretaries according to their office of origin:

> … If they are originally from the Board of Revenue, then they will serve in customs-related affairs; if they are originally from the Board of Rites or the Court of Dependencies, then they will work on dispatches; if from the Board of War, then on border patrol transmissions. If they are Grand Council secretaries, they will work on memorials that concern the two offices, as they are very

familiar with these and can manage them without error and causing complications.[34]

The only real obstacle the proposed secretarial structure encountered concerned the secretaries from the Grand Council. The memorialists had suggested that secretaries from the Grand Council staff serve concurrently in both offices. However, the January 20 edict stated that Grand Council secretaries appointed to serve on the Zongli Yamen would need first to relinquish their Grand Council posts. The edict ran counter to the commissioners' plans for building a comprehensive communications network. It also diverged from a temporary edict of January 13 issued in response to requests for Grand Council confidential information. In this case, Wenxiang was allowed to order Grand Council secretaries to copy any memorial received before September 21, 1860, and kept in the Military Archives (*fang lue guan*).[35] Secretaries from the Grand Council were crucial if the Zongli Yamen were to have quick access to confidential memorials and files kept at the Grand Council. The compromise finally reached on February 15 allowed for sixteen secretaries from various offices, none of them to serve concurrently at the Grand Council. Eight additional supernumerary secretaries in the Grand Secretariat would also be assigned to work on relevant secret foreign affairs documents and be available to go to the Zongli Yamen as needed.[36] Although the grand secretaries and their staff could access extensive sensitive information that flowed through regular bureaucratic channels, they did not have access to the secret palace memorial system. Only grand councilors and their staff were privy to this information. The absence of Grand Council secretaries on the Zongli Yamen staff consequently decreased access to information; however, the presence of first Grand Councilor Wenxiang and then other grand councilors helped mitigate the setback. Over the years, as the number of grand councilors increased on the Zongli Yamen, the barriers to transmitting sensitive Grand Council information disappeared.

The second article concerned chain of command and information gathering. The Yamen hoped to receive reports of foreign affairs–related issues directly from provincial officials. Expressing awareness of the dangers of not collecting information or of collecting inaccurate information, the article laments that in the past provincial officials in Jilin and Heilongjiang concealed Russian border infringement and Russian occupation of Chinese lands from the central government to the point that "we can no longer prevent it from happening."[37] By requiring the accurate submission of information from the provinces as events unfolded, commissioners hoped that the central government would be better positioned to regulate outcome.

By requesting that officials managing affairs in Tianjin and Shanghai send separate reports to the Zongli Yamen, Article Two also makes clear that the memorialists planned for the Zongli Yamen to be superior to the new post of superintendent for the three ports at Tianjin and the now expanded post of imperial commissioner for the five ports in Shanghai. During negotiations with the West, the Tianjin post had been subordinate to Prince Gong. However, the article as proposed and as implemented sufficiently diverged so as to set up a potential break in the hierarchy of command. As of the January 20 edict, both the Shanghai and the Tianjin officials could directly memorialize the throne; they did not need to report through Prince Gong or the Zongli Yamen. Prince Gong had considered these posts to be the commercial extensions of the foreign office. They were to handle minor trade matters locally and report major ones to the Beijing office. As established, however, they were not closely attached to the Zongli Yamen. Instead of memorializing all or even only important affairs to the Yamen, they were ordered to memorialize routine matters to the Board of Rites, and important matters to the Grand Council.[38] The information would then be passed on to the Yamen by those two organizations. This arrangement obtained for more or less all provincial officials.[39] In terms of general administrative structure, the separation of the superintendent for the three ports and the imperial commissioner of the five ports from the Zongli Yamen and the provincial administration from the Zongli Yamen meant that the foreign affairs hierarchy would become another one of the nonintegrated parallel hierarchies within the Qing system. As such, it would be subjected to the limits of a relatively narrow domain defined outside of the Yamen by the information conveyed to it by the Grand Council and Grand Secretariat.

Such an arrangement constituted a blow to the envisioned information structure. Not only did the Zongli Yamen move away from a position of integrative power, but it also moved, in terms of communication flow, to a subordinate position in relation to the Board of Rites, as well as to the Grand Council. Since the Board of Rites was responsible for tributary affairs, this was a major setback for the new foreign affairs structure. The divergence of the memorial and the edict is the most striking for the second article.

The third article concerned arrangements for customs collections at the treaty ports and along the Russian frontier. The imperial commissioners proposed a reorganization of responsibilities for customs collection. By aiming to place the new superintendent of trade for the three ports in charge of customs revenue at Tianjin and having the governors, as head of the territorial administration, work with the superintendents of trade in selecting men to run customs in the new treaty ports, the memorialists envisioned an arrangement that linked the well-established territorial administration with the relatively new Customs Administration, which would be under the purview of the new foreign affairs administration headed by the Zongli Yamen. By centralizing the new tariff structure, the Qing government, through the Zongli Yamen, could bring the hitherto loose processes of tariff collection under more standardized control. The memorialists noted that "Customs officials have looked at this [collection of duties] as a way to make profit. Embezzlement, fraud, smuggling, and a hundred malpractices arose. ... Now that we will collect twenty percent of customs [for the central government] it is especially important to clear accounts to avoid complications from developing."[40] The collection of Imperial Maritime Customs revenue ranked high on the ministers' list of priorities; disputes that threatened that collection would attract the Zongli Yamen ministers' attention. The January 20 edict, however, kept the administrations distinct, with information flowing up to the Court, but not horizontally between the Imperial Maritime Customs and the Zongli Yamen. The superintendents of trade, as established, answered to the throne and not to the Yamen. To overcome these shortcomings, Zongli Yamen ministers over the course of the next decade centralized foreign affairs through the realignment of the new customs administration with a spatially reorganized territorial administration focusing on the positions of circuit intendant or daotai as well as the superintendents of trade. The next chapter details this effort.

The fourth article discussed the protocol for the reporting system, the provincial officials' sharing of information on foreign affairs and the setting up of archives for successors. In this article, the memorialists addressed the parallel and vertical nature of the Qing bureaucracy when they noted "… hitherto, the Grand Council has not issued copies of letters, edicts, and communications that concern the management of foreign affairs to provincial officials; nor have the provincial officials kept each other informed." Because of the gaps in knowledge that resulted from this lack of coordination, the Zongli Yamen proposed that the Court "instruct the officials concerned with foreign trade in the provinces and the imperial commissioner to send regular reports to the Zongli Yamen in the capital" and that "Military generals, the prefect of the Metropolitan Prefecture,[41] and the governors-general should now all keep each other regularly and mutually informed of events in their jurisdictions …"[42] Thus, the memorialists proposed that provincial officials not only memorialize the Zongli Yamen regarding foreign affairs, but also apprise each other in order to avoid misunderstandings.

Communication flow in the Qing system was usually directed toward the throne, with the throne responding to the reporting party. While it could be relayed by the emperor to a particular office or by a grand councilor to a Board to which he had a concurrent appointment, information disclosed in the communications sent to the throne was not routinely disseminated to other parties, not even necessarily to those involved in the reported affair. Consequently, an imbalance of intelligence weighted toward the center resulted. Provincial officials were often unaware of events and information that might prove useful if shared with them because the source belonged to a different parallel hierarchy and information did not automatically flow back down from the center in a general manner. Even within a single province there was no assurance that information would be disseminated among the various branches of the provincial government. In stating their case for greater communication, the memorialists quoted the former governor-general of Liang Jiang, He Guiqing:

> Hitherto, all matters have been memorialized to the throne secretly, without officials keeping each other informed. Furthermore, there have been no files that an official could check. Even those serving in the same office do not necessarily know the details of each other's affairs. This situation causes misunderstandings and discrepancies and gives rise to abuses of the system. Your servant requests that officials be instructed to mutually inform one another in order to unify practice.[43]

With its proposal for cross-communication, the Zongli Yamen would help increase awareness of foreign affairs problems and solutions, leading to a more consistent, empire-wide approach. In order to create institutional memory, the memorialists also suggested in the same article that files be maintained at each yamen and that when one official left a post, he hand over his files to his successor. Through these measures, the Zongli Yamen placed itself at the top of a pyramidal, regular network of communications. Different levels would communicate among themselves for the sake of efficiency, and the Zongli Yamen would retain directional and integrative control of the process. Over the course of the 1860s, Yamen ministers worked to overcome the limitations of the establishing edict by forging more direct information-gathering tools vis-à-vis the provinces.

The response to these concerns and requests in the January 20 edict was mixed; the edict read:

> All communications with foreign countries, along with matters concerning trade, must be reported to the throne directly. Moreover, original communications should be turned over [to the throne] for inspection. Officials should

> communicate with the Board of Rites, who will, in turn, hand communications over to the Zongli geguo tongshang shiwu yamen. In addition, the respective military governors, governors-general, and governors should keep each other informed.

While the edict accepts the need for greater communication among high provincial officials, it kept the flow of communication directed through existing channels; the Zongli Yamen did not become the collection and dissemination point for information. Nor were the provincial officials instructed as to how they should keep each other informed. The need for more institutional memory within an office was clearly heard as the edict went on to include instructions for an official to "hand over his archives to his successor." Again, over the course of the 1860s, Zongli Yamen ministers worked on developing techniques for overcoming the limitations in their access to information.

The fifth article addressed the need for foreign-language training. The memorialists recognized that the lack of Chinese officials who were conversant in or had a reading knowledge of Western languages contributed to misunderstandings of the West in general and to communication barriers in negotiations in particular. As a corrective measure, the provincial officials in Jiangsu and Guangdong were to pick four men from the merchants in Shanghai and Guangdong (two from each city) who had become familiar with Western languages to send foreign books to Beijing. In addition to this, promising young boys from each of the Eight Banners were to be selected to study the English and French languages. Although the edict did not address the article, by suggesting that dependable and capable men be sent to the capital as language instructors and boys be selected to study the languages, the memorialists laid the foundation for the subsequent establishment of the Tong wen guan or Foreign Languages College.[44]

Last, the sixth article asked that governors-general, governors, military generals, and the prefect of the Metropolitan Prefecture each send monthly reports to the Zongli Yamen on foreign news and the commercial situations in their areas in order to ensure complete coverage, in the event that the imperial commissioner was not aware of a potentially important event or problem. Recognizing that foreign newspapers had sprung up in all of the old treaty ports and would probably soon start in the new ports, the memorialists hoped to take advantage of the information contained therein. They recognized that "foreign newspapers are not necessarily accurate; nonetheless, through careful reading it is possible to obtain the general idea (of events)." Besides, the ministers admitted, efforts to gather information secretly had not been fruitful. Thus, the memorialists requested that foreign newspapers published in the treaty ports, whether in Chinese or in a foreign language, be sent along with the reports to Beijing.[45] With a better understanding of happenings in the treaty ports, the Zongli Yamen would be able to maintain awareness of issues presenting potential problems and foreign perceptions.

Contained within this article was the identification of the very local nature of many of the events that belonged to the category "foreign affairs." The memorialists state that "in the handling of foreign affairs, it is all the more important to prepare to know the smallest details, for in such matters, the periphery can move the center." Here, we see advanced recognition of how foreign policy can be a bidirectional process, a reaction of the central government to events that are initially handled at the local level. Collection of information and shared knowledge of events at both the capital and treaty ports was essential to standardizing approaches at each of the ports through the application of the centralized new treaty-abiding direction of foreign policy. Success in this required the education of local officials and broad and detailed knowledge of how affairs were handled on site.

Shifting Change

Prince Gong, the main proponent of the Zongli Yamen—and author of the memorial proposing it—figured prominently in the Qing government as an imperial advisor. He worked with two others to establish China's first Foreign Office: Wenxiang, a grand councilor, and Guiliang, a grand secretary. The Grand Council and princely imperial advisors, owing to the integrative function of the former and the advisory role of the latter, had access to all important issues. The Grand Secretariat, as coordinator and drafter of edicts of the routine memorial system, had access to routine memorials. The grouping of an imperial prince, a grand councilor, and a grand secretary as the founders of a central-level government office is significant as together they represented the three most powerful organs at the apex of the Qing hierarchy. Their regular access to the emperor and influence on him imparted the three with imperial authority and helped grant legitimacy to the fledgling Zongli Yamen. Their knowledge of their respective offices, government functioning, and precedent informed their proposal for structuring the new Foreign Office.

Memorials containing proposals for new policies were not unusual during the Qing; rather, they were a major component of the Qing machinery. Despite limitations on information received through their particular bureaucratic regular channels, officials in any part of the bureaucracy could attempt to participate in the decision-making process through the submission of their own proposals via memorial. Flexibility in officials was not only desirable, but it was also imperative for long-term dynastic survival. As with Prince Gong's new foreign office, suggestions often simultaneously reflected a changed reality while acknowledging the importance of established practice and precedent for legitimacy. The wise official not only comprehended the fundamental order, but he also understood how to meet the needs of changing situations in acceptable ways.[46] Short-term resistance to the new foreign policy was overcome by military exigencies. Once the emergency receded, long-term support had to be cultivated by building a consensus over time. The hope of opponents that the new strategy was temporary made the actions of the three imperial commissioners all the more critical. "Institutionalizing" a new government office, however, was a process that during the Qing required patience and a long-term approach.

All six articles outlined in the memorandum accompanying the proposal for the Zongli Yamen touched on issues of access to information. In the world of the Qing government, access to information translated into power. By situating the new Zongli Yamen near the top of a communications network, the six articles aimed to position the new organization within the highest rung of the Qing bureaucracy. As a whole, the articles threatened to shake up the status quo by shifting information and expertise to the Zongli Yamen by allowing it to share Grand Council personnel and by becoming the command center for foreign affairs and the clearinghouse for related information. Had all of the articles been approved exactly as proposed, the Yamen's role as a comprehensive, deliberative body would have been achieved directly. Instead, the Court made modifications that immediately weakened the intended role of the new institution and threatened to isolate it in a new parallel administrative hierarchy that was dependent on the more comprehensive nature of the Grand Council and Grand Secretariat for information. Their knowledge of bureaucratic functioning derived from their years of experience as imperial advisors and high officials guided the three memorialists' subsequent shaping of the Foreign Office into a workable and powerful new institution. The three ministers went to work to mediate the changes decreed in the edict and situate the Yamen in the integrative position envisioned in the original proposal. For the first three years, the organization and staff responsibilities fluctuated; a reorganization in 1864 made the internal staffing more stable. The establishment of a foreign affairs field administration and foreign affairs communications network over the course of the 1860s worked to place the Zongli Yamen at the top of a foreign affairs hierarchy in terms of function and helped it overcome the gaps between the Yamen as envisioned by the memorialists and that decreed by edict in 1861.

NOTES

1. The following treaties comprised this system: the 1842 Treaty of Nanjing with Great Britain, along with the Supplementary Treaty of the Bogue; the 1844 Treaty of Wangxia with the United States; the 1844 Treaty of Whampoa with France; the 1845 Exchange of notes with Belgium granting the right to trade under the procedure established by existing treaties; the 1847 Treaty with Sweden and Norway; the 1858 Treaties of Tianjin with the United States, Russia, Great Britain, and France; the 1860 Conventions of Beijing. Treaties with additional powers that contributed to this system were 1861: the Treaty of Prussia; 1862: the Treaty with Portugal (ratification refused by Chinese government); 1863: the Treaty with Denmark and the Treaty with the Netherlands; 1864: the Treaty with Spain; 1865: the Treaty with Belgium; 1866: the Treaty with Italy; 1869: the Treaty with Austria-Hungary; 1871: the Treaty with Japan. Supplemental negotiations with the treaty powers continued throughout the remainder of the dynasty. Peru, Brazil, Portugal, and Mexico also negotiated treaties with China. See C.F. Remer, *The Foreign Trade of China*, (Shanghai: The Commercial Press, 1928), 5. For the English text of the four Treaties of Tianjin (with Great Britain, the United States, France, and Russia), as well as the Chinese version of the Treaty of Tianjin with Great Britain, see S. Wells Williams, *The Chinese Commercial Guide, Containing Treaties, Tariffs, Regulations, Tables, Etc., Useful in the Trade to China and Eastern Asia; with an Appendix of Sailing Directions for those Seas and Coasts*, 5th edition (Hong Kong: A. Shortrede & Co., 1863; reprinted by Ch'eng-wen, Taipei, 1966), 1–61. For the Chinese versions of all of the treaties, see *Qing chao tiaoyue quanji*, Tian Tao, ed. (Heilongjiang People's Press, 1999). Many historians of China have written on the unequal treaty system. A classic in this regard is John King Fairbank's, *Trade and Diplomacy on the China Coast*.

2. The "most-favored-nation" clause first appeared in the Treaty of Nanjing in 1842. The right to extra-territoriality was first negotiated by the British and the Qing as part of the "General Regulations of Trade" signed in July 1843, as well as included in the "Supplementary Treaty of the Bogue" of October 8, 1843. It was subsequently included in treaties with other powers, with the Treaty of Wangxia, signed by the United States and the Qing Court in 1844, being the first in this category.

3. The others were Russia, Belgium, Germany, Portugal, Denmark, the Netherlands, Spain, Italy, Austria-Hungary, Japan, Peru, Brazil, Mexico, Switzerland, Norway, and Sweden.

4. Michael Lazich provides the view from the other side, examining the response of American missionaries to the opium trade and the pressure they exerted on the U.S. government in shaping U.S. policies toward China. See Michael C. Lazich, "American Missionaries and the Opium Trade in Nineteenth-Century China," *Journal of World History* 17, no. 2 (2006): 197–223.

5. In the British Treaty of Tianjin, formally known as the "Treaty of Peace, Friendship, Commerce and Navigation between Her Majesty and the Emperor of China" (signed June 26, 1858, with ratifications exchanged October 21, 1860), the most-favored-nation clause is Article LIV; in the American Treaty it is Article XXX; in the French Treaty, Article XL, and in the Russian Treaty, Article XII. See Williams, *The Chinese Commercial Guide*, 13–14, 40, 55, 59. See also H.B. Morse, *The International Relations of the Chinese Empire*, vol. 1, 557–70, for a discussion of the various terms of the Tianjin Treaties.

6. For an example of a case in which local officials seek treaty rights clarification, see ZYDFJS, Hubei, 01-16/7-2.8-16.

7. H.B. Morse details the duties of the American consul in regard to extra-territoriality. In addition to presiding as police magistrate for crimes committed by Americans, he also acted as civil and criminal judge in suits brought against Americans not only by Chinese, but also by other Americans and foreigners as well. See Morse, *The Trade and Administration of the Chinese Empire*, 184–86.

8. Eileen Scully provides a very useful analysis of extra-territoriality (also known as extrality) in terms of American citizens in Shanghai and U.S. citizenship, exploring the privilege not only in terms of being a tool of imperialism, but also in terms of being part of a "citizenship regime" that was critical to a nation-state's equal and sovereign participation in the international world of nineteenth-century geopolitics. Scully also points out that most cases that reached the extra-territorial tribunals of Great Britain and the United States, the two largest such tribunals in China and Japan, were disputes between foreigners, not between foreigners and Chinese. See Scully, *Bargaining with the State from Afar: American Citizenship in Treaty Port China, 1844–1942* (New York: Columbia University Press, 2001), especially 2–8.

9. Pär Cassel argues that the development of the Shanghai Mixed Court derived from Qing traditions and institutions, yet because of Shanghai's position as the center of all things modern and as the premier treaty port,

this connection with existing practices and traditions has been overlooked. See Pär Cassel, "Excavating Extraterritoriality: The 'Judicial Sub-prefect' as a Prototype for the Mixed Court in Shanghai," *Late Imperial China* 24, no. 2 (December 2003): 156–82.

10. See Remer, *The Foreign Trade of China*, 8–10, for a more detailed discussion of the differences among the different types of ports open to foreigners.

11. The Maritime Customs was an outgrowth of the Shanghai Customs. In 1853, the Small Sword Society (*Xiao dao hui*) took over Shanghai, forcing the daotai to flee. Because the daotai had been in charge of collecting the duties required of the foreign merchants by treaty, the foreign consuls were left in a dilemma. In order to enforce the treaty terms, the American and British consuls made their nationals record their goods, both imports and exports, at the consulates. Bonds to ensure eventual payment of the duties were also required of the merchants. Once the area was pacified and the daotai returned, the involvement of foreign nationals in the collection of customs was formalized with an agreement signed on June 29, 1854. This arrangement expedited customs collection by adding personnel with foreign language skills to the customhouses. In 1858, with the Treaties of Tianjin, the system of foreign involvement in Shanghai customs was extended to the other treaty ports. H.N. Lay served as the first head of the Imperial Maritime Customs. All foreigners working for the Chinese Maritime customs were in the employ of the Qing government. For more on the origins of the Maritime Customs, see the introduction by L.K. Little in *The I.G. in Peking: Letters of Robert Hart, Chinese Maritime Customs, 1868–1907,* John King Fairbank, ed. (Cambridge: Belknap Press of Harvard University Press, 1975), vol. 1, 3–34. See also Stanley F. Wright, *The Origin and Development of the Chinese Customs Service, 1843–1911: An Historical Outline* (Shanghai: 1936).

12. The likin or lijin was first introduced during the Taiping Rebellion, probably in 1853, as a way to raise money for the provincial troops organized under Zeng Guofan, Zuo Zongtang, and Li Hongzhang. Zeng was first to use the new tax, which was an ad valorem transit or sales tax. After the suppression of the Taiping, provincial officials retained the lijin as a source of provincial income. For more on the origins of the lijin, see Luo Yudong, *Zhongguo lijin shi* (Shanghai; Shangwu yinshuguan, 1936); and Edwin George Beal, Jr., *The Origin of the Likin, 1853–1864* (Cambridge: Chinese Economic and Political Studies, Harvard University Press, 1958). For more on the new armies raised by regional figures like Zeng, Zuo, and Li, see Richard J. Smith, "Chinese Military Institutions in the Mid-Nineteenth

Century, 1850–1860," *Journal of Asian History* 8, no. 2 (1974): 122–61. For biographical information on Zeng Guofan, see *QSG, juan* 405, liezhuan 192, 11,907–08; and Hummel, vol. 2, 751–55. For more on Zuo Zongtang, see *QSG juan* 412, liezhuan 199, 12,023–24; and Hummel, vol. 2, 762–67.

13. See Fairbank, *Trade and Diplomacy*, vol. 1, 317. See also Yen-p'ing Hao, *The Commercial Revolution*, for an account of how the treaties affected trade along the coast, 259–63.

14. Articles XXXVIII, XXXIX, XL, and XLV-XLIX of the British Treaty of Tianjin; Articles XIV, XIX, XXI, XXIII, XXVI of the American Treaty of Tianjin; Articles VII, XXIV, XXV, XXVII, XXVIII, of the French Treaty of Tianjin; and Article IV of the Russian Treaty of Tianjin. See Williams, *The Chinese Commercial Guide*, 10–13, 35–39, 44–51, and 57.

15. See Rules 3 and 5 of the "Rules Respecting Trade and Dues" from the British supplementary treaty signed in Shanghai in November 1858 as reprinted in Williams, *The Chinese Commercial Guide*, 70–71.

16. See William Mesny, *Mesny's Chinese Miscellany*, 43, 164.

17. Before the Grand Council developed into its powerful integrative position, the Grand Secretariat played an integrative role at various times throughout the Qing, , especially in routine matters.

18. The Six Boards were the Boards of Revenue (*hu bu*), War (*bing bu*), Personnel *(li bu)*, Rites (*li bu*), Punishments (*xing bu)*, and Works (*gong bu*). Each board had two presidents, one Manchu and one Chinese, and sometimes a superintendent (*zongli*) overall; each board also had four vice presidents, two Manchu and two Chinese. In addition, boards were staffed with various support personnel.

19. All provinces except Shanxi, Shandong, and Henan had a governor-general in charge of their provincial administration. In 1850, there were nine governors-general, with most overseeing two provinces. The governor-general was also usually the governor of one of the provinces under his jurisdiction. There were governors-general for the Manchurian provinces; for Hubei and Hunan; for Shaanxi, Gansu, and Xinjiang; for Guangdong and Guangxi; for Yunnan and Guizhou; for Jiangsu, Anhui, and Jiangxi; for Zhili; and for Sichuan. The last two positions required the governor-general to administer only one province.

20. Kenneth Lieberthal and Michel Oksenberg discuss a similar vertical/horizontal hierarchy phenomenon in relation to the twentieth-century PRC government. The PRC's government requires both formal and informal mechanisms for integration. This need is filled by a variety of comprehensive organs just below the apex of power, in which individuals play a crucial role. See

Lieberthal and Oksenberg, *Policy Making in China: Leaders, Structures, and Processes* (Princeton, NJ: Princeton University Press, 1988), chs. 1–3.

21. The Kangxi emperor inaugurated the use of the palace memorial as a secret method of gathering provincial information from officials whom he personally knew and trusted. These select, few officials sent memorials directly to the Kangxi emperor, bypassing official bureaucratic channels. The Yongzheng emperor greatly expanded the use of secret palace memorials in order to enhance secrecy and his control of information, policy-making power, and the power of the Inner Court. During the Yongzheng reign, more and more officials were permitted to send palace memorials. The Inner Court Ministers (who would soon become the grand councilors) aided the emperor in reading palace memorials and advised him on how to respond. See Beatrice Bartlett's *Monarchs and Ministers*, especially chapter one, for a thorough discussion of the development of the palace memorial system and its links to the Grand Council's development. Silas Wu discusses the structure of the memorial system in "The Memorial Systems of the Ch'ing Dynasty," *Harvard Journal of Asiatic Studies* 27 (1967): 7–75.

22. *DQHD*, Guangxu, *juan* 2.9.

23. The memorial and memorandum translated in full can be found in Appendix A, and the translated edict can be found in Appendix B.

24. *YWSM-XF* 71.19.

25. *YWSM-XF* 72.1–2.

26. *YWSM-XF* 72.22.

27. Tseng-tsai Wang states both seals were used regularly; see *Tradition and Change*, 108. In my own research, I came across the office title without the term "*tongshang*" or commerce far more often than with it.

28. Luo Bingmian in "Zongli yamen yu Manzu benwei zhengce" (The Zongli Yamen and the basic policy of the Manchus) raises the possibility that the Zongli Yamen and its founders were infused with Manchu thinking. The basic Manchu policy, Luo asserts, made the Manchus at Court fearful of assimilation and careful to keep leadership of organizations, especially those like the Grand Council and Zongli Yamen that dealt with military matters, in the hands of Manchus and close to the interests of the Manchu Imperial household. See Luo Bingmian, 163–75.

29. The clause was not, as has been asserted by Immanuel Hsu and Mark Mancall, intended to make the Yamen a subcommittee of the Grand Council. Hsu, *China's Entrance*, 107–25; and Mark Mancall, *China at the Center: Three Hundred Years of Foreign Policy* (New York: The Free Press, 1984), 173.

30. *YWSM-XF* 72.20.

31. Beatrice Bartlett in *Monarchs and Ministers* convincingly argues that concurrent positions contributed to the grand councilor's accrual of power. See Bartlett, 186–90, 261–62. Pao Chao Hsieh also noted the advantages of concurrent postings as a way to reduce friction between two offices with overlapping duties. See Pao Chao Hsieh, *The Government of China (1644–1911)* (Baltimore: The Johns Hopkins Press, 1925), 80.

32. Ministerial membership of the Zongli Yamen and Grand Council significantly overlapped, especially through 1884. For every year from 1862 until 1884, at least 50 percent of the grand councilors served concurrently on the Zongli Yamen. For the first half of the 1870s, four of the five grand councilors were also Zongli Yamen ministers each year; for the second half of the decade, all of the grand councilors were Zongli Yamen ministers concurrently. This heavy representation of grand councilors continued, even after the 1884 cashiering of Prince Gong and the rest of the Zongli Yamen ministers. For each of the years from 1887 until 1892, two of five grand councilors were Yamen ministers. Most years the Yamen still had at least 50 percent of the grand councilors on board. The year with the smallest representation is 1901 with only one of the four grand councilors on the Yamen. These figures attest to the continuing importance of the Zongli Yamen, even after Prince Gong's fall from power.

33. *YWSM-XF* 72.22.

34. *YWSM-XF* 72.19–22.

35. *YWSM-XF* 71.26–27.

36. *YWSM-XF* 73.10–12.

37. *YWSM-XF* 71.17–26.

38. *YWSM-XF* 72.1–2.

39. *YWSM-XF* 72.35–36.

40. *YWSM-XF* 71.17–26.

41. This was the equivalent of the mayor of Beijing.

42. *YWSM-XF* 71.17–26.

43. Ibid. The provinces of Jiangsu, Anhui, and Jiangxi constituted the jurisdiction of the governor-general of the Liang Jiang region.

44. After a search for qualified foreign-language teachers among the merchants of Canton and Shanghai ended in failure, the Zongli Yamen ministers proposed that foreigners be employed as the instructors. The students would also be taught Chinese subjects by Chinese teachers. See *YWSM-TZ*: 8.29–30. For more information on the Tong wen guan, see Knight Biggerstaff, *The Earliest Modern Government Schools in China* (Ithaca: Cornell University Press, 1961), chapter 2, and Su Jing, *Qingji tongwen guan ji qi laosheng* (Taipei: Su Jing, 1984).

45. *YWSM-XF* 71.17–26.

46. Thomas Metzger in *The Internal Organization of the Ch'ing Bureaucracy* discusses access to information as determining participation in decision making in the Qing dynasty. He also stresses the normative flexibility of the Qing system, which allowed officials to memorialize outside their domain. See Metzger, *Internal Organization,* 57, 168–77.

4

MAKING CHANGE WORK—
INSTITUTIONAL NEGOTIATIONS

ONCE IT WAS FORMALLY ESTABLISHED IN EARLY 1861, the Zongli Yamen assumed responsibility not only for central-government-level diplomatic efforts, but all activities and endeavors associated with foreign affairs arising at any level. The original mandate of the Yamen, as presented in the edict that created the new office, was limited and temporary and fell short of that envisioned by Prince Gong, Wenxiang, and Guiliang. Yet the Zongli Yamen did not prove to be temporary; it lasted through the last decade of the century. Moreover, it functioned within the many external and internal realms associated with the Western Affairs Movement (*yangwu yundong*) and the Self-Strengthening Movement.[1] The new office accrued power through institutional processes of reorganization by which the Zongli Yamen went from being a temporary institution to one of the most important offices of the late Qing. Prince Gong, Wenxiang, and Guiliang, now Zongli Yamen ministers, established a framework to extend the new Foreign Office's control beyond Beijing—a necessary step for a jurisdiction as broad as that of the new office—and in the process, altered Qing administrative organization and decision making by adding horizontal links to the parallel vertical hierarchies that had previously comprised Qing governmental structure.

In order to assume its foreign affairs responsibilities and its place in the institutional hierarchy, the new Zongli Yamen had to coordinate with other offices that had been previously charged or were newly charged with such duties. Because of the pivotal roles they were to play in the operation of the new foreign affairs machinery, two offices in particular received attention from the new foreign office. One, the office of *daotai* or circuit intendant, had long belonged to the regular territorial provincial administrative structure as the official heading a circuit (*dao*). The Zongli Yamen made the daotai a key position for controlling and monitoring Chinese interactions with the foreigners in the treaty ports. Philip Yuen-sang Leung has already convincingly demonstrated how the daotai's foreign affairs role in Shanghai expanded in the latter part of the nineteenth century.[2] Building on Leung's work, here I argue that the Zongli Yamen played a critical role in this expansion of power. For the Zongli Yamen, the challenge was to shift the existing circuit daotai's office from the territorial hierarchy into the jurisdiction of the Zongli Yamen, which did not have responsibility for territorial administration.[3] The Zongli Yamen ministers accomplished this through a reorganization of circuit seats to locate them in and coordinate them with the treaty ports, thereby making the circuit intendant a shared resource for territorial as well as foreign affairs administration. Once circuit seats were moved to treaty ports, daotais in essence and title became treaty port daotais. As such, they played a dual role in the developing Customs Administration and in the well-established system for provincial administration.

The second post that Zongli Yamen ministers turned their attention to was the superintendent of trade. Having been created along with the Zongli Yamen, the office of superintendent of trade was an outgrowth of the imperial commissioner tradition. From the memorial proposing the office, it is clear that Wenxiang, Prince Gong, and Guiliang initially intended the superintendents of trade to be institutionally subordinate to the new foreign office. However, as the office of superintendent of trade was actually established, the hierarchical relationship was not clearly defined in favor of the new Foreign Office. Rather, Zongli Yamen ministers asserted Zongli Yamen influence over the superintendents of trade through other institutional channels and through the use of overlapping personnel.[4] Through cultivating links between each of these positions and the Zongli Yamen, Zongli Yamen ministers helped strengthen the ties between the treaty port daotais and the superintendents of trade, resulting in both offices being closer to the Zongli Yamen. In short, the Yamen altered the structure of the Qing administrative hierarchy in order to create a foreign affairs administration with the Zongli Yamen at the apex of its hierarchy and outposts in the provinces.

Powers at Creation

The new Zongli Yamen had responsibility for the general handling of all matters concerning foreign countries. Interestingly, only five lines of the much longer six-point memorandum that outlined the structure of the new organization discuss the actual establishment of the Zongli Yamen. The bulk of the memorandum focuses on issues surrounding the creation of the Yamen; more specifically, it explores the potential relationship of the Zongli Yamen with other levels of officials and the communications process. Inserting a new organ into the Qing administrative machinery would prove to be a complicated affair, and the memorialists clearly recognized this. Thus, the memorandum outlines how the new office would interrelate and interact with other offices and existing policies. In this regard, Articles Two, Three, and Four are the most significant. Each of these details a different aspect of the conduct of foreign affairs at the provincial or local level. Each also ties local and provincial level interactions with foreigners to the central government and to the Zongli Yamen.

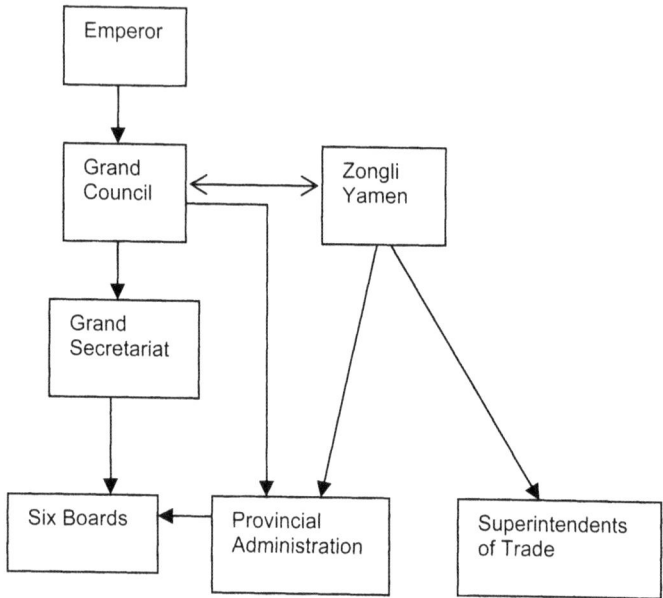

Figure 1. The Zongli Yamen's place in the Qing administrative structure as proposed by Prince Gong, Wenxiang, and Guiliang in initial memorial and memorandum.

Figure 1 provides a sketch of the proposed links, as detailed in the six-point memorandum, between the Zongli Yamen and other government organs. The superintendents of trade, the governors-general, and the governors were to send regular and monthly reports directly to the Zongli Yamen according to the arrangement in Article Two. The significance of this lay in the flow of communication. The Zongli Yamen was to be the main repository of the information, enabling it to have a comprehensive view of diplomatic affairs throughout the empire. The discussion of Article Three centered on Customs administration, the most meaningful aspect of the article being that the Zongli Yamen ministers had started to rearrange Customs personnel. The Maritime Customs Bureau, which had its roots in foreigners' efforts during the Taiping Rebellion to collect duties, had been expanded and systematized in the Treaties of Tianjin of 1858. Article Three attempts to make officials in charge of customs in each of the treaty ports responsible to the superintendents of trade. Combined with the second article, Article Three put the Zongli Yamen in a position superior to the Customs administration through the superintendents of trade. This became more important as the Zongli Yamen worked to make daotais in the treaty ports also responsible for foreign customs.[5] In Article Four, the memorialists proposed a system by which horizontal communications were to take place between offices of equal rank that belonged to different parallel hierarchies, in order to facilitate communications and avoid misunderstandings. Significantly, this extra communication was to be in addition to regular reports sent to the Zongli Yamen, creating additional information gathering mechanisms for the new office.

The edicts issued in response to the memorials formalized the existence of the Zongli Yamen; however, they also modified its proposed structure in significant ways. Instead of an institution that clearly headed a new arm of the government, the Zongli Yamen in its initial stages was not necessarily superior to the two superintendents of trade (this will be discussed more fully below). Just as important, provincial officials were not instructed in the edicts to report all of their matters concerning foreign affairs directly to the Zongli Yamen. Instead, officials were to "communicate with the Board of Rites, who will, in turn, hand communications over to the Zongli geguo shiwu yamen." In the same edict, the military governors, governors-general, and governors are told to "keep each other mutually informed," but the means by which they were to do so remained unclear. More important in this regard, the provincial officials did not receive orders to send their communications to the Zongli Yamen as well. Thus, no clearinghouse of information was specified.[6] Figure 2 sketches the ambiguous ties between the offices that resulted from the edicts establishing the Zongli Yamen.

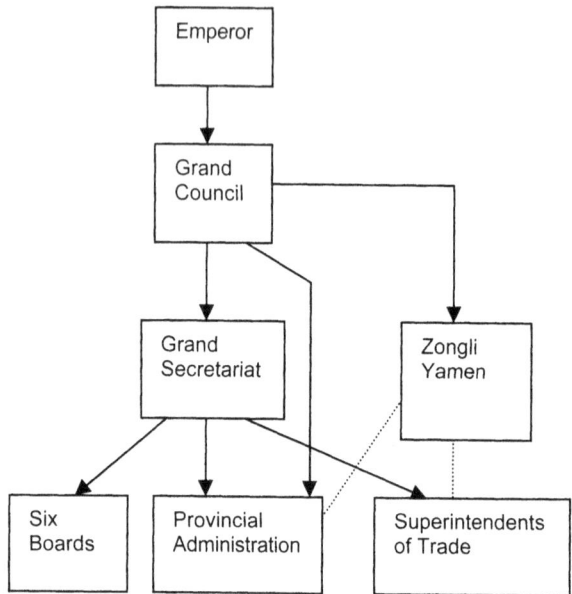

Figure 2. Place of Zongli Yamen in Qing administrative structure as determined by the edict establishing the Yamen.

Because the links between the Zongli Yamen and the Grand Council were not clear, and because communications did not flow directly to the Zongli Yamen, the Yamen at its inception held an ambiguous position in the hierarchy. Moreover, despite the high standing of the Grand Secretariat on paper, it had already been functionally displaced by the Grand Council, making the new Zongli Yamen's position more difficult to outline. One of the first calls to action, then, was for the Yamen ministers to sort out and clarify the relationships between the Yamen and the superintendents of trade, governors-general, and central government institutions. As the edicts left the hierarchy indefinite, subsequent practice determined the actual role and position of the Yamen in the Qing administrative structure.

Powers of Reorganization

Because of the debate behind its creation, asserting and enforcing its jurisdiction was among the Yamen's first priorities; it needed to gain control of foreign affairs within the central government and within the provinces. Only then could it turn its attention to the rapidly increasing contacts with Westerners along the coast. Instead of directly handling lower-level disputes with foreigners in the provinces, the Yamen brought the local and provincial offices that handled such matters into the new foreign affairs institutional hierarchy. In fact, Yamen ministers allowed many treaty-port-level contacts with foreigners to continue unhampered by central government intervention. Since interaction with foreigners preceded its establishment, the new Zongli Yamen had first to standardize existing practices among the provinces, as well as establish new procedures to bring these practices under central control.

While the superintendents of trade evolved and developed as the regional heads responsible for foreign affairs duties, the Zongli Yamen worked to establish more direct lines with another office— that of *daotai*. Daotais, or intendants, were an important part of the regular provincial administration. Some held specialized responsibilities, such as the salt or grain intendants, while most had more general administrative responsibilities. The latter were designated *fen xun dao* or *fen shou dao* or daotais; these officials headed the administration of two or more prefectures, independent subprefectures, or departments.[7] Daotais were also responsible for the administrative supervision of prefects, subprefects, and county magistrates (the lowest of the official postings in the Qing system) within their circuits. The number of counties within the domain of each daotai ranged from a few to more than fifteen. On the provincial level, each province consisted of anywhere from two (Anhui province) to eight (Zhili and Gansu provinces) circuits, each with a daotai in charge, who was, in turn, responsible for the offices within the jurisdiction of that particular circuit. Even in the provinces with relatively large numbers of circuits, a daotai's physical area of responsibility was large. Table 1 illustrates the relative positions and rankings of offices within the provincial administration structure. Although the number of officials in each category from daotai to magistrate varied within each province and within each circuit, the administrative structure for all of the provinces was similar.

Table 1.   Official Hierarchy of a Province with Territorial Jurisdictions of Lower Officials

Governor-general (*zongdu*) (ranked 1B)
Governor (*xunfu*) (2A)
Provincial treasurers (*buzheng shi*) (2B); and Provincial judges (*ancha shi*) (3A)
Superintendant / Daotai (circuit or *dao* level) (4A)
Prefects / Zhifu (prefectural or *fu* level) (4B)
Subprefects / Tongzhi (5A) (subprefectural or *ting* level)
Magistrates / Zhixian (7B) (county or *xian* level)

In addition to regular administrative duties, daotais in circuits with foreign contact also had a number of foreign-affairs-related responsibilities. With no institutional framework for foreign relations, however, each daotai resolved issues concerning foreigners within his jurisdiction according to his own experience and vision. Thus, until the arrival of the Zongli Yamen there was no institutional means of assuring consistency of approach to problems and issues related to foreign contact in the provinces. Consequently, Zongli Yamen ministers ranked centralizing the daotais' individual policies among their priorities. By extension, a unified approach implemented by daotais in the treaty ports would provide county magistrates, the most local of Qing officials, with better guidance for actions involving foreigners.

The daotais communicated with the central government in Beijing through the office of the provincial governor or governor-general. For the most part, a daotai submitted reports to the provincial government, which would, in turn, forward information to the throne through the Grand Secretariat or the Grand Council. Owing to the distance between places like Fujian or Sichuan and Beijing, regular communications between the center and provinces could take upward of a month or two, although there were means in place for faster service. With the arrival of steamships, however, communications between the southeast coast or ports along the Yangzi and Beijing took less than a week. After Qing authorities authorized the construction of a telegraph line between Beijing and Shanghai in 1880 and 1881, the process became yet faster.[8] Not surprisingly, the new technologies contributed to a more coordinated and centralized approach to foreign affairs.

In his work on county governments, John Watt argues that the Qing experienced a long-term rationalization and centralization of government that extended to the local level. He associates these trends with the urbanization that occurred throughout the Qing. Most important for this discussion is Watt's assertion that the Qing central government strove to keep a balance between administrative and economic centers and to keep those with administrative power in control of those with economic power.[9] With the establishment of the treaty ports, the Zongli Yamen faced a similar challenge. The new treaty ports were either long-established economic centers or they were chosen to become trade centers, but they were not necessarily administrative centers. The gulf had to be bridged, and the Zongli Yamen brought its nascent administrative weight to bear on the situation to assert its presence in distant hubs of foreign activity by aligning economic and administrative powers.

After the Treaty of Nanjing, but prior to the establishment of the Zongli Yamen, the Qing Court used two types of officials for the conduct of foreign affairs in the treaty ports: daotais whose circuits had jurisdiction over the newly created treaty ports or officials specially charged with management of foreign affairs in treaty ports.[10] Whether or not a daotai assumed this role depended on the location of the seat of the circuit and the experience of the particular official. Examining the case of each of the original treaty ports is instructive. Two of the original treaty ports, Fuzhou and Xiamen, both in Fujian, were circuit seats. Nonetheless, in 1842 the Fujian provincial treasurer, Xu Jiyu, not the circuit daotai, was ordered to handle relations with foreigners.[11] After the Conventions of Beijing, however, the circuit daotais located in each of the two cities took over foreign affairs duties. Xu Jiyu continued working in the area of foreign affairs as a Zongli Yamen minister, starting in 1865. In two of the other five ports, Shanghai and Ningbo, the daotai was charged with diplomatic responsibilities. In the last, Canton, the imperial commissioner, the governor-general, and the provincial treasurer shared this responsibility.

The Treaties of Tianjin (1858) and Conventions of Beijing (1860) opened an additional eleven Chinese ports to foreign trade.[12] Of these, only one, Jiujiang, was already a circuit seat when it became a treaty port. Within a few years, however, each of them became the seat of a treaty port daotai. Administrative reorganization, while not unheard of in the Qing, was not the norm. The reassignment of circuit seats to treaty ports in the early 1860s reflected a policy on the part of the Zongli Yamen to associate treaty ports with circuit seats. The Yamen ministers' desire to do so indicated the importance of developing a centralized policy, as well as their recognition of the ports' growing economic significance. The volume of trade at the ports contributed to their growing economic significance. By 1865, Shanghai, Fuzhou, and Hankou had all surpassed Canton—the foreign trade center under the pretreaty cohong system—in terms of duties collected.[13]

Reassigning daotai yamens to treaty ports was an effort on the part of Zongli Yamen ministers to keep the balance between economic and administrative nodes of power. On a more practical level, the relocation of circuit seats was necessary to centralization efforts, since the treaty ports stipulated in the Treaties of Nanjing and Tianjin belonged to different levels of Qing spatial administrative hierarchy. Fuzhou, for instance, was a provincial capital and circuit seat while the northern city of Niuzhuang was a subprefectural seat.[14] Niuzhuang, a relatively minor city, became a treaty port in 1861. In the same year, the prefect was ordered to move the prefectural seat to the city of Yingkou, though the superintendent of customs at Shanhaiguan handled foreign affairs. In 1864, the city of Yingkou, thirty miles to the south of Niuzhuang, started to serve as the treaty port instead of Niuzhuang. In 1866, the Zongli Yamen abolished the office of Shanhaiguan superintendent of customs. Then the seat of the circuit daotai was moved from Shanhaiguan to Yingkou. Thus, Yingkou's level in the administrative hierarchy was brought to that of circuit seat in a series of reorganizations. Such restructuring of the administrative hierarchy at the treaty ports was an important part of central government efforts to streamline and restructure foreign affairs.[15] Only after the treaty port administration was standardized could the Zongli Yamen structure have regular channels of communication. With this done, the Zongli Yamen assigned treaty port daotais the task of handling foreign relations in the treaty ports. In fact, in 1870 the Zongli Yamen recognized that treaty port daotais fell into a different category than regular circuit daotais; specifically, treaty port daotais had foreign relations duties in addition to their traditional duties.[16] This accrual of responsibilities had been orchestrated by Zongli Yamen ministers to channel on-site interactions with foreigners to the office of treaty port daotai in order to ease communication between the central government and localities.

The Superintendents of Trade

The Southern Superintendent of Trade

The origins and development of the superintendents of the northern and southern ports were very closely related to the use of imperial commissioners and to the establishment of the Zongli Yamen. During the period of the First Opium War, the Qing Court dispatched an imperial commissioner to manage the negotiations with the British, resulting in the Treaty of Nanjing. After the Treaty of Nanjing was concluded, however, the Court did not dispense with the appointment; rather, it retained an imperial commissioner to manage the commercial affairs of the five newly opened treaty ports. The imperial commissioner title, however, was changed to include the designation of superintendent of the five ports (*wu kou qinchai dachen*), with the governor-general of the Liang Jiang region concurrently holding the post of superintendent of the five ports.[17] In 1844, the governor-general of the Liang Guang area became the concurrent holder of the superintendent of the five ports title.[18] For the next fourteen years, the post of superintendent remained associated with the Liang Guang governor-general; after which it moved back to the governor-general of the Liang Jiang region. The changes of association of the post from Nanjing to Canton and back again were connected to the amount and location of foreign trade and negotiations. Nanjing, as the site of the treaty negotiation, initially played a more strategic role, but the amount of contact and trade in Canton soon caused the Qing Court to move its commissioner there. Only with another round of treaty negotiations and the naming of Nanjing as a treaty port did the post move back to Nanjing.[19]

With the ratification of the Conventions of Beijing came eleven new treaty ports along the coast and rivers. Because the superintendent of the five ports could not simultaneously serve as governor and track the events in numerous dispersed treaty ports, subgroupings emerged. Initially, all except the three northernmost new ports were grouped with the original five treaty ports and put under the jurisdiction of the acting superintendent (and imperial commissioner) and governor of Jiangsu, Xue Huan.[20] Although the government still used the name "superintendent of the five ports," many people and documents referred to the post as the "Shanghai superintendent of trade" (*Shanghai tongshang dachen*), because of the superintendent's residence in Shanghai. The larger number of ports and the need for easier management soon dictated further changes. On March 24, 1862, Xue Huan, by orders of the central government, gave up his duties as governor of Jiangsu and solely focused on his duties of superintendent of trade.[21] In the summer of that year, the term "southern superintendent of trade" (*nanyang tongshang dachen*) started to appear. This was the beginning of the division into the superintendent of trade for the northern ports and the super-intendent of trade for the southern ports. The initiation of the southern superintendent as an independent post reflected the evolution of the imperial commissioner tradition that had been utilized for the negotiation of treaties. Central government officials increasingly recognized the importance of trade issues, but hoped to keep the majority of these dealings limited to the treaty ports. By relieving Xue Huan of his duties as governor, the throne extended the practice of granting imperial commissioners more independence and stature. The rest of the administrative structure, however, did not support the functioning of the superintendent of trade for the southern ports as an independent post, as it was not part of regular bureaucratic functioning.

Before long, Xue Huan sent a memorial to the throne. Frustrated, he complained that although the superintendent had been charged with foreign affairs, his responsibility was in name only. In the two years that he had been posted to Shanghai as superintendent, he had not performed distinct duties; instead, his duties fell under the domain of and were actually carried out by the governor of Jiangsu. He wrote that by itself the post of superintendent of trade for the southern ports had limited power and hard-to-meet expenses; thus, he suggested that the post revert to being held concurrently by the governor-general of the Liang Jiang region.[22] In response, the Zongli Yamen consulted Zeng Guofan (the governor-general of Liang Jiang),

Guanwen (the governor-general of Hu Guang),[23] Li Hongzhang (the acting governor of Jiangsu), and Xue Huan himself. In February of 1863, the Zongli Yamen determined that Li Hongzhang would assume the post concurrently with his responsibilities as governor of Jiangsu.[24] When Li assumed the post of governor-general of Liang Jiang in summer of 1865, he kept his assignment as superintendent of trade of the southern ports, and from this point, the post became more permanently associated with the post of governor-general of Liang Jiang.[25] During the earlier periods of treaty negotiation, the imperial commissioners had carried seals of the same designation as governors-general or governors, but did not necessarily hold an official post.[26] The close link to the position of the governor-general of Liang Jiang was a step toward formalizing the post of southern superintendent of trade and making it a regular part of the bureaucracy.

The duties of the superintendent of southern trade included managing trade in the open ports along the Yangzi River and the southeast coast, as well as a variety of diplomatic responsibilities. According to the *Qing Statutes*, the superintendent "had responsibility for foreign affairs for the port of Shanghai and those ports inland along the Yangzi. For the treaty ports in Fujian, Guangdong, and Zhejiang, the superintendent had shared responsibility," along with the governors-general and governors.[27] The terseness of the passage is misleading. A more complete and correct description would be that before the Second Opium War, the superintendent of trade managed the negotiation process with foreigners, but without much in the way of independent powers. In addition, his role was limited to specific projects. After 1858 the Qing Court dispatched a more highly placed imperial commissioner in order to expedite negotiations. Although the Court had increased the standing of the imperial commissioner and taken a step toward making the commissioner the equivalent of his Western counterparts, the commissioner's discretion and power remained limited to discrete assignments. In close relationship to the establishment of the Zongli Yamen and a regular place for foreign affairs, the responsibilities of the imperial commissioner, in the form of superintendent of trade, broadened. The mandate of the new Zongli Yamen as the main organization for foreign affairs provided the framework for the post of the new superintendents of trade as a more permanent fixture in the bureaucracy and as an arm of the foreign affairs machinery. The rest of the *Qing Statutes* entry reveals the connection of the superintendents to the Yamen. In resolving matters within his region, the superintendent was to settle minor affairs on site either on his own or by consulting with provincial and local officials. For more important matters, the superintendent was to inform the Zongli Yamen or report directly to the throne. Being cognizant and informed of matters large and small formed the basis of the superintendent's responsibilities.[28] In addition to his diplomatic role, the superintendent was also to be active in the realm of customs and duties by sending reports on such matters to both the Zongli Yamen and the Board of Revenue.[29] He thereby was to play a key role in keeping the central government and the Zongli Yamen informed of happenings in the treaty ports.

By making the superintendent of the southern ports a concurrent title to be held by the governor-general of Liang Jiang, the Zongli Yamen altered the structural hierarchy in its favor. The governor-general of Liang Jiang, as superintendent of trade, now reported on foreign affairs to the Zongli Yamen. In addition, the treaty ports that were not under the sole jurisdiction of the southern superintendent were part of his shared jurisdiction with other involved governors; by extension, the Zongli Yamen had established administrative lines to those governors.

Regularizing conflict resolution and communication of urgent matters ranked high among the priorities of the Yamen and the Court, and the southern superintendent of trade played a crucial function in creating a working system. The parallel nature of the Qing hierarchy presented challenges in this regard in that the superintendent often received word of noteworthy events and conflicts involving foreigners, but he was informed not as the person responsible for resolving the problems, but as the collector of information. Customs or provincial officials, each legitimately claiming responsibility for affairs with foreigners, informed the superintendent sometimes only after informing the central government in Beijing—and not necessarily the Zongli Yamen. Linking the superintendent to a powerful provincial post and pulling him into the nascent foreign affairs administration contributed to the solution of the Zongli Yamen's information problem. By channeling information flow to the Zongli Yamen, the Yamen, not the superintendency of trade or other central organs, could evolve into the highest-ranking institution for foreign affairs.

The Northern Superintendent of Trade

In contrast with the southern superintendent of trade, which had its roots in the Treaty of Nanjing, the northern superintendent of trade, also known as the superintendent of trade for the three northern ports (*beiyang dachen* or *san kou tongshang dachen*), had its roots in the Treaty of Tianjin. The throne named a special official to manage trade in the newly opened ports in 1860.[30] Article Two of the six-point memorandum called for the formalization of this post along with that of the Zongli Yamen. Despite the fact that the Foreign Office and the northern superintendent were conceived of together, the creation of the northern superintendent of trade challenged the new Foreign Office in a number of ways. From the outset, Zongli Yamen ministers recognized the need for highly placed officials with regional responsibilities for the north and south. Prince Gong, Wenxiang, and Guiliang suggested that Heng Qi and Chong Hou be posted to Tianjin as the superintendents of the three northern ports, while Xue Huan be posted in the south.[31] The Zongli Yamen planned to have the regional officials play a crucial role in the conduct of foreign relations. Without access to the information in these newly opened ports, the proposed Zongli Yamen would be ineffective. By utilizing the superintendents, however, the Yamen could have more local eyes and ears. As proposed by the Zongli Yamen architects, the new posts were to be subordinate to the Zongli Yamen. As established, however, the posts acquired a certain amount of independence from the Yamen.

After ratification of the Conventions of Beijing, the French and British troops retreated from Beijing to Tianjin. Winter approached and the allied commanders and ministers remained skeptical that the Qing Court intended to uphold the new treaties; therefore, the British and French ministers decided to station their forces in Tianjin until spring, instead of retreating altogether. As a result of the British and French decision, Tianjin became not only open to trade by treaty, but the allied troops immediately created a significant foreign presence. Consequently, the Court expected foreign commerce and contact to increase quickly, as merchants and missionaries were sure to follow the soldiers. With the military presence and the expected influx of other foreigners, Prince Gong and his cohort suggested that the throne dispatch Heng Qi to accompany the Western troops to Tianjin and remain there to manage the new affairs. Chong Hou, too, went to Tianjin to assist Heng Qi. The Xianfeng emperor clarified Prince Gong's suggestion by declaring that the two officials stationed in Tianjin were the subordinates of Prince Gong, the head of the new Zongli Yamen. The edict continued with instructions to Heng Qi to manage less important matters on site, without assistance from Beijing. Significant matters, on the other hand, warranted a report to Prince Gong and the Zongli Yamen. The prince would then notify the throne with a memorial.[32] Significantly, Heng Qi and Chong Hou did not have direct access to the throne, revealing that the two officials assumed a set of responsibilities connected and subordinate to the new Zongli Yamen. This particular arrangement lasted only two and a half months, but it served as the starting point for the more permanent post of the northern superintendent of trade, the northern counterpart of the superintendent of trade of the southern ports.

While the treaty ports along the Yangzi and the southeast coast belonged to the jurisdiction of the previously established imperial commissioner of the five ports, the northern ports of Niuzhuang (later Yingkou), Tianjin, Dengzhou (later Yantai) were assigned to the superintendent for trade for the three ports. Unlike the title for the commissioner in the south, the northern title did not include the term "*qinchai*" or imperial commissioner. The absence of the term was perhaps indicative of the relative importance of the two posts in their early stages. The southern superintendent had already played a role in diplomatic affairs, and the expectation at Court and the Zongli Yamen was that he would continue to do so. The northern superintendent, on the other hand, was in charge of an area with fewer harbors conducive to foreign trade; perhaps more important for the post's standing, the Court did not want to encourage foreign traders to operate close to Beijing. Consequently, the northern post had not played and was not expected to play as important a role as its southern counterpart, as was demonstrated by its funding. In order to save expenses, the post of Changlu salt intendant was to revert to the governor-general of Zhili, and the monies used for the newly defunct salt intendant would go to the superintendent of trade for the three ports. In other words, the northern position was not deemed worthy of allocation of new funds.[33]

Chong Hou's instructions indicated that he should cooperate with the governors-general, governors, and military officials of the port areas. He had plenty of opportunities to do so, as he served in the position for nearly ten years until 1870. Within this period, he left to serve as acting governor-general of Zhili, during which time the Zongli Yamen minister Dong Xuan assumed responsibility for the three northern ports. Significantly, the two posts remained separate through-out this time.

This changed in the summer of 1870 when the hostility many Chinese residents of Tianjin felt toward foreigners exploded into violence. Many local Chinese viewed the presence of the Catholic Church and Christian missionaries with suspicion; many believed rumors circulating that the missionaries horribly mistreated Chinese children in their care. The construction of the huge Catholic cathedral on the site of an imperial temple in Tianjin added to the animosity. The general situation was tense with crowds gathering frequently to protest the foreign presence. When the French consul Henri Fontanier decided to confront the magistrate over his seeming indifference toward the aggressive crowds, he did so by arriving at the magistrate's yamen with a drawn sword and two pistols. Angered by the magistrate's attitude, Fontanier fired one of his pistols, and although he missed the magistrate, he killed a bystander. The furious crowd killed Fontanier and his companion; they then continued to a Catholic convent where they killed ten Sisters of Mercy. Altogether, nineteen foreigners—three Russians and sixteen Frenchmen—lost their lives that day, and foreigners of the time quickly dubbed the event the Tianjin Massacre.[34]

The killings in Tianjin and the foreign uproar that followed prompted the Court to recall Chong Hou and send him to France as the Chinese government representative deputed to bear reparations and apology. Before his departure the Court increased Chong Hou's standing by bestowing on him the title "imperial commissioner to France," indicating the perception that his title of superintendent of trade was insufficient for the task at hand.[35] First Zongli Yamen minister Mao Changxi and then Cheng Lin took over as acting superintendent for the three northern ports for Chong Hou while he was in France.[36] The overlap of Zongli Yamen ministers serving as superintendent of the northern ports indicated the increased prominence given to the position by the central government.

In addition, the mob action in Tianjin and the settlement with France prompted some in the Qing Court to criticize the lack of real power of the superintendent of trade of the northern ports. Mao Changxi suggested that the post's separation from the regular provincial government and its "responsibility for maintaining local peace while having no military power" had contributed to the outbreaks of violence in Tianjin against foreigners, especially since local officials did not always relay the severity of discontent and disturbances to Beijing.[37] After Mao returned to Beijing from Tianjin, the Zongli Yamen sent a memorial to the throne with Mao's suggestions that the post be abolished in its current form and be re-created on the model of the commissioner of trade for the southern ports. The memorial also suggested that the post be held concurrently with the office of governor-general of Zhili. According to Mao and the memorial, the post had only developed separately as a result of rebellions demanding the governor-general's attention and preventing him from handling coastal defense and foreign affairs.[38] Prince Gong and the other Zongli Yamen ministers reported that they agreed with Mao's assessment. Their memorial proposed that "Commerce in the three [northern] ports did not require a separate official. The governor-general of Zhili should manage the foreign affairs and coastal defense of the ports. Moreover, as in the case of the commissioner of trade of the southern ports, a seal with the words 'Imperial Commissioner' [*qinchai*] should be issued." The instructions went on to say that the governor-general should rotate between residence in Tianjin and Baoding, depending on the season.[39] The Court approved the recommendations. Less than three months after he had become governor-general of Zhili, Li Hongzhang was appointed superintendent of the northern Ports, but with "*qinchai*" added to the title, making him an imperial commissioner.[40] This latter designation broadened the duties of the northern superintendent, as it had for the southern superintendent. From this point on, the governor-general of Zhili held the title of superintendent of trade for the northern ports as an imperial commissioner, thereby allowing the post of superintendent access to the regular provincial administration.

As listed in the *Statutes of the Qing Dynasty*, the duties for the superintendent of trade for the northern ports ranged from attending diplomatic matters in the ports to controlling coastal defense to managing customs for the Jinhai, Donghai, and Shanhaiguan customs houses. He also managed cases of merchant or industrial activity. When deemed of national scope or importance, the superintendent was to set up a bureau dedicated to specific industrial activities, such as mining or telegraphy, and appoint an official as manager.[41] Li Hongzhang as the superintendent of the northern ports utilized this charge by assuming responsibility for the China Merchants' Steam Navigation Company.[42] The broad range of duties in the north exceeded the scope of the southern superintendent of trade, who was also in charge of coastal defense and foreign affairs, but did not become involved to the same degree as the northern superintendent.

Li Hongzhang's authority as northern superintendent grew to the point that one scholar has described him as a one-man challenge to the Zongli Yamen.[43] Li indisputably acquired power and influence; however, his loyalties remained true to the central government, and he remained in its service throughout his career. Thus, although Li's clout increased through his posting as superintendent of trade, he did not as a result of his growing influence eclipse the functions of the Zongli Yamen. Rather, the structure of the superintendent post contributed to both Li's rise to power and the office's subordination to the Zongli Yamen. Further, his role as superintendent of trade has been overlooked in estimations of Li's remarkable career. Philip Yuen-sang Leung explains the broad role in modernization efforts of men like Li Hongzhang as a result of the absence of precedent for and the general lack of interest in modernization projects, allowing officials like Li who were interested to retain control of projects outside their regular jurisdiction. Li's assignment as northern superintendent of trade broadened his administrative and regional jurisdiction even further by aiding his transition from a provincial official to a metropolitan and national official, providing him a national stage for his projects. This extension of opportunity was especially important for officials who had been responsible for Self-Strengthening projects who were transferred to different regions and continued working on both ongoing and new projects. Moreover, in the case of Li his modernization efforts in the north were linked to those in the south.[44]

Many scholars have attributed the strength and breadth of the northern post to the person of Li Hongzhang.[45] The needs of the Qing Court, however, also contributed to the strength of the two superintendents. While the south appeared to be the main arena for interaction with the foreigners, the southern superintendent out-weighed the northern superintendent in prestige and position. Once that arena moved to the north, the situation reversed. Li Hongzhang maneuvered the various responsibilities of his two concurrent positions so that they reinforced each other and expanded in the process. Moreover, through his accrual of duties, he simultaneously helped connect and distance the superintendent of the northern ports in relation to the Zongli Yamen.

Roles of the Superintendents

When contemplating the northern and southern superintendent posts, Prince Gong and his colleagues envisioned officials who not only aided in commercial matters in the new ports, but officials who would also act as agents and representatives of the Zongli Yamen in conducting local foreign affairs responsibilities on site. Even while the Zongli Yamen was still in the process of negotiating its own establishment, Prince Gong was already instructing Xue Huan, as superintendent, to negotiate with the foreigners and prevent the lesser Western powers seeking to forge unequal treaties of their own from doing so. Such a responsibility exceeded a purely regional duty and clearly had national and international implications. Because of the consequences of the outcome, the Qing Court hoped that Xue Huan could employ the assistance of the existing treaty powers in maintaining the status quo as far as the number of treaty signatories was concerned. Foreign representatives from England, France, and the United States, however, all refused to meet with Xue Huan on the matter, not because of the issue, but because of the procedure. With their new treaty rights of access to the central government, they would not negotiate with a post they viewed as regional. Even the smaller Western countries that did not yet have treaty rights bypassed Xue Huan and sent representatives straight to Beijing.[46] Thus, although the Zongli Yamen hoped that the southern superintendent would take over some of the diplomatic duties of the Foreign Office in the South, the Yamen and the Court did not grant him sufficient powers and prestige to convince Western representatives that he was more than a regional official.

For the northern superintendent, the situation was different. In the summer of 1861, Prince Gong sent a communication to the French and British envoys stating that when foreigners wished to go to Beijing, they needed to go first to their consulate. There they would request a certificate of permission, which would then be sent to register the request with the superintendent of trade for the three ports. The superintendent would then instruct the Tianjin prefect to affix his seal; at which point, the superintendent would give instructions to inform the Chongwen Gate. Only then could the foreigners proceed with their journey to Beijing.[47] The British and French did not object to this arrangement. The Zongli Yamen then attempted to have Chong Hou deny nontreaty powers the right to enter Beijing to seek treaties, but these efforts faltered. As a result, the Yamen appointed an additional minister to assist Chong Hou, and at the same time, made both men "imperial commissioners" (*qinchai dachen*) to aid them in their negotiations. The two imperial commissioners then negotiated treaties in Tianjin with Denmark and Holland in 1863, Spain in 1864, and Belgium in 1865. Moreover, the Zongli Yamen successfully informed treaty countries that new foreign ministers arriving in China had to first stop in Tianjin and inform the superintendent of the three ports. The superintendent would then inform the Zongli Yamen of the arrival, meaning foreign envoys had to communicate initially through the superintendent of the three ports in order to proceed to Beijing.[48] In effect, Chong Hou, as superintendent, was an on-site foreign affairs representative of the Zongli Yamen and the central government. In the twenty-five-year period from 1870 to 1895 when Li Hongzhang held the position, the post became even more important, and Li, as superintendent, played an increasingly large role in foreign affairs and treaty negotiations with Japan, England, France, Russia, Korea, Peru, and Brazil. Under the guidance of Li Hongzhang and the Zongli Yamen, the post of northern superintendent of trade became an integral part of the Zongli Yamen's foreign affairs machinery.

The Zongli Yamen's relationship with the northern and southern superintendents of trade centered on diplomatic and commercial affairs. The diplomatic efforts of both posts made the positions of the offices vis-à-vis the Zongli Yamen hard to determine definitively. This was especially the case for Superintendent Li Hongzhang, since his activities covered such a broad range. Despite any overlap of activities, however, the superintendents clearly belonged to the new foreign affairs hierarchy that was established by Prince Gong and his cohort and was headed by the Zongli Yamen, with the central government granting the superintendents a certain amount of disc-retion and authority. As noted earlier, the superintendents were to resolve minor diplomatic and commercial affairs with the assistance of provincial and local officials, without guidance from the Zongli Yamen. They did, however, have to keep the Yamen informed with regular communications. Major incidents and problems were handled differently. For significant matters that concerned the Qing Court or were of urgency, the superintendents were to send a memorial or telegram. The Zongli Yamen, after rendering a recommendation, would inform the superintendent how to proceed.[49]

Because the superintendents maintained decision-making power for many minor matters, they have been portrayed as equal in stature to the Zongli Yamen. The fact that they turned to the Zongli Yamen in accordance with the statute for guidance in serious matters demonstrates that the superintendents belonged to a lower rung in the emerging foreign affairs hierarchy. Even Li Hongzhang revealed in his letters that he consulted regularly with the Zongli Yamen ministers. In addition, when starting in 1872 he traveled to Beijing for his yearly audience with the throne, he also met with the Zongli Yamen ministers.[50]

More telling perhaps was the vocabulary of communication used between offices. Despite the ambiguous standing of the Zongli Yamen at its birth, all its ministers had high standing within the central government. Communications that arrived at the Zongli Yamen from governors-general and the superintendents of trade reflected the reality of the Zongli Yamen's standing. A common form of written communication for nonroutine matters from the super-intendents and provincial officials to the Zongli Yamen was the *zicheng*, denoting communication to a superior.[51] Provincial officials kept the Zongli Yamen informed of routine matters through regular reports sent to both the Board of Rites and the Yamen. Thus, in its operations the Zongli Yamen overcame the ambiguity of its position as it was sketched in its founding edict.

The superintendents of trade and the Zongli Yamen shared a close relationship, borne out by the career paths of the superintendents. Both Xue Huan and Chong Hou received promotions to Zongli Yamen minister shortly after their tenures as trade superintendents. Conversely, Dong Xun, Mao Changxi, and Chang Lin—all Zongli Yamen ministers—served as northern superintendent of trade for a short time. In addition, Li Hongzhang, Wang Wenshao and Rong Lu, who served concurrently as northern superintendent of trade and governor-general of Zhili, entered the Zongli Yamen.[52] The throne issued these promotions and transfers, yet if there had not been close ties between the Zongli Yamen and the superintendents, the exchange of personnel between the provincial officials and the metropolitan Yamen would surely have taken place less often.

Conclusion

Zongli Yamen ministers overcame their office's initial institutional shortcomings through reorganizing offices key to the development of a foreign affairs field administration. In the case of the daotai, the ministers relocated circuit seats to the treaty ports. By virtue of its mandate to handle foreign affairs, the reorganization brought the daotais within the reach of the Zongli Yamen by linking the otherwise parallel and separate territorial and foreign affairs administrative hierarchies. The Zongli Yamen also needed to establish through practice a superior position to the superintendents of trade. Because of the superintendents' regional jurisdiction and responsibility for foreign affairs in the treaty ports, treaty port daotais reported to them. The dual nature of the treaty port daotai, belonging both to the regular provincial and the new foreign affairs administrations, meant that the daotais worked with both provincial officials and the superintendents of trade. Provincial governors and superintendents both reported to the Zongli Yamen on foreign affairs, resulting in treaty port daotais further falling within the domain of the Zongli Yamen. The superintendents of trade along with the treaty port daotais comprised the Zongli Yamen's main regional operatives. By focusing in its early years on the reorganization of the key positions of superintendents of trade and treaty port daotais, Zongli Yamen ministers created the personnel base necessary to make the nascent foreign affairs administration operative.

NOTES

1. Western affairs (*yangwu*) included the handling of diplomatic matters with the West, as well as efforts to strengthen China through the building of a modern military, navy, mining industry, arsenals, etc., in an effort to strengthen all of Chinese society. For a discussion of Chinese-language works on the Western Affairs Movement, see Jiang Chen, "Recent Chinese Historiography in the Western Affairs Movement: Yangwu Yundong ca. 1860–1895," *Late Imperial China* 7, no. 1 (1986): 112–27.

2. For a discussion of the growing role of the Shanghai daotai in late Qing foreign affairs, see Philip Yuen-sang Leung, *The Shanghai Taotai: Linkage Man in a Changing Society, 1843–1890* (Honolulu: University of Hawaii Press, 1990), especially chapters 4 and 5.

3. The word "yamen" is a generic term that refers to the official residence and office of a government official. Each magistrate had a yamen, each daotai a yamen, etc. Thus, some cities that served as seats for multiple counties or that were seats for multiple levels of imperial governance would have multiple yamens, one for each office or official.

4. For an interesting discussion on the intersection of the offices of daotai and superintendent of trade of the northern ports as well as a discussion of personnel selection in Shanghai, see Yuen-sang Leung's "The Shanghai-Tientsin Connection: Li Hung-chang's Political Control over Shanghai," in Samuel C. Chu and Kwang-Ching Liu, eds., *Li Hung-chang and China's Early Modernization* (Armonk, NY: An East Gate Book, M.E. Sharpe, 1994).

5. For foreign goods one had only to pay duty at the tariff rate one time at the treaty port at which the goods entered China. After that, as long as the

goods traveled only from treaty port to treaty port, they were exempt from further duties and tariffs and transit fees. If the goods traveled inland to a place that did not have treaty port status, they were then subject to transit fees. See Morse, *Trade and Administration*, 204–5.

6. *YWSM-XF* 72.1.

7. Daotais held the rank of 4A. In addition to salt, grain, and circuit daotais, there were also river and customs daotais. For a listing of new types of daotais added at the very end of the dynasty as well as the older forms, see Brunnert and Hagelstrom, *Present Day Political Organization of China*, 419–25.

8. Morse, *Trade and Administration*, 55–56. For a history of telegraphy in China, see Erik Baark, *Lightning Wires: The Telegraph and China's Technological Modernization, 1860–1890* (Westport: Greenwood Press, 1997).

9. See John R. Watt, "The Yamen and Urban Administration," in G. William Skinner, ed., *The City in Late Imperial China* (Stanford: Stanford University Press, 1977), 353–59.

10. Philip Yuen-sang Leung provided much of the background information for this section. His discussion of the Shanghai daotai as part of a new foreign relations system helped shape my own research. For the discussion of the treaty port daotais and foreign affairs responsibility, I have relied in part on the very useful chart Leung provides. See Leung, *The Shanghai Taotai*, 74–75. I have also relied on the *YWSM*. More recently Leung has written on the Qing government's extensive use of "expectant" or "irregular" officials during the late nineteenth and early twentieth centuries in Shanghai and other major treaty ports as a way of handling the extraordinary circumstances that often accompanied the high volume of matters related to foreigners and modernization in these cities. See Leung, "Crisis Management in Late Qing China: Changing Roles of the Expectant Officials," *Hong Kong Journal of Modern Chinese History* (Hong Kong) 1 (2003): 95–112.

11. Xu Jiyu (1795–1873) was subsequently appointed governor of Fujian; he retained his foreign affairs duties in this post. With his foreign affairs experience, Xu became a Zongli Yamen minister in 1865. He retired in 1869 because of old age and ill health. The Zongli Yamen tried to get experienced people to be in charge at the treaty ports and to serve on the Yamen itself. Xu is a good example of both. See Hummel, *Eminent Chinese*, vol. 1, 309–10, and *QSG, juan* 422, *liezhuan* 209, p. 12,182, for Xu's biography; for his offices, see Wei Xiumei, *Qingji zhiguanbiao fu renwu lu* [Offices and personnel in the Late Qing period: metropolitan officials and high officials in provinces and

dependencies, 1796–1911]. (Taipei: Institute of Modern History, Academia Sinica, 1978).

12. These were Tianjin, Taiwanfu (or Tainan), Hankou, Jiujiang, Shantou (Swatow), Qiongzhou, Danshui (Tamsui), Dengzhou (Chefoo), Nanjing, Niuzhuang (Newchuang), and Zhenjiang. Different treaties with the various Western nations opened different ports, but through the most-favored nation clause present in all of the treaties, when a port became open to one treaty signatory, it became open to all. Nanjing, because it was first occupied by the Taipings and then deemed by British and French officials as not conducive to trade, did not actually open until 1899. After declaration as a treaty port in 1858, Qiongzhou only opened in 1876, owing to a lack of interest on the part of the merchant community. En-sai Tai describes each of the individual treaties and what was gained from each for all of the Western powers. See En-sai Tai, *Treaty Ports in China (A Study in Diplomacy)* (Arlington, VA: University Publications of America, Inc., 1976; reprint of 1918 original), ch. 3.

13. See Yen-p'ing Hao, *The Comprador in Nineteenth Century China: Bridge between East and West* (Cambridge: Harvard University Press, 1970), 50. Elsewhere, Hao makes an argument for the emergence of a Chinese commercial nationalism as a response to increasing Western encroachment. Just as the Zongli Yamen hoped to manage China's relations with the Western countries by using the rules of Western international law, officials and compradors hoped to fight the West with the economic and commercial rules by which the West drew its strength. See Yen-p'ing Hao, *The Commercial Revolution in Nineteenth-Century China: The Rise of Sino-Western Mercantilism* (Berkeley: University of California Press, 1986), ch. 7.

14. *YWSM-TZ* 44.4–6.

15. *YWSM-TZ* 82.3.

16. Ibid.

17. The Liang Jiang region consisted of the provinces of Jiangsu, Jiangxi, and Anhui.

18. The Liang Guang region was comprised of the provinces of Guangxi and Guangdong.

19. Brief descriptions of the responsibilities and development of the superintendents of the northern and southern ports appear in the *Da Qing hui dian: DQHD, juan* 100, 909–10; the *Qingchao xu wenxian tongkao* (A supplement of the Qing classified historical documents; hereafter cited as *QXWT*), Liu Jinzao, comp. (Taipei: Xinxing Publishers, 1963 reprint), *juan* 337, 10,781.

20. *YWSM-XF* 72. For an account of Xue Huan's career, see *Qing shi lie zhuan* (hereafter cited as *QSLZ*) (Taibei: Qi ming shu ju, 1965), *juan* 53, 22–25.

21. *YWSM-TZ* 5.

22. *YWSM-TZ* 6.

23. The provinces of Hubei and Hunan made up the Hu Guang region.

24. *YWSM-TZ* 6.

25. Occasionally the governor of Jiangsu held the post, but it was considered the standard practice from this point on for the governor-general of Liang Jiang to hold the position concurrently with his governor-generalship.

26. Brunnert and Hagelstrom, *Present Day Political Organization*, nos. 330 and 984.

27. *DQHD, GX, juan* 100, 909. It is also worth mentioning that the superintendents of trade, both Northern and Southern, appear in the Zongli Yamen section of the *Statutes*. Neither of the superintendents has a listing separate from that of the Zongli Yamen.

28. *DQHD, GX, juan* 100, 909.

29. *DQHD, GX, juan* 100, 909–10.

30. *YWSM-XF* 68.17.

31. Chong Hou, Heng Qi, and Xue Huan received their official assignments in an edict of January 20, 1861. For more on Chong Hou, see *QSG, juan* 446, *liezhuan* 233, pp. 12,476–77.

32. *YWSM-XF* 68.17

33. *YWSM-XF* 71.17–26, article 2.

34. John K. Fairbank has argued that the local officials were in an untenable position. Although they frequently encountered demands by foreign officials residing in their cities, they did not necessarily have the authority to meet those demands. Moreover, if the local officials did accommodate foreign requests, they risked alienating the local gentry. See John K. Fairbank, "Patterns Behind the Tientsin Massacre," *Harvard Journal of Asiatic Studies* 20 (1957): 495–99. Joseph Esherick makes a similar argument in his *The Origins of the Boxer Uprising*. Esherick maintains that the increasing strength that the Catholic Church gathered through extrapolation of treaty rights increasingly angered and alienated residents in areas with strong missionary presence. Local officials risked further angering Chinese residents by strictly and aggressively upholding treaty rights. See Joseph W. Esherick, *The Origins of the Boxer Uprising* (Berkeley: University of California Press, 1987), especially 83–86.

35. Chong Hou's mission preceded the regular sending of legations to Western countries, which started in 1875.

36. See Qian Shifu, ed., *Qingdai zhiguan nianbiao* [Table of Qing dynasty officials], 4 vols. (Beijing: Zhonghua Shuju, 1997), 3019.

37. *YWSM-TZ* 77.

38. The Nian rebels who roamed northern China were not fully suppressed until 1868.

39. *YWSM-TZ* 78.28. Once the waters thawed, he was to reside in Tianjin; once the river froze in the winter, he was to stay in Baoding, the traditional site of the governor-general's yamen.

40. *YWSM-TZ* 18.25. Li's mentor, Zeng Guofan, held the post of superintendent of trade for the southern posts until his death in 1872. The Zongli Yamen recommended both officials for their posts.

41. *DQHD, GX, juan* 100, 910.

42. Li Hongzhang established the China Merchants' Steam Navigation Company in 1872. The question of Li's goals and aims in this endeavor has been debated. What is of concern here is that his role as the superintendent of trade for the northern ports certainly aided him in his Self-Strengthening projects. For a biography on Li, refer to Hummel, vol. 2, 464–71; and *QSG, juan* 411, *liezhuan*, 198, pp. 12,011–13. For more on Li and his involvement in the Foreign Affairs Movement and the Strengthening Movement, see Yi Li, *Chinese Bureaucratic Culture and its Influence on the 19th-century Steamship Operation, 1864–1885: The Bureau for Recruiting Merchants* (Lewiston, NY: E. Mellen Press, 2001).

43. See Liu Xinxian, "Zhongguo waijiao zhidu de yange" [The evolution of Chinese diplomatic institutions] in *Zhongguo jindai shi lunzong*, vol. 3, ch. 5, 23–28.

44. See Leung, "The Shanghai-Tientsin Connection: Li Hung-chang's Political Control over Shanghai," 114–15. This article presents an important description of the interactions between the offices of the circuit intendant and superintendent of trade of the northern ports.

45. Li Hongzhang was certainly the most remarkable of the men to hold the position. His place in the Self-Strengthening Movement and influence at the Qing Court is noteworthy. Although a discussion of Li Hongzhang and his role in the Self-Strengthening Movement and late Qing history exceeds the scope of this work, a mention of the contribution the position of the superintendent of the northern ports made to Li's success is warranted. Li Hongzhang with his strong leadership certainly bolstered the position of superintendent of the northern ports; conversely, holding the post of an

imperial commissioner increased the breadth of Li's responsibilities and provided him with a venue for his Self-Strengthening projects. For works that attribute the influence and power of the position of northern superintendent to Li, see the selections in *Li Hung-chang and China's Early Modernization,* Samuel C. Chu and Kwang-Ching Liu, eds. (Armonk, NY: An East Gate Book, M.E. Sharpe, 1994) that mention Li in his capacity of northern superintendent of trade, especially Kwang-Ching Liu's "Li Hung-chang in Chihli: The Emergence of a Policy, 1870–1875," 49–75, and Part IV, which addresses Li's role as diplomat. Earlier works presented Li Hongzhang as a force for regionalism that worked against central government efforts like the Zongli Yamen; for an example, see Stanley Spector's *Li Hung-chang and the Huai Army* (Seattle: University of Washington Press, 1964).

46. *YWSM-TZ* 6.

47. *YWSM-TZ* 1.

48. *YWSM-TZ* 24.

49. *DQHD, GX, juan* 100, 100.

50. See Li Hongzhang, *Li Wenzhong gong quanji* [Complete works of Li Hongzhang], *Pengliao hangao* [Letters] (Nanjing: 1905), 12.26; 13.3–4, 6–8, 32, 15, and 16.

51. For a brief guide on the various forms of official correspondence, see William Frederick Mayers, *The Chinese Government: A Manual of Chinese Titles,* 3rd edition (Shanghai: Kelly and Walsh, 1897; reprinted by Ch'eng-wen, Taipei, 1970), 138–41.

52. See Wu Fuhuan, *Qingji Zongli Yamen Yanjiu* [A study of the Qing Zongli Yamen] for brief accounts of the careers of each of these Zongli Yamen ministers. For Heng Qi, p. 236; for Dong Xuan, p. 237; for Xue Huan, pp. 237–38; for Mao Changxi, pp. 240–41; for Cheng Lin, p. 241; for Chong Hou, pp. 241–42; for Wang Wenshao, pp. 244–45; for Rong Lu, p. 258; and for Li Hongzhang, pp. 259–60. See also the section on Zongli Yamen ministers in Qian Shifu, ed., *Qingdai zhiguan nianbiao,* vol. 4, 3018–26.

5

BRIDGING THE BUREAUCRACY—
LINKING COMMUNICATION AND POWER

IN JUNE OF 1877, TWO BRITISH BUSINESSMEN WENT HUNTING in the hills around Jinkou, Hubei province. When one of them shot at a rabbit, a piece of buckshot ricocheted off of a rock and hit a woodsman, who was partially obscured by a tree, in the leg. The injured woodsman, Liao Xuanfa, was within sight of the road, and a crowd quickly gathered around him. After Liao fainted, the crowd demanded on his behalf that the British nationals make restitution and a dispute broke out. The townspeople accused the hunters of irresponsibility and demanded money for Liao's medical treatment, while the hunters suspected extortion and doubted whether one piece of ricocheted buckshot could incapacitate a rabbit, let alone a man. Fearing that the British businessmen would go on their way without satisfactory resolution to the dispute, the crowd locked up the marksman until he paid 100 foreign dollars. At this point, the other still-free business-man went to the yamen office of the subdistrict magistrate, who managed to obtain the release of the marksman after thirteen hours of incarceration.[1]

On the twentieth day of the fifth month of the third year of the Guangxu emperor's reign (June 30, 1877), the Hu Guang governor-general[2] submitted a report prepared by the Han-Huang-De daotai[3] to the Zongli Yamen that recounted the case. Although everyone involved agreed that the shooting was unintentional, the incident set off a series of events that ultimately involved Zongli Yamen ministers, the British consul, the daotai, the subdistrict magistrate and the village head-man,[4] as well as the parties directly involved in the shooting. The seven-page case report sent to the Zongli Yamen contains no fewer than nine summations of the events in the form of petitions, interrogations, investigations, letters, reports, and replies. This level of detail for a seemingly minor case raises several questions. First among these is: Why did this episode warrant reporting to the central-government-level Zongli Yamen and ow was it relayed? Once reported, why would Zongli Yamen ministers concern themselves with the accidental shooting of a commoner in one of the provinces? And finally, why would so many layers of government become involved?

Answering these questions helps illuminate the process by which the Zongli Yamen carved a place for itself within the Qing bureaucratic structure. For not only did its ministers face the prob-lem of creating a workable organizational structure for foreign affairs at the central government level, but they had to extend the Yamen's reach past Beijing and into the provinces and counties in order to fulfill their responsibility to centralize foreign affairs. To be effective, the Yamen required de facto, rather than merely de jure, control over all foreign matters, including cases like the one above in the provinces. With the Yamen's central government directive to manage all foreign affairs, contact with foreigners in the provinces fell under its jurisdiction. Because much of the everyday contact with foreigners occurred far from Beijing, however, treatment of foreigners and foreign affairs differed from locality to locality, thus complicating the Yamen's charge.[5] In addition, Qing society at the local level was largely self-governing; active involvement in county affairs by a central-level organization was highly unusual. Nonetheless, the Zongli Yamen attempted to penetrate lower levels of government and society to achieve supervisory control in the provinces and regularize the conduct of foreign affairs throughout the Empire.

Contact between Chinese and foreigners at the local level occurred with increasing frequency in the late nineteenth century. Responsi-bility for supervising this contact to ensure consistency and treaty enforcement belonged to the Zongli Yamen. Impressively, its ministers succeeded in their efforts to centralize local negotiations with foreigners, not through micro-management of all contact with foreigners, but through a managerial style that kept the Yamen abreast of local contact and developments and in charge of general policy direction. By bringing all contacts with foreigners under its nominal domain, the Yamen was able to advance the general goal of treaty enforcement by standardizing the management of cases. The Zongli Yamen extended its reach to the provincial and local levels through the collection of information on cases involving foreigners in the provinces that covered a variety of subjects. These included complaints foreign businessmen lodged with the local foreign consuls involving disputes with local businesses or residents, as well as complaints lodged with local magistrates by Chinese against foreigners, ranging from debts overdue and bankruptcy to infringements on well use and murder.[6]

By collecting information and monitoring cases that had implications for treaty interpretation or central government aims, the Zongli Yamen successfully inserted itself into the process of negotiations with foreigners at the local level. With this, it reinforced its emerging central government position as the determining force behind foreign policy initiatives and policy directions.

Information and Power

In the realm of traditional management of foreign affairs, the Board of Rites and the Court of Dependencies managed everyday matters of the tributary states and dependencies, but important matters were memorialized directly to the Grand Council for policy determination (*da shi shang zhi, xiao shi ze xing*).[7] Before the establishment of the Zongli Yamen, the Grand Council was the destination and repository of many memorials from governors regarding foreign affairs. In addition, grand councilors had access to reports to the emperor from the imperial commissioners appointed prior to 1861 to conduct negotiations with foreigners and to serve in an advisory role to the emperor in foreign affairs.[8]

As demonstrated by Silas Wu in his discussion of the evolution of the secret palace memorial system and the Grand Council in the early Qing period, access to information brought power since information allowed for control of the decision-making process through determination of the choices recommended to the emperor.[9] Officials in the Qing thus paid much attention to lines of communication: who received information from whom was a mark of hierarchical position and power. Creating channels of communication and directing them toward a specific office played an important role in the evolution of decision-making power for particular offices in the Qing system.

The lack of horizontal ties within the Qing hierarchy compounded the importance of establishing links from one's own office to subordinate offices. Despite this, or even because of it, most of the high-level central government offices had overlapping responsibilities and no way of definitively ascertaining that a given office had access to all communications pertinent to its charge. The Zongli Yamen founders realized this and aimed to approach the Grand Council's status as a repository of information. Gaining access to as many sources of information from as many offices as possible was critical, because the overlapping nature of foreign relations was quite extensive.

Linking Localities

The Zongli Yamen, although heading the foreign affairs machinery, did not unilaterally command the information flow to it, especially in its earliest years. Rather, pertinent communications from various central and provincial offices continued to be directed to the throne alone. The Grand Council then disseminated memorials and edicts as deemed appropriate. Thus, many memorials from provincial officials concerning foreign affairs continued to flow to the Grand Council along well-established lines, even after the founding of the Zongli Yamen. Memorials addressed to the throne could not be diverted to the Yamen first, no matter how closely related to Yamen responsibilities. In fact, communication from the provinces directed to the Zongli Yamen, as proposed in the January 13 memorial, usually went to it at the discretion of the Grand Council.[10] Overlapping personnel between the Grand Council and the Zongli Yamen at times made the original destination of information immaterial. Nonetheless, from an institutional perspective, the arrangement was inefficient.

The significant reorganization of the daotai system, which created treaty port daotais as a link between the new foreign affairs (and customs) administrations and the territorial administration, helped build a communication channel to the provinces. The treaty port daotais were vertically linked to the Yamen through the Customs Administration, and their role within territorial governance provided a necessary horizontal link for foreign affairs administration to the provinces. Their presence in both administrations set the stage for new regularized channels of intelligence collection; the treaty port daotais could, according to Qing practice, send information directly to the Zongli Yamen, as they were the designated officials to manage foreign contact in their localities. Reports, originating with the daotais and sent to the Zongli Yamen, apprised the Yamen ministers of situations in various localities and problems that specific magistrates and daotais experienced. Such means aided the Yamen in acquiring control of the process of local negotiations with foreigners, since they provided the Yamen ministers with knowledge of cases involving foreigners, cases that could have repercussions for all of China.

In the larger picture of institutional reform, by creating systematic and regular channels of communication with local and provincial officials and creating means for information gathering at the local level, the Zongli Yamen forged new links within the communication hierarchy. The actual mechanisms of this involved establishing horizontal communication bridges, which changed the nature of information gathering and, therefore, decision making in China.

In 1866, the Yamen ministers ordered local and provincial officials to gather and record information on disagreements brought to the local yamen's attention for the purpose of keeping the Zongli Yamen abreast of foreign affairs at the local level.[11] The standing order for the reports stated:

> Every three months, all incidents of negotiations with Westerners should be reported to the Zongli Yamen for investigation. This applies to all provinces. Realistically speaking, there are many such cases that do not concern the affairs of the daotais and of the Customs Bureaus. The superintendents of trade cannot manage these situations from afar. Therefore, these instructions [to investigate and report] go to every province ... One and all they [the cases] must be investigated ... Each one must be stated in detail so that the case can be re-created from the report. The reports should be then be submitted for further investigation.[12]

With this order, local reports were to be submitted quarterly from all provinces.[13] The act of requiring the reports and tracking the individual cases within the reports were indicative of how the Zongli Yamen positioned itself as the overseer of the local process of on-site negotiations with foreigners. Just as importantly, the reports provided a mechanism for systematizing foreign affairs and implementing central government directives. Whether on the coast or inland, analysis of cases involving disputes between native Chinese and foreigners demonstrates how the Yamen kept abreast of and broadly controlled local negotiations. As consistency in approach and operation was imperative in presenting a unified approach to the Western nations, the Zongli Yamen ministers took an active role in matters they deemed critical to Beijing's foreign policy aims. The quarterly reports served as a technique for extending Beijing's reach into the provinces and a tangible method for the Yamen to establish itself as the functional head of the foreign affairs hierarchy.[14]

Using documents as a means of management and control in local governments was not new. Daotais and prefects supervised magistrates through the medium of documents. Although the amount of paperwork involved could be burdensome and might distract the magistrate at times from more pressing work, their requirement and preparation were essential to the Qing policy of controlling localities. While supervision came from above, the local-level officials carried out the business of government and reported back up the institutional ladder. Presenting the Zongli Yamen in this light of supervision and involvement contradicts how it has been presented in past scholarship. In his classic work on the Zongli Yamen, S.M. Meng states that the Yamen's role was limited to only that of a supervisory one in regard to local affairs. According to Meng and the traditional view, the Zongli Yamen became involved only if contacted by a Western representative. Meng adopts this view, in part, from the general Western attitude toward the Qing central government at the end of the nineteenth century, as presented by William Frederick Mayers in his work on the Qing administration. On the contrary, by requiring the reports and by becoming involved in select cases, the Zongli Yamen demonstrated a more activist nature than presented in either Meng or Mayers.[15]

As the new quarterly reports were to be sent to the Zongli Yamen from the provincial governors and governors-general, they forged a new horizontal link between the territorial and foreign affairs administrations and helped establish Yamen power at the provincial level. As a consequence, the reports contributed to solidifying the Zongli Yamen's preeminent position in the area of foreign affairs. The mandatory reports were to originate with the daotais and be sent up the hierarchy to the provincial governors; from there, they went to the Zongli Yamen in Beijing. Because the reports were lateral communications between Yamen ministers (heads of foreign affairs administration) and governors (heads of provincial territorial administrations), they, unlike memorials, did not have to first travel to the Grand Council. The vocabulary used in lateral communications, which were not referred to as memorials, but as *han, gong han, zi,* and *ziwen,* reflects the relatively equal status of the offices involved. The Zongli Yamen's efforts to create communication links with offices sharing in foreign responsibilities followed the established chain of command, while also linking the previously separated hierarchies.

Although all provinces submitted quarterly reports, Fujian and Hubei are highlighted here; both provinces had a high level of foreign activity and a consistent record in submitting the reports.[16] For Fujian, reports cover the years from Tongzhi 3 (1864) through Guangxu 26 (1900), though the reports do not seem to have been necessarily filed every three months as ordered.[17] Reports were sometimes filed biannually, for fall and winter or spring and summer.[18] In such instances, the cases included appear to be routine in nature. For example, in 1875, Li Haonian, the governor-general of Fujian and Zhejiang, submitted a report listing twenty-one unresolved cases in Fuzhou, Xiamen, and Taiwan for the spring and summer of 1874. Most of these involved a simple debt or dispute concerning goods between a foreign company and a Chinese individual or a Chinese company. The expectation was that each of the cases would be settled without cause for alarm at the local level, with no need to rise above the daotai level. Many of the cases included in the provincial reports were routine in nature, and consequently, the only record of them is in the Zongli Yamen reports. Thus, there is no definitive way of knowing that all cases from all provinces were faithfully reported to the Yamen. However, one can surmise by the routine nature of so many of the cases that most cases were included, at least in the provinces that regularly submitted the quarterly reports.[19]

As interactions with foreigners increased, however, so did the complexity of the reports, as noted by a commissioner of trade in 1888, "Those that come [to Fujian] as traders and missionaries increase daily and go everywhere. Cases reporting negotiations between Chinese and foreigners have become increasingly complicated as the contact has increased."[20] Chinese and Western merchants alike quickly responded to the increased opportunities for trade along China's coast and rivers that accompanied the treaties.[21] With the rise in contact came an increase in disputes between natives and foreigners. As a result, the number of disagreements and altercations brought to the magistrates' attention rose. Because of Fujian's distance from Beijing and the southern superintendent of trade's residence in Nanjing, local officials had to perform a balancing act of getting the job done while maintaining proper channels of decision making.[22] Fujian has been depicted as a place more traditional in outlook and practices than other provinces because of its distance from the capital. In the realm of foreign affairs, however, Fujian did not appear to be more traditional than other provinces; in fact, the opposite argument can be made, since the frequency of contact gave local officials more experience. In my view, the quarterly reports reveal no evidence of attitudes in Fujian that were significantly different than those in the capital.[23]

Hubei, on the other hand, is located inland. Nonetheless, commerce flourished in the Wuhan cities of Hankou, Wuchang, and Hanyang at the confluence of the Yangzi and Han Rivers. By 1800 Hankou had become the great inland commercial hub of China. Radiating from it were connections to all the major regions of China and eastern Central Asia and, after 1842, via Shanghai, to the rest of the world. By the mid-nineteenth century Hankou dominated a market that was truly national in scope and in which foreign trade started to play a role in the 1860s.[24]

The first documented trip of Westerners to Hankou occurred in 1842, well before the city became a treaty port, when Captain Collinson of the British Navy sailed up the Yangzi River to investigate river routes and Qing fortifications. In the years between Captain Collinson's voyage and the designation of Hankou as a treaty port in 1858, a few foreigners did venture to that city. For the most part, their presence was peaceful and not contentious.[25] When treaties first designated the city as an open port, Taiping rebels still held much of the area. Nonetheless, some enterprising foreign businessmen took advantage of price disparities between Taiping areas and Qing areas to trade items such as salt and tea to earn quick money.[26] Catholic missionaries were the first foreigners to take up residence in Hubei, setting up churches, hospitals, schools, and orphanages in Hankou, Wuchang, and Shashi in 1858.[27] The establishment of first a British then a French consul in Hankou in 1861 aided foreign business and missionary transactions. From the 1880s on, the foreign presence grew and interactions between natives and Westerners became more frequent, especially along the major river routes, as foreign businessmen tried to enter the prosperous markets. For Hubei, the first report in the archives, dated Tongzhi 1 (1862), is a summation of earlier cases concerning disturbances with the British in Hankou, and the last report is dated Guangxu 25 (1899).[28]

Examination of the quarterly reports reveals a significant amount of interaction between Hubei locals and foreign businessmen, missionaries, and government representatives. Like Fujian, Hubei was also a considerable distance from the capital. Unlike Fujian, Hubei did not have decades of experience with foreigners. The reports submitted by Hubei officials reflect their receptivity to Zongli Yamen initiatives and also how the Zongli Yamen extended its reach beyond the coast into China's interior. Despite the different circumstances of Fujian and Hubei, the local governments in both places encountered a similar range of problems in their foreign contact, and both provinces, in accord with Zongli Yamen hopes and orders, deferred to higher level of government involvement when stakes were high.

The very scope of the Yamen's domain meant that much of the local contact with foreigners had to be handled by lower levels of government, that is to say, by prefects, magistrates, and daotais. As in the case of Liao Xuanfa (the man injured in the hunting accident), immediate action was taken by the magistrate and submagistrate. In this particular case, their actions served to ensure that Liao was taken care of and the British national released. The case was then reported to the daotai, and resolved at that level. The daotai allowed Liao Xuanfa to keep the money paid him, asked the British consul to urge common sense on gun-wielding British subjects, and put the local headman, who had incited the crowd, in the cangue. The daotai took this last measure after he had determined that the headman had been drunk when he initially caused the ruckus; thus, the headman's punishment was meant as an admonition to all to uphold the peace. The involvement of the British consul meant that the Zongli Yamen also had an interest in the case. Regular transmission of such case information to the Yamen worked in its favor, not only in terms of controlling international repercussions of cases, but also in terms of internal functioning. With the involvement of so many localities and so many levels of the Qing bureaucracy, consistency in approach and methods throughout the Empire was essential. Effective use of information contributed to the systematization of foreign contact to the daotai level and below.

Although the governor-general and governors submitted the reports to the Yamen, circuit- and county-level officials compiled the cases and defined their substance. The magistrate and the daotai comprised the local level officials with whom Chinese and foreigners alike in the provinces had the most contact. These "father-mother" officials (*fumu guan*), as they were commonly known among the Chinese, were the first recourse for local Chinese with a complaint against a foreigner. Filling the lowest officially appointed office in the Qing bureaucracy, magistrates served in the posts closest to the people, positioning them to know more about local conditions than other Qing officials. In practice, the magistrate learned about disputes when one party approached his yamen. He would accept a petition and then investigate as he saw fit. If a foreigner wished to bring a disagreement to the attention of the local Chinese government, he would first approach his respective consul, who would then contact the daotai. The daotai would contact the magistrate of the county concerned, who would then collect petitions and conduct interrogations and investigations as he deemed necessary. Consequently, the magistrate was best able to supply information on the disagreements between locals and Westerners.

To stress the importance of foreign affairs management, a recapitulation of the 1866 order began each report. For instance, a report compiled by the Fuzhou daotai and submitted by the Fujian Manchu general-in-chief Xiyuan[29] to the Zongli Yamen gives a typical rendering; the daotai explains his report was "in response to the Zongli geguo shiwu yamen's communication that all provinces should handle negotiations with foreigners in a timely manner and every three months make a list reporting the cases already resolved and those not yet resolved and send it to this [Zongli Yamen] office to keep on file."[30] The language of the initial order reveals that the Yamen was ultimately responsible for all foreign relations and contacts, while the intent of the order was to gain access to county- and provincial-level foreign relations. The summary that began each report reinforced the Zongli Yamen's assertion of jurisdiction in local negotiations with foreigners, while the compilation of case material included in each report indicated that the Yamen did indeed gain access to the information it sought.

In addition to establishing control vis-à-vis the Qing bureaucracy, the Zongli Yamen had to convince foreign governments that it controlled foreign affairs. Consuls stationed in the various treaty ports contacted their ambassadors in Beijing when requesting intervention at the local level. Zongli Yamen ministers, to be credible, needed to be apprised of these events prior to contact with foreign representatives. Through the reports, Zongli Yamen ministers hoped that "if in the event the ambassador of one of the Western countries [brings up one of the cases], then the Zongli Yamen can conveniently explain to him the situation as documented in the reports. [In this way] potential mutual misunderstanding can be avoided."[31] In other words, Zongli Yamen ministers would be informed in advance and not caught in the embarrassing situation of not having on record cases referred to by foreign consuls and ambassadors. For the daotais and lower-level officials, knowing that their cases would be reviewed by high ministers, even if it were after the fact, served as incentive to resolve problems in manners deemed appropriate and consistent by the central government.[32] The reminder at the beginning of every report of the need for regular submissions and the importance of procedure served to reinforce the power hierarchy being created by the Zongli Yamen.

By requiring the reports, the Zongli Yamen staked its jurisdictional and institutional claim to the new duties and the office of the treaty port daotais. In the reports, daotais were to document contacts, usually though not always contentious, with foreigners at the local level, far from Beijing and far from the Zongli Yamen. From the resolution of cases, we see the process of multilevel institution building, culminating in Zongli Yamen control. The reports demonstrate how the Zongli Yamen as a new central government agency institutionalized these multilevel interactions in foreign affairs. Because the Yamen was to be informed of all cases, it was able to determine which ones affected national foreign policy and should therefore be settled at the central level and which ones were routine matters to be settled on site without interference. In the event of sensitive or important cases, a mechanism for higher involvement was thus already in place. In addition, the Zongli Yamen could ensure that lower officials approached local negotiations and conflict resolution with foreigners in the various provinces in manners consistent with central government aims.[33] It did this by responding to certain reports with orders for actions to be carried out.

A mid-Tongzhi era request for a lease of land from the American Consul in Xiamen demonstrates how the reports could attract Zongli notice and trigger action. Xiamen, off the southern coast of Fujian, was one of the earliest treaty ports. Involved in this brief case were a subprefect (*tongzhi*), a circuit intendant (*daotai*), a governor-general (*zongdu*), and the Zongli Yamen, as well as the American consul. Xiamen itself was a subprefecture (*ting*) belonging to the Xing-Quan-Yong Circuit. In the reported case, the American consul contacted the subprefect in Xiamen, as the local government representative, to lease land. The subprefect, determining that the strip of beach requested for lease by the Americans was too remote, reported this to the daotai. The daotai, in turn, channeled the subprefect's report to the governor-general's office. The governor-general's staff after reading the report, reported back to the subprefect through the intermediation of the daotai. The subprefect was ordered to "prepare and pick out on a map all the places that could be chosen or leased and present them for consideration." Reacting to the order, the subprefect sent attendants to a stretch along the coast to find a suitable place and discovered that a Chinese local had built five appropriate buildings. These buildings, the subprefect suggested, should be presented to the American Consul as choices. The case was reported to the Zongli

Yamen with the subprefect's recommendation to the higher authorities for approval and a decision.[34] The Yamen ultimately approved of the choices and sent word of its decision to the American consul in Xiamen.

This process was in accord with Zongli Yamen directives on arranging foreign affairs and controlling foreigners as much as possible in places and manners that could be more easily tracked, if necessary, from the center. Because of its implications, the leasing of land to foreigners required the subprefect and provincial officials to seek Zongli Yamen approval before making a final decision. Cases involving issues of land use or serious noncommercial issues or crimes often went to the Yamen for decision making or at least decision approval.

In the Hubei case of Liao Xuanfa and the British hunter, neither the daotai nor the provincial governor deemed a demand made by local villagers for the British national to pay for Liao's medical expenses to be unreasonable. The villagers had incarcerated the British national until he had paid; this, too, did not strike the daotai or governor as unreasonable. The issue, rather, was convincing the British consul that the matter was resolved with the acceptance of the payment and the punishment of the village headman. Also, at the end of the report, the daotai wanted to know if the treaties allowed foreigners to hunt in the Chinese countryside. If hunting was not clearly written into the treaty, then the two businessmen had broken the terms of the treaty when they ventured into Jinkou to hunt. By the time the report was submitted, however, the village headman had already been punished with the cangue and a letter had been sent by the daotai to the British consul detailing the investigation and its results. The only reason the case was submitted to the Zongli Yamen as "unresolved" was for the clarification of treaty terms—clearly an item for central-level determination. Once the daotai learned that the British consul was satisfied and that hunting was indeed allowed under terms of the treaties, the case was deemed "resolved."

In some cases, the daotais and magistrates tried to protect their charges from demands for punishment by foreign consuls. For example, in a Hubei case from November 1876, the British consul complained on behalf of an employee of the Baoshun Company who was attacked by squatters when he went to survey the land on which they were living and attempted to expel them. The consul wanted the magistrate of Hanyang to dispatch someone to expel the squatters and he requested that the magistrate severely punish the attackers. Thereupon, the daotai gave instructions to the magistrate to drive out the squatters and investigate the matter. The magistrate reported back that his yamen runners had driven away the illegal squatters and that the runners had found that the perpetrators of the violence were "unbearably worthless old men," who were crippled and poor. The magistrate then requested that "deep investigation" be foregone. The concern here was that the British consul would push for further action; the magistrate, wishing to end the matter while it was still within his control, expelled the squatters, but punished no one.[35] Because no clarification of treaty terms or other foreign policy question was at stake, higher-level participation was unnecessary, and the Zongli Yamen did not become involved.

Reports also contain numerous examples of debts and undelivered goods that were resolved at the county level by the magistrate or at the subprefect level. In these cases, even when a problem was included in the unresolved section of a report, there was no request for assistance from higher levels, and none was forthcoming.[36] This was because such cases were not viewed as sufficiently complicated or important to warrant higher-level intervention.

Most financial disputes were solved without provincial- or central-level intervention, as well. For example, in 1878 when a dispute over 300 yuan erupted between Quanfa, a Chinese bank, and a Spanish missionary on Xiamen, the subprefect received orders from the Xing-Quan-Yong daotai to seize Chen Da, the person in charge of the bank, for questioning. However, by the time the orders were issued to the subprefect, the daotai had received another communication from the Spanish consul stating that Chen Da had already paid back 200 yuan and all subsequent action was unnecessary.[37] This case is representative of the mundane nature of many of the events recounted in the reports.

Even cases involving the beating of a missionary did not necessarily advance past the daotai. In 1879, a British missionary society legally rented a building in Jianning Prefecture to establish a church. Once the church was ensconced in the village, a man named Shi Siming tried to extort money from the resident missionary. When the missionary refused, he was beaten, and some church property was destroyed. The magistrate and prefect quickly issued proclamations of protection and peace, thus resolving the incident and reinforcing already well-established Zongli Yamen responses toward missionary cases.[38] Such cases were included in the reports not to receive input from the Yamen, but to keep the Yamen abreast of developments. Had the magistrate acted differently, the case would have most likely incurred higher-level involvement. The inclusion of the cases in the Yamen reports reinforced the position of the Zongli Yamen as ultimately responsible for the cases, even though local level officials were often the ones to resolve them.

Incidents involving Western military might and Chinese territorial sovereignty could not wait for reports to be filed before being settled and moved quickly up the institutional hierarchy for resolution. For example, on March 12, 1867, the American ship *Rover* ran aground along the Taiwan coast. Taiwanese aborigines killed thirteen sailors, their captain, and his wife. The American consul at Xiamen, upon hearing about the incident from the British Consul in Danshui, went to Taiwan to negotiate a settlement, but the local official—the Taiwan-fu prefect—only offered the view that "aborigines, or 'savages', were not under his jurisdiction."[39] The American consul then despatched a gunboat to deal with the "savages." The Zongli Yamen immediately told the governor-general of Fujian and Zhejiang provinces to order the Americans to halt military action against Taiwan. The Yamen instructions stated that "although the 'savages' acted against the law, Taiwan is Chinese territory."[40] The case started out following field administration procedures outlined by the Zongli Yamen, with the American consul seeking out officials in Taiwan; but in this instance, events quickly moved beyond local control. When emergencies such as military expeditions were impending, the reports were too slow a mechanism for resolution, though they did serve to document the case later. Thus, the reports have their limitations, but they are useful in analyzing the smooth operation of the field administration. They are a good source for understanding the process of routinization that occurred in creating an operating system.

The quarterly reports required by the Zongli Yamen of its provincial and local officials served two important purposes and contributed to a significant change. First, the reports provided a mechanism for central government monitoring of foreign affairs at the local level. Through this venue, the Zongli Yamen was kept apprised of both significant and less significant interactions with foreigners on the local level throughout the Empire. The Yamen was able to use the tool of the reports to inject itself into the local foreign affairs scene. By being knowledgeable about unresolved cases, the Zongli Yamen could become involved in local cases of significance and keep local affairs consistent with national policy aims. Issues of territorial sovereignty and questions of commercial rights attracted central-level notice, for such issues affected treaty interpretation and rights. Issues that were individual in nature were left for local resolution. Magisterial handling of simple debt and altercation issues demonstrated the Yamen's willingness to allow such cases to be resolved without interference. By distinguishing among the cases to determine their importance and impact, the Yamen was able to work toward centralizing the conduct of local negotiations with foreigners and set the agenda for foreign policy aims, while not becoming embroiled in the everyday details of foreign contact.

Second, with the details of the accounts available to it, the Yamen could serve as a repository for case information and thus acquire power through its access to that knowledge. With the reports, the Beijing Zongli Yamen had an established line of communication to counties and prefects in the various provinces that bypassed the routine and palace memorial systems. Indeed, since magistrates and daotais did not have the privilege of submitting secret memorials to the throne, the reports provided an important central government means for information gathering from the county and prefect level. The submission of the reports to the Zongli Yamen, rather than to the Grand Council, gave the Yamen more room for maneuvering at the highest levels of government. Having direct access to these local sources through the lateral communication of the quarterly reports allowed the Yamen to claim its position at the top of the new foreign affairs hierarchy, and thus claim institutional space in the crowded Qing bureaucracy.

In addition, the reports provide a valuable window into late Qing multilevel governmental functioning. Cases that made their way up to the Zongli Yamen involved all levels of local and provincial government. Magistrate and daotai questions concerning the exact nature of treaty clauses and privileges reflect the utilization of the reports as a vehicle for central government clarification of treaty terms. Examination of the reports illuminates how the Yamen functioned within the greater Qing institutional structure in terms of leading the foreign affairs administration.

Just as significantly, the reports also contributed to the linking of hierarchies, both parallel and horizontal, and thereby contributed to a shift in the decision-making process in the Qing bureaucracy. The institutional peculiarities and limitations that led Prince Gong to join with Grand Councilor Wenxiang and Grand Secretary Guiliang in forming the Zongli Yamen were over time partially overcome by the forging of horizontal connections among the parallel vertical hierarchies. The Zongli Yamen overcame its institutional shortcoming, in part, by tapping into the power of communication, thereby establishing itself as the head of the foreign affairs administration and integrating multiple hierarchies. In proposing to control the information process and serve as a repository for communications on foreign matters, the Zongli Yamen ministers did not employ a totally novel approach for power and control in the Chinese system; earlier Qing emperors and the Grand Council had done the same.[41] However, in placing horizontal communication linkages between vertical Qing hierarchies in order to manage foreign affairs through control of information, Zongli Yamen ministers did put in place new measures with far-reaching implications.

NOTES

1. ZYDFJS, Hubei, 01-16/7-2.8-16. The dispute centered on whether the treaties allowed hunting, whether the hunters had been irresponsible, whether the townspeople were extorting the businessmen or honestly trying to get medical expenses paid, and finally, whether indeed one piece of ricocheted buckshot could incapacitate a person.

2. Li Hanzhang (1821–1899) served as governor-general of Hu Guang (Hunan and Hubei provinces) from 1876 until 1882. See Wei Xiumei, vol. 2, 63, 549.

3. The Han-Huang-De daotai was responsible for the prefectures of Hanyang, Huangzhou, and De'an, all located in Hubei. The daotai in this account was He Weijian.

4. The subdistrict magistrate was Du Shaofang, and the village headman was Hou Deming.

5. For a discussion of how widely treatment of a particular affair could vary in different localities, see Bradly Ward Reed, *Talons and Teeth: County Clerks and Runners in the Qing Dynasty* (Stanford: University Press, 2000). Reed demonstrates that the central government often did not know the specifics of local administration. The Zongli Yamen faced a situation such as Reed describes. Its goal, however, was not to control the details of local contact with foreigners, but the overall general direction.

6. Not all the cases are disturbances. Some request rewards, as in a case reporting a commercial English vessel saving ten Chinese fishermen adrift at sea after their boat was damaged by high winds. See ZYDFJS, Fujian, 01-16/19-2.26-27 (1866).

7. *DQHD*, Guangxu, *juan* 63, 586.

8. The memorial and memorandum of January 13, 1861, proposing the establishment of the Zongli Yamen pointedly mentioned the overwhelming amount of documents on Western affairs that the Grand Council received. It was the view of the memorializers that this new area of responsibility, in addition to the Council's already expansive responsibilities, would over-

extend the councilors, and important matters would inevitably be over-looked or misunderstood. *YWSM-XF* 71.17–26.

9. Silas Wu, *Communication and Imperial Control*, ch. 8. Wu's work focuses on the evolution of the Grand Council and the role of information control through the evolution of the secret memorial system. From his research and from that of Beatrice Bartlett, we see how the Grand Council's power was closely linked to access to and control of the information in the palace memorials.

10. *YWSM-XF* 71.19.

11. The Local Negotiations section of the Zongli Yamen archives, housed in the Ministry of Foreign Affairs archives at the Institute of Modern History at the Academia Sinica in Taipei, holds a report from as early as October 1862, but this is in the form of a letter from Sir Robert Hart, the Imperial Maritime Customs Commissioner, to the Zongli Yamen concerning disturbances in Hankou and the local officials' handling of the affair. See ZYDFJS, Hubei, 01-16/4-1. There are also records of other cases that occurred before the standing order was given, but the reports of these cases were submitted after the 1866 order so as to give the Zongli Yamen a complete account of past negotiations and cases. For some examples, see ZYDFJS, 01-16/4-2, Hubei; 01-16/1-1, Jiangsu; 01-16/12-1 and 01-16/17-3, both Fujian.

12. ZYDFJS, Hubei, 01-16/7-2.8; see also ZYDFJS, Fujian, 01-16/17-2.2.

13. Each report, regardless of province of origin, had two sections: first, cases already resolved (*yi jie*) and then, cases not yet resolved (*wei jie*). The combination of the two categories proves extremely useful, as an unresolved case in one report might appear as resolved in the next, thereby allowing the researcher to track developments and involvement of various parties from initial appearance through settlement. In addition, the reports sometimes contained additional information that the Zongli Yamen would find pertinent, such as lists of the foreign consuls living in a particular treaty port. Reports range in length from one or two pages describing one case to well over a hundred pages depicting scores of cases. A brief summary tag begins each case, with a more detailed recapitulation of events following. Some of the more complex cases consist of fifteen to twenty pages, though most are only a few pages.

14. T'ung-Ts'u Ch'ü discusses the use of documents as a means of supervision in local governments. See Tung-Tsu Ch'ü, *Local Government in China under the Ch'ing* (Stanford: Stanford University Press, 1969), especially chapters 2 and 3.

15. See Meng, ch. 8, for his discussion of the inefficiencies of the Yamen. See also William Frederick Mayers, *The Chinese Government*, 14, for views on the central government role in provincial and local affairs in general, and 15–17, for his views on the Zongli Yamen.

16. Reports from these two provinces include cases involving British, American, German, Dutch, Spanish, Russian, Japanese, and Danish nationals. These reports are housed in the Zongli Yamen archives at the Institute of Modern History at the Academia Sinica in Taiwan. They are all recorded in the section devoted to foreign negotiations at the local level (*difang jiaoshe*), *ZYDFJS* 01-16.

17. Nor do the archives in Taiwan hold all reports that were submitted. For example, for the negotiations with the French in Fujian, there are reports for the years Tongzhi (TZ) 8, and TZ 9 to 13, Guangxu (GX) 2 to 4. Local negotiations occurred with the French in other years as well, as French businessmen continued to be active in Fujian. The breakdown of coverage of years and countries for Fujian reports is as follows: with the British, TZ 3 to 26; with the Americans, TZ 4 to 13; GX 1 to 4, and 15; with the Japanese, TZ 13, GX 9, 12, 19, and 23 to 26; with the French, TZ 8 to 13, GX 2 to 4; with the Swiss, Danes, and Dutch, TZ 8 to 13; with the Germans, TZ 8 to 13, and GX 2; with various countries grouped together, GX 17 to 21; and with Spain, a smattering from the late Tongzhi reign to the mid-Guangxu reign.

18. For examples of reports submitted for two seasons, see ZYDFJS, Fujian, 01-16/17-2 and 01-16/17-3.

19. ZYDFJS, 01-16/17-2. Some provinces did not regularly submit reports; Xinjiang, for example, which became a province in 1884, seems to have submitted reports sporadically, mainly when there was a spate of diplomatic or foreign activity. The provinces that had continual contact with foreigners throughout this period submitted reports regularly and consistently.

20. ZYDFJS, 01-16/23-1.2. Report dated GX14.9.12 (1888).

21. Yen-p'ing Hao in *The Commercial Revolution in Nineteenth-Century China* asserts that there was significant foreign trade along the Chinese coast even before the breakdown of the cohong system and the establishment of the treaty ports. Spaniards, for instance, could legally trade in Xiamen before it became a treaty port, but British businessmen did as well. See Hao, 1986, 14–16.

22. In other instructions, we see that the treaty port daotais had to submit reports to the appropriate superintendent of trade as well as to the Zongli Yamen. ZYDFJS, Fujian, 01-16/17-2.3-4. In the cases of Fujian and

Hubei, this meant the superintendent of trade for the southern ports residing in Nanjing. After 1870, this office was a dual appointment with the governor-generalship of the Liang Jiang region.

23. For Fujian portrayed as a more traditional province, see Li Guoqi, *Zhongguo xiandaihua de quyu yanjiu: Min Zhe Tai diqu, 1860–1916* (Modernization in China, 1860–1916: A regional study of Fujian, Zhejiang, and Taiwan) (Taipei: Institute of Modern History, Academia Sinica, 1985), 99–103.

24. See William Rowe, *Hankow: Commerce and Society in a Chinese City, 1796–1889* (Stanford: Stanford University Press, 1984), for a description of the scale of Hankou commerce and government policies toward it, especially chapters 1–6.

25. See Su Yun-feng, *Zhongguo xiandaihua de quyu yanjiu: Hubei sheng (1860–1916)* (Modernization in China, 1860–1916: A regional study of Hubei), 2nd edition (Taipei: Institute of Modern History, Academia Sinica, 1987), 96–97. Su cites as his source the *Journal of the North China Branch of the Royal Asiatic Society*, No. 2 (May 1859): 231.

26. William Mesny was one such foreigner. He arrived in China in 1860 and stayed through the end of the century. He gives an extended, if self-righteous, account of his own experiences running boats up and down the Yangzi under the British flag in 1862. He first served on the *Rob Roy*; he then commanded his own boat, the *Hailongwang*, for a Chinese comprador in Hankou. According to Mesny, native lorchas and junks looked to convoy with boats flying a foreign flag. Even with the flag as protection, traveling was dangerous; Taiping and imperial troops routinely tried to stop boats. In addition, native customhouses would try to get the boats to pay transit dues, but according to the treaties, foreign boats only had to stop at treaty ports and not at every native customhouse. See the "Adventurer" accounts throughout William Mesny, *Mesny's Chinese Miscellany: A Test Book of Notes on China and the Chinese*, vol. 1 (Shanghai: China Gazette Office, 1896).

27. Su Yun-feng, *Zhongguo xiandaihua de quyu yanjiu*, 98–106.

28. The breakdown for years covered for Hubei's negotiations on site with nationals of the various foreign countries is as follows: with the British, TZ1 to GX 17; with the Americans, TZ 5 to 13 and GX 5; with the Japanese, GX 17 and GX 22 to 24; with the French, TZ 4, TZ 6 to 9, TZ 11 to 13, and GX 1 to 5; with the various countries grouped together, GX 15 to 25.

29. Xiyuan (d. 1894) served as Manchu general-in-chief in four of the eight provinces that had the office of Manchu general-in-chief: Zhejiang (Hangzhou), Hubei (Jingzhou), Fujian (Fuzhou), and Jiangsu (Nanjing). He

also served as military governor in Heilongjiang. See Wei Xiumei, *Qingji zhiguanbiao*, vol. 2, p. 130.

30. ZYDFJS, Fujian, 01-16/24-6.2.

31. ZYDFJS, Hubei, 01-16/7-2.8.

32. ZYDFJS, Hubei, 01-16/7-2.16. On the last page of the Liao Xuanfa case, for instance, the daotai raises the issue of the legality of hunting under the treaties. He demonstrates that he is aware that both sides, the Chinese and the foreign, are supposed to be upholding the treaty clauses.

33. At first the primary aim of the government was strict adherence to treaties in order to protect further infringements by Western powers. Over time this came to include the protection of Chinese territorial and commercial rights. See Wu Fuhuan, *Qingji Zongli Yamen yanjiu*, ch. 7, for a description of the aims of the Zongli Yamen. For a discussion of the guiding principles during the Self-Strengthening Movement, see David Pong, "The Vocabulary of Change: Reformist Ideas of the 1860s and 1870s," 25–61.

34. ZYDFJS, Fujian, 01-16/17-2.138 (1864).

35. ZYDFJS, Hubei, 01-16/7-2.6 (1876).

36. There are literally thousands of examples of cases like this. For some examples in one report, see ZYDFJS, Fujian, 01-16/19-2.134-139; all the reports I have looked at, however, contain such examples.

37. ZYDFJS, Fujian, 01-16/17-2.137.

38. ZYDFJS, Fujian, 01-16/23-1.3-4.

39. ZYDFJS 01-16/35-4 and *YWSM-TZ* 57

40. *YWSM-TZ* 57.

41. Beatrice Bartlett discusses the roles of the Kangxi and Yongzheng emperors in the development of the secret memorial system and the Grand Council. See Bartlett, *Monarchs and Ministers*, chs. 1–4.

6

NEGOTIATED SOLUTIONS—
MULTILEVEL RESOLUTIONS

THE NOVEL AND COMPLEX REGULATIONS OF THE UNEQUAL treaty system and the diversity of local circumstances contributed to an atmosphere that generated regular challenges for local and provincial officials in treaty interpretation and enforcement. At the central level, the general goal of the Self-Strengthening Movement to limit further foreign demands through strict application of treaty terms made consistency of approach of primary importance. Together, local and central needs contributed to a context that shaped foreign policy at all levels of government. While the quarterly reports helped monitor foreign contact and disputes with Chinese in treaty ports, they did not cover conflict that concerned activities clearly prohibited by the treaties. In order to discern government priorities in terms of security and foreign policy goals and the application of a coherent foreign affairs approach, this chapter explores activities prohibited by the treaties and how the Chinese government handled infringements.

Zongli Yamen ministers could use the quarterly reports discussed in the last chapter to detect potential problems and operational discrepancies, making them a valuable troubleshooting mechanism. However, even with its administrative position established through such reporting patterns, the Zongli Yamen faced the reality that the treaty ports and their hinterlands served as the stage for most non–central-level foreign contact. The extent of the territory and the range and degree of foreign contact in various localities prevented direct ministerial-level involvement in most common affairs, even if the government had such interventionist desires. Thus, although the Zongli Yamen, conducting the new foreign affairs machinery from Beijing, wanted information and overall control, it did not concern itself with local details on an active basis. In fact, owing to the vastness of the Qing Empire, no central government organization could hope to be informed of and involved in all local affairs. As long as affairs remained unproblematic, local and provincial officials operated relatively free from central control. In general, the central-level Zongli Yamen operated consistently with this tenet; nonetheless, ministers made it clear that the Zongli Yamen held the power to determine policy directions and retained the ability to insert itself on site when necessary to achieve its aims. For the vast majority of cases, this was neither feasible nor advantageous. For issues that held implications that went beyond simple disturbance resolution, however, Zongli Yamen ministers became involved through the exchange of correspondence with and orders for the local and provincial officials.

Despite the value of the quarterly reports to overall coherence in structure and purview, they were periodic by design and not meant to be the primary tool for dispute resolution. Daily management of affairs required mechanisms for timely attention, in addition to the coherence of a centralized structure. As seen in Chapter Five, county magistrates, daotais, prefects, provincial governors and governors-general, as well as superintendents of trade, all became involved in local cases. This chapter examines the dialogue that took place between the various levels of government in the resolution of disputes with foreigners in the provinces and how that interaction, in turn, flowed up the administrative hierarchy and helped form foreign policy at the center.

The treaties of the unequal treaty system set out the broad parameters of the diplomatic and commercial relations between China and the signatory states. In addition, the treaties outlined the conduct of trade, specifying limits on activities in which foreigners could engage;

for instance, they restricted access to hinterland travel for foreigners. For pleasure travel to the interior of China (more than 100 *li* or 33 miles from treaty ports), foreigners were obligated to apply to their consuls for passports, which required the countersignature of the local Chinese authorities.[1] The treaties and regulations by themselves, however, did not indicate how the Chinese interpreted and applied these rules. It is in the Chinese record that a better picture of trade and behavior in the ports and hinterland emerges.

Prohibited Activities

Many disputes with foreigners required a certain amount of interpretation to determine whether or not they fell within the terms of the treaties, with investigation of particular contested activities determining which were legal and which were illegal, resulting in further definition of treaty regulations. The treaties and subsequent trade regulations, however, clearly outlawed other activities; the Zongli Yamen archives are the repository for a wealth of material detailing cases involving foreign participation in activities prohibited by treaty and resultant Qing seizures of foreign property. The "Prohibitions and Seizures"[2] section of archives details these cases, documenting such infringements as the sailing of foreign ships in closed areas, the opening of foreign warehouses or businesses in nontreaty port cities, and the illicit trade of monopoly goods or contraband. Case reports also cover Qing actions and reactions to illicit activities, including license revocation or seizure of goods. Analysis of this information reveals efforts on the part of Qing officials to limit the scope of foreign activity, to enforce existing treaty terms, and to prevent the expansion of treaty rights through private and individual foreign initiatives.

  While geographic region and the involved foreign power determined the grouping of the local negotiations quarterly reports, the 2,052 pages of cases in the "Prohibitions and Seizures" section of the archives are divided roughly by year, and only occasionally by foreign power. Ranging from 1861, the last year of the Xianfeng reign, to 1901, the year in which the Zongli Yamen became the Foreign Ministry, cases hold abundant information on what types of activities were initially reported as illicit and what activities were later determined legal or illegal. Because officials at the circuit level or lower initiated most of the cases, while higher officials tended to determine their outcome, case resolution can be traced up the institutional ladder. Understanding the involvement of the different levels of officials allows us to assess the specific roles for particular officials or offices in the field administration of foreign affairs.

In contrast to the summaries of correspondence and related documents presented in the quarterly reports, all correspondence concerned with a particular case is grouped together in the "Prohibitions and Seizures" section. Copies of the various letters to and from the foreign consuls as well as the correspondence to and from the Zongli Yamen are included (over twenty pages of documentation for most cases), making it possible to trace the progress of a case from its origin to its conclusion.[3]

The cases reveal that local and provincial officials, through their investigations and recommendations to the Zongli Yamen, contributed to foreign policy formation in the provinces. The nature of the events covered contributed to the prominent roles played by on-site officials. Much of the illegal business activity took place in areas closed to trade, demanding the immediate involvement of local officials acting without recourse to superiors and requiring their coordination with the foreign affairs field administration. Despite the urgent nature of many of the cases and first action taken by local officials, the role of the Zongli Yamen ministers as final arbiter is made clear through the deferral of local officials to the Yamen's ultimate decision-making power in sensitive cases and their status as final interpreters of treaty terms.

Issues and Resolutions of Cases

Travel to closed areas:

Especially in the Zongli Yamen's early years during the 1860s, but extending well into the Guangxu reign, many reports of illegal foreign activity concerned travel to closed ports, which often veiled trade operations or the intent to set up trading operations.[4] The participation of Sir Robert Hart, the inspector general of the Chinese Maritime Customs,[5] and the various treaty port daotais in these cases indicates an awareness on the part of contemporary officials of the commercial nature of the contested foreign travel, as well as a concern on the part of the Qing central government and the Zongli Yamen for customs revenue collection. The practice of treaty port daotais simultaneously performing the duties of superintendent of customs (*haiguan jiandu; haiguan dao*) reinforced the close relationship of the offices and the awareness of the amount of illegal trade being conducted and the resulting lost revenue. In their customs capacity, treaty port daotais reported to the Imperial Maritime Customs, under the direction of Hart, who answered to the Zongli Yamen. Indeed, the Imperial Maritime Customs personnel figured prominently in such cases. The resolution of a case involving a British ship caught in a closed coastal area of Guangdong illustrates the importance of customs revenue to the Qing government.

In 1867 when local authorities caught a British ship near the Qing army encampment of Shuidong, a closed area of Guangdong, the regional Canton Maritime Customs House notified the British consulate in Canton and the headquarters of the Imperial Maritime Customs.[6] As allowed by the Treaties of Tianjin, the Imperial Maritime Customs confiscated the British ship. A combination of officials—daotai, foreign consul, and inspector general of customs—then investigated. The ship's captain claimed that his boat had accidentally entered the Shuidong area as a result of strong winds and his related efforts to save a faltering Chinese vessel. Although the captain asked for leniency because of the accidental entry into closed waters, the ship remained in Qing control. Deliberations on the case took place between the Canton treaty port daotai, Robert Hart as the inspector general of the Imperial Maritime Customs, and the British consul through a series of written communications. In the end, both Qing and British officials concurred that the ship had been rightfully confiscated by the Chinese government. The Zongli Yamen received reports from Hart and from the Canton superintendent of customs (the Canton treaty port daotai). In turn, the Zongli Yamen ministers issued responses to Hart and to the British consulate and gave orders to Hart and the Canton superintendent of customs. The Yamen ministers also relayed the results of the case to the superintendent of trade of the three northern ports, and the governor of Guangdong and the governor-general of Liang Guang. The final determination was that the British ship had entered Shuidong illegally and that the Qing authorities had rightfully confiscated it and its goods. By resolving the case and disseminating the results to a wider audience, the Zongli Yamen served as the dispenser of information, guiding by precedent officials in other areas who might encounter similar circumstances. Dissemination of such intelligence contributed to empire-wide policy coherence.[7]

Although the Zongli Yamen ministers and their subordinates were concerned with enforcing the terms of the existing treaties in order to prevent further encroachments on Qing sovereignty, they were also concerned with the collection of revenue for the central government. This concern contributed to the interest in the above instance of alleged weather-related intrusion into a closed area and manifested itself in the backing of the decision to confiscate the goods that might have been intended for sale. The impact of the local decision to confiscate first and investigate later on the Zongli Yamen resolution of the case is discussed below.

Early in the case, the Canton superintendent of trade reported that for a number of years foreign ships from Hong Kong and Macao had sailed the Guangdong coast in order to sell their goods in closed areas, evading the Imperial Maritime Customs. Because these merchants neither reported their goods to Customs as required by treaty, nor paid duty on them, the official practice was to confiscate the boats and their goods when possible.[8] Pleas for leniency from the ship captain in this instance eventually resulted in the Zongli Yamen decision to allow the ship to be redeemed for the price of 4,000 silver dollars.[9] The payment satisfied both Qing government demands for collecting customs revenue and upholding treaty terms. The main force in the negotiations for this case was the Maritime Customs official who provided much of the background information and the initial course of action, with the Zongli Yamen ministers acting as ultimate judges. Just as important as the Zongli Yamen's role as arbiter was its role as conduit and coordinator of information. By passing the results of this case to Hart, the Canton Maritime Customs daotai, the British consul, as well as the superintendent of the three northern ports, the Zongli Yamen ministers clarified concerns about ship seizure, determining when it was legal.[10]

Daotais assumed more central roles in other types of cases. In 1871 a British ship docked at Suzhou and loaded both goods and passengers in violation of treaty regulations, since Suzhou was neither a treaty port nor an open port. The Jiangnan Customs daotai handled the case, sending Imperial Maritime Customs officials to investigate.[11] After reporting his results to Zeng Guofan,[12] the superintendent of the southern ports and the governor-general of Liang Jiang, Zeng reported to the Zongli Yamen. Subsequent communications between the Zongli Yamen, the British authorities, and the superintendent of southern trade each referred to the daotai's report and his continued investigation. None of the higher authorities contested the daotai's findings that the ship had entered an area closed to foreigners and illegally taken on passengers in Suzhou. In addition, all agreed that Article 47 of the British Treaty of Tianjin had been violated, as pointed out by the daotai. But the point of contention was whether or not the ship also took on goods in Suzhou. If this was the case, the goods on the ship were liable to confiscation, having been loaded illegally without the required duty first being paid. The daotai, in his role as investigator and initial assessor of the situation, set the tone for the debate; his words were repeated in all of the subsequent communications. More importantly, his findings held firm over the objections of the British company. His place in the foreign affairs machinery provided him with the stature and means to handle disputes. The superintendent of southern trade also played a significant coordinating role in this case. Interestingly, the Zongli Yamen addressed Zeng Guofan in his capacity as superintendent of trade, rather than as governor-general of Liang Jiang. In this way, the matter was retained within the jurisdiction of the Zongli Yamen as a maritime customs matter and not as part of the Qing territorial administration. Thus, the problem could be managed by the treaty port daotai field administration the Zongli Yamen had put in place. The concurrent duties of Zeng Guofan allowed the Zongli Yamen to bridge administrations and utilize the resources of both.[13]

Cases involving the illegal transport of foreign munitions or the presence of Western gunboats concerned not customs revenue, but national security; hence, the Imperial Maritime Customs did not investigate or become involved in such matters. Rather, the governor or governor-general of the area, in his territorial administration capacity, cooperated with the Zongli Yamen to enforce the treaty terms. In these cases, magistrates or daotais initiated investigations by reporting the presence of gunboats or suspected illegal transport or sale of foreign arms within their jurisdictions. Because a foreign military presence could cause unrest among local inhabitants, the local officials acted quickly to keep the peace. Lei Qida, the daotai of the Gao-Lian-Qin Circuit in Guangdong Province, reported that a French naval ship entered his area's waters during a surveying expedition in February 1891 and sailors came ashore to plant a flag. As a result of the French sailors' actions, "the residents of the countryside were alarmed and agitated." The daotai traveled to the area to keep the people from violence and restore peace. Lei then reported the incident to the governor-general of Liang-Guang, Tan Zhonglin,[14] who then reported it to the Zongli Yamen and asked for instructions. The French sailors had acted in a locale that remained closed by treaty; French interests in Annam (Vietnam), which abutted Lianzhou Prefecture, one of the three prefectures comprising the Gao-Lian-Qin

Circuit, most likely explain the French presence in and attention to the area and would justify Zongli Yamen suspicions that France might be trying to expand its influence and activities in a Chinese area. Once the Zongli Yamen knew of the incident, it approved of the daotai's peacekeeping actions in a communication to the governor-general. Yamen ministers also sent a despatch to French Ambassador Gérard apprising him of the situation and asking him to order the French navy to cease surveying the waterways.[15]

Illegal opening of warehouses or businesses:[16]

When local authorities, trying to prevent illegal foreign business activities within their jurisdictions, reported their efforts to their superiors, they were recorded. Five of the eleven *han* in the "Prohibitions and Seizures" section of the archives contain documents describing the efforts taken by both local and higher officials to stop non–treaty-authorized commercial operations.[17] While the majority of documented cases in the "travel to closed areas" subsection dated to the end of the Xianfeng reign or the beginning of the Tongzhi reign, most cases regarding the illegal opening of foreign warehouses occurred during the Guangxu reign (1875–1908), reflecting the changing reality that treaty negotiations continued to open China to foreign trade and, as a result, fewer areas of interest to foreign merchants were off limits.[18] As more areas opened to Western trade, greater Western commercial expansion took place throughout Chinese coastal and inland ports, and a growing number of foreign traders looked for opportunity in Chinese markets. In the 1880s and 1890s, the most common causes for complaint included the establishment of foreign warehouses, the long-term rental of residences, the opening of banks, and the illegal operation of businesses.[19] Cases of factories being illegally opened also received attention.[20] Because such cases might include questions relevant to the proper interpretation of treaties that affected both its Chinese subordinates and the foreign community, they could warrant Zongli Yamen attention.

In these instances, local and provincial officials looked to the Zongli Yamen to provide guidance and knowledge of precedent for interpreting treaty terms. In 1886, Zhang Zhidong,[21] governor-general of the Liang Guang region, sent a memorial to the throne regarding the illegal opening of a warehouse. Within the memorial, Zhang referred to a precedent set by the Zongli Yamen in a similar case in 1861, an indication of the information-sharing taking place between the Zongli Yamen and its field administration throughout the Empire. In that instance, a British firm had opened a warehouse in the closed area of Zhangjiakou in Zhili Province. [22] According to Zhang's memorial, the Zongli Yamen resolved the problem by instructing the local daotai to inform the offender that his shop must be closed; the Yamen ministers also sent a letter to the British ambassa-dor demanding that he order the British merchant to close shop. In the straightforward circumstances of the case, such action succeeded in making the British merchant adhere to treaty terms. The strategy of applying the treaty terms directly and through foreign ambassadors and consuls proved effective. Although Zhang Zhidong had mentioned the precedent, the situation about which he currently wrote had already exceeded the former case in complexity. Four local officials, representing three different offices—a department magistrate, an acting prefect, and a magistrate (the fourth official was an expectant magistrate)—had already tried the direct approach of the 1861 case. Three of the Chinese officials had personally gone to investigate the circumstances of two warehouses opened by a German merchant in two different areas of Guangdong and Guangxi.[23] Invoking the precedent had proven futile; the merchant was not cooperative. Instead the broader foreign affairs field administration was utilized; local officials coordinated with provincial and central-level officials to ensure the merchant was not issued the permits necessary to conduct trade. The Chinese superintendent of customs for Canton (*Ao haiguan jiandu*)[24] was ordered by the Zongli Yamen to cease issuing permits permanently to the merchant. If the merchant continued operation without permits, he clearly did so illegally. Such illegal operation would clear the way for the Zongli Yamen to instruct the local officials to confiscate the native products in the merchant's possession in accordance with the treaties.[25]

Zhang's choice to submit a memorial about the matter to the throne, instead of directly communicating the matter to the Zongli Yamen, raises the ongoing question about the Yamen's formal position vis-à-vis the Qing institutional hierarchy, and especially the Grand Council. Why, after the Yamen had been in place for twenty-five years, did Zhang not send the matter directly to the attention of the Foreign Office? The institutional hierarchy of the Qing government determined communication flow. The emperor, at this point the very young Guangxu emperor, remained at the apex of the Qing hierarchy. All memorials were addressed to him; and all matters were theoretically in his domain. Governors-general reported to the throne as subordinates; they reported to the Zongli Yamen as equals. Despite the efforts put forth by the Zongli Yamen ministers to solidify the office's institutional ranking, the fact remained that the Foreign Office did not formally rank above governors-general. To a certain extent, the Zongli Yamen's status as head of the foreign affairs administration relied on the cooperation and recognition of other metropolitan and provincial officials. Cases in the provinces that were not reported directly to the Zongli Yamen, however, did get turned over to the office at the central level, owing to the effect of the process of power accrual in the area of foreign affairs that the Zongli Yamen had practiced over the preceding two decades. In the above instance, the Grand Council responded by directing the memorial to the Zongli Yamen for action. From the concern voiced by the local officials, Zhang was most likely worried about security in the countryside—a traditional concern of the territorial administration; thus, he reported the event in his capacity as a member of that administrative hierarchy. By submitting a palace memorial, he apprised the throne of the potential danger to Chinese territory. Because of the close relationship of the Zongli Yamen and the Grand Council through overlapping personnel and more importantly, because of the de facto standing of the Zongli Yamen in the foreign affairs administration, he was also in effect requesting Zongli Yamen involvement.

In a different report received by the Zongli Yamen from the Acting Superintendent of Trade of the Northern Ports Li Hongzhang on November 11, 1883,[26] there was a more detailed reference to the same Zongli Yamen precedent referred to by Zhang Zhidong. This time, the Jinhai Customs daotai, Zhou Fu,[27] made the reference on behalf of one of his subordinates, the subprefect Chen Jinshi. Chen noted that the actions of a British merchant who had rented space and opened shop in Duolunnuoer[28] in Zhili ran counter to treaty terms, as the subprefecture remained closed to foreign trade. Chen, like the local officials in the 1886 case, worried about the effects of the illegal business on his responsibilities, rather than solely about treaty terms and illegal business operations. Because the subprefect was charged with taking care of commercial affairs, the arrival of the British merchant's comprador Xu Baoshan from Tianjin to open the Sha Sheng Foreign Company (*Sha Sheng yang hang*) alarmed him. Xu had done so openly, without qualms or concerns; he had even advertised his flouting of the law by hanging a sign outside the shop proclaiming, "This shop sells Western goods and buys native products." At this point, Subprefect Chen Jinshi submitted his report with the request that the Zongli Yamen, according to the 1861 precedent, instruct the British ambassador to order the British merchant to cease operations. He couched his alarm not only in terms of the flouted treaty regulations, but also in terms of tax shortfall, by stating that he, the subprefect,

> collects the taxes from Chinese businessmen, but because of the [situation with the Sha Sheng Foreign Company], I am coming up short on taxes. In addition, my jurisdiction falls outside of the treaty ports; moreover, it is not a port open to trade. I further fear that if [the British company] stays too long, there will be trouble. I have considered this [problem], and I can only request that [the Zongli Yamen] send a communication to the British consul requesting an order be issued stating that the foreign businessman, Lao Shasun, should stop conducting business in a place not

open to commerce. He should be ordered to return to Tianjin immediately, in order to be in accord with the regulations.[29]

Tax revenue and security ranked prominently among Chen's, and by extension Zhou's and Li's, reasons for petitioning the Zongli Yamen.[30] The British company, by setting up shop in an area without customs representation, avoided paying duties. Moreover, by protection of the treaties, the firm was not subject to regular transit duties. Besides these concerns, Chen also feared that the presence of the business would agitate the local populace. Thus, his worries covered revenue, security, and treaty terms. Zongli Yamen ministers responded to the above matter by sending a letter to the British ambassador requesting that he transmit an order to the said businessman to operate according to the treaties. After a series of petitions and investigations, the business finally ceased operations in Duolunnuoer.[31]

Not all matters were so readily agreed upon by the foreign governments' representatives in China. Western merchants who felt unfairly treated had their authorities initiate on their behalf roughly one in four of the investigations covering the establishment of warehouses. In these cases, the local foreign consul usually directly contacted the customs daotai to start an investigation. When satisfaction was not obtained, the dispute went up the chain of command, first to the superintendent of trade and then to the Zongli Yamen.[32] The matter would then be handled by the Yamen ministers and the respective ambassador, both sending their decisions back to their subordinates.

The above cases illustrate that the Zongli Yamen did indeed achieve the three memorialists' early aim of information sharing. Local and provincial officials' references within cases to precedent and to cases in other provinces demonstrate that familiarity with case resolution in other parts of the Qing Empire informed how local and provincial officials framed their presentations to the Zongli Yamen. Information sharing resulted in better-informed local and provincial officials, fulfilling another related early goal of the Zongli Yamen. The ability of provincial officials to refer to cases similar to the ones they were handling demonstrates that through the availability of information they were prepared to treat incidents within their own jurisdictions in a manner consistent with Zongli Yamen directives and goals.[33]

Although responsible for illegal trade, the Zongli Yamen seemingly ceded responsibility for one type of illegal good to the territorial administrative hierarchy: contraband firearms. Illegal foreign sale of firearms meant there were Chinese buyers involved in the transactions, making the trade an overt threat to regional stability. For this reason, the Zongli Yamen took a secondary role to the provincial administrations in this type of illegal trade; in fact, although a section of the archives is devoted to cases of such sales, very little is reported.[34] Western dealers certainly traded illegally in arms, especially in areas of unrest.[35] Either collusion with local officials kept such trading out of the official record of reported illegalities or they were reported elsewhere. Most likely a combination of the two occurred.

The other type of arms case reported in the archive that garnered the attention of the Zongli Yamen had less to do with Chinese operatives and more to do with foreign rivalries. Spain issued a complaint to the Zongli Yamen that illegal shipping of arms to the Philippines originated on the southeast coast of China in Fujian. The Zongli Yamen issued orders to the northern and southern superintendents of trade, the Imperial Maritime Customs, and the governors-general of Liang Guang and Min Zhe to try to stem the smuggling of arms from their jurisdictions to overseas Chinese.[36] The Spanish government had a legitimate complaint since the rules for trade that formed a part of the Tianjin Treaties prohibited both the import and export of arms.[37] Other treaty terms, however, worked against the Spanish government's claim. Because the ships used for the smuggling were registered to British merchants and flew the British flag, the Zongli Yamen and its subordinate officials had little recourse in stopping the trade. Issuing orders reiterating the prohibition was the extent of their sway. Yamen ministers relayed this fact to the Spanish ambassador.[38]

Roles and Goals

Officials who became involved in the investigations of complaints of prohibited activities did so because of their growing responsibilities in the foreign affairs administration. Officials from the Zongli Yamen ministers to the treaty port daotais and customs supervisors shared the tasks of upholding treaty terms and interacting with foreigners. Because violations of treaty and trade terms most often took place in the provinces rather than in Beijing, local officials necessarily figured prominently in investigations and solutions. After the Zongli Yamen had reorganized the administrative structure to accommodate its foreign affairs role, it was able to cast a supervisory net and practice ultimate decision-making power through rank over the local officials from its center in Beijing.

Local and provincial officials, out of practicality and from recognition that their presence on site counted considerably, also had a say in policy formation. Chinese contact with foreign businessmen in the counties involved magistrates, prefects, and daotais. Although the treaties complicated their duties by adding new dimensions to them, their traditional responsibilities of maintenance of peace and stability and revenue collection did not change or diminish with the Western treaties. At least initially, the treaties left local officials with little local recourse in dealing with new foreigner-related problems. As foreign affairs became national, as well as local, in scope and implication, the Zongli Yamen served as the local official's main resource for best practice and precedent and his chief recourse for resolving foreign conflicts. The fact that local officials sometimes couched their concerns about foreign affairs cases in terms of the traditional priorities of revenue collection and stability perhaps indicates the transition taking place in roles. The daotai, in his long established role of circuit daotai and his new functions as both treaty port and customs daotai, would have felt the ambiguity which centered on the growing responsibilities that accompanied service in two of the Qing's parallel hierarchies and his entry onto a larger stage. The treaty structure and establishment of the Zongli Yamen compounded the complexities of the daotai's local responsibilities by adding to them national and international ramifications.

In cases involving prohibited activities, the Zongli Yamen ministers worked to coordinate efforts in the provinces to accord with treaty terms. In addition, the Zongli Yamen ministers tried to provide leadership in setting the direction of policy for important matters of national security and treaty enforcement. For their part, local officials worked to maintain order in the treaty ports and country-side and keep the flow of revenue constant. The governors-general, the inspector-general of the Imperial Maritime Customs, and the superintendents of trade provided intermediary and coordinating offices. The combined efforts and interactions of the various levels of Qing government in these matters led to bidirectional foreign policy formation, a departure from the formerly unidirectional approach taken by the Qing.

Through disseminating the resolutions of complicated situations to its subordinate offices, the Zongli Yamen created a more uniform awareness among provincial and local officials as to how to interpret the treaties. Including provincial officials and the superintendents of trade increased the efficiency of the network in dispensing decisions and information. The coordinating efforts of provincial-level officials and the superintendents of trade aided in the formation of an increasingly unified network. The cross-referencing of precedent and cases within the communications indicates the growing coherence of a foreign affairs network headed by the Zongli Yamen. The range of the issues handled by the foreign affairs network, too, point to a growing capacity. The Zongli Yamen's ability to coordinate the various levels of the Qing government involved in foreign affairs at all levels ultimately resulted in its effectiveness.

NOTES

1. British Treaty of Tianjin, Article IX; French Treaty, Article VIII. See Williams, *The Chinese Commercial Guide*, 4, 18, 44. See also Morse, *International Relations*, vol. 1, 563.

2. Prohibitions and Seizures *(jjnling jibu)* refers to the 01-31 section of the Zongli Yamen archives, hereafter referred to as ZYJLJB, 01-31. The subdivision titles are *jinzhi yang chuan si dao fei tongshang kou'an* (01-31, 1, *ce* 1 to 5); *jinzhi yang chuan si dao buzhun tongshang kou'an* (01-31/2, *ce* 1 to 9 and 01-31/3, *ce* 1 to 5); *jinzhi yangshang li hang chan* (01-31/4, *ce* 1 to 6, 01-31/5, *ce* 1 to 6, 01-31/6, *ce* 1 to 7, 01-31/7, *ce* 1 to 4, and 01-31/8, *ce* 1 to 7); *jinzhi fan yan* (01-31/9, *ce* 1 to 9); *jin yun junhuo* (01-31/10- *ce* 1 to 6); *jinling jibu* (01-31/11, *ce* 1 to 5); *gexiang jinling* (01-31/12, *ce* 1 to 13). For a better idea of the scope of the "Prohibitions and Seizures" section, refer to the catalogue of the Yamen archives, Jindai lishi suo (Institute of Modern History), *Waijiao dangan mulu huibian: zongli geguo shiwu yamen, 1861–1901; waiwu bu, 1901–1911* (Taipei: Institute of Modern History, Academia Sinica, 1991), vol. 1, 226–28.

3. Each of the reports from the daotais was included, along with reports from such superiors as the inspector-general of the Imperial Maritime Customs, governor-general, and superintendent of trade. In the "Local Negotiations" *(difang jiaoshe)* section of the Zongli Yamen archives (01-16), daotai reports were included in summary form within reports from the governor-general. For the most part, each of the 81 *ce* in the Prohibitions and Seizures section of the archives covers one case. Exceptions are *ce* covering the late Xianfeng and early Tongzhi reigns; see ZYJLJB, 01-31/1-1; ZYJLJB, 01-31/1-2; ZYJLJB, 01-31/3-4; ZYJLJB, 01-31/9-1 for *ce* covering more than one case.

4. Nearly eighty percent of the materials in the subsection concerning travel to closed areas in the "Prohibitions and Seizures" section of the archives dates either to the last year of the Xianfeng reign or to the Tongzhi reign. The vast majority of incidents during the Guangxu period huddle in the mid-reign, from Guangxu 15 to Guangxu 17 (1889–1891). See ZYJLJB, 01-31, *han* 1–3.

5. Sir Robert Hart (1835–1911) served as inspector-general in China's Imperial Maritime Customs for fifty years; he was appointed by the Qing Court after H.N. Lay was dismissed in 1862, following the Osborne flotilla debacle. For a chronology of Hart's life, see Chen Xiafe and Han Rongfang, eds., *Archives of China's Imperial Maritime Customs: Confidential Correspondence*

between Robert Hart and James Duncan Campbell, 1874–1907, vol. 4, 522–53. For a discussion of his role in the Maritime Customs, see the introduction by L.K. Little in *The I.G. in Peking: Letters of Robert Hart, Chinese Maritime Customs, 1868–1907,* vol. 1, 3-34; and Stanley F. Wright, *Hart and the Chinese Customs.* See also his biography in the *QSG, juan* 435, *liezhuan* 222, pp. 12,362–12,364.

6. Shuidong was a *ying* or army camp, located in Leizhou Prefecture. Its closed status resulted from its military connection.

7. The documentation for the case can be found in ZYJLJB, 01-31/2-1.7-24.

8. ZYJLJB, 01-31/2-1.7.

9. ZYJLJB, 01-31/2-1.23.

10. ZYJLJB, 01-31/2-1.24.

11. *Qianshou* is best translated as tidewaiter, a Customs official with the responsibility of collecting duties on goods unloaded from merchant vessels.

12. For biographies of Zeng Guofan, see Hummel, vol. 2, 751–56, and *QSG, juan* 405, *liezhuan* 192, pp. 11,907–11,908.

13. The documentation for the case includes two communications from the superintendent of trade for the southern ports to the Zongli Yamen; a letter from the Zongli Yamen to the British ambassador, Thomas F. Wade; and a dispatch from the Zongli Yamen to the superintendent of trade for the southern ports. See ZYJLJB, 01-31/2-5.

14. For a synopsis of Tan Zhonglin's career, see Wei Xiumei, vol. 2, 51. For a biography, see *QSLZ,* juan 61, 45–48.

15. ZYJLJB, 01-31/3-5.2-8. Two seemingly similar cases involving American and British gunboats are recorded in the index to ZYJLJB, 01-31/3-4, but the documents for the cases are not included in the archives.

16. Warehouses or godowns were places of business; they were not merely for the storage of goods.

17. These are ZYJLJB, 01-31, *han* 4–8.

18. Nearly forty percent of the documentation dates to the end of the Xianfeng reign or to the Tongzhi reign, and over sixty percent to the Guangxu reign.

19. For examples of foreign warehouse establishment, see ZYJLJB, 01-31/6-1; ZYJLJB, 01-31/6-2; ZYJLJB, 01-31/6-5; and ZYJLJB, 01-31/8-1; for banks, see ZYJLJB, 01-31/8-2 and ZYJLJB, 01-31/8-3; for illegal business operations, see ZYJLJB, 01-31/6-5; ZYJLJB, 01-31/6-6; ZYJLJB, 01-31/8-2; ZYJLJB, 01-31/8-3; and ZYJLJB, 01-31/8-7.

20. See ZYJLJB, 01-31/8-6 for a particularly well-documented case.

21. For biographies of Zhang Zhidong, see Hummel, vol. 1, 27–32, and *QSG, juan* 437, *liezhuan* 224, pp. 12,377–12,381.

22. Zhangjiakou, a subprefecture, was located in Xuanhua Prefecture, which was part of the Koubei Circuit in the province of Zhili. Zhangjiakou was also known as Kalgan.

23. The warehouses were located in Luoding in Guangdong Province and Pingnan County in Guangxi Province. The documents refer to the Guangxi location as Pingnanrong County, a variation of Pingnan County.

24. The superintendent of maritime customs was in charge of collection and recording of duties and dues within his district. Usually, the circuit daotai assumed these responsibilities at the circuit level, contributing to the treaty port circuit daotais' participation in the foreign affairs administration.

25. ZYJLJB, 01-31/8-4.4-7.

26. ZYJLJB, 01-31/8-1.2.

27. Zhou Fu (1837–1921) went on to serve as provincial judge in Zhili from 1888 to 1895, provincial treasurer of Sichuan from 1899 to 1900, governor of Shandong from 1902 to 1904, governor-general of Jiangnan and Jiangxi from 1904 to 1906, and then briefly as governor-general of first Fujian and Zhejiang and then Guangdong and Guangxi from 1906 to 1907. See Qian Shifu, *Qing dai zhiguan nianbiao*, vol. 2, 1501–1502, 1741–1742; see also Wei Xiumei, *Qingji zhiguan biao*, 146.

28. Duolunnuoer Subprefecture was located in Xuanhua Prefecture in Koubei circuit in the northwestern part of Zhili Province. The selection of Duolunnuoer by the businessman is curious, since it was far removed from a coastal treaty port. It was close, however, to a number of Qing banner garrisons.

29. ZYJLJB, 01-31/8-1; quotations from pp. 2–3.

30. For a good discussion of the relationship between merchants and officials, see Susan Mann, *Local Merchants and the Chinese Bureaucracy, 1750–1950* (Stanford: Stanford University Press, 1987). See also Wellington K.K. Chan, *Merchants, Mandarins and Modern Enterprise in Late Ch'ing China* (Cambridge: Harvard University Press, 1977).

31. ZYJLJB, 01-31/8-1; ZYJLJB, 01-31/8-2.

32. *Han* 4-8. See ZYJLJB, 01-31/6-1.3-5; ZYJLJB, 01-31/8-4.9-10 for examples.

33. See ZYJLJB, 01-31/7-4.8-9.

34. In Guangxu 18 (1892), the governor of Henan, Yu Kuanwen, sent a memorial recounting events of a rebel group that must have purchased arms; see ZYJLJB, 01-31/10-2. According to the index, the year before,

Superintendent of Trade Liu Kunyi reported an instance of a foreign ship selling guns; see ZYJLJB, 01-31/10-1.

35. Mesny mentions such activity. See his *Miscellany*. Also, Milton Osborne in *River Road to China*, in recounting the adventures of a team of French explorers also discusses the French arms dealer Jean Dupuis. Dupuis was based in Hankou and busied himself with selling arms unofficially to officials in Yunnan, which was suffering from Muslim rebellions. See Osborne, *River Road to China: The Search for the Source of the Mekong, 1866–1873* (New York: Atlantic Monthly Press, 1996; first published in 1975 by Allen and Unwin, London as *River Road to China: The Mekong River Expedition, 1866–1873*), 181–83, 194–95, 200–03. The "Prohibitions and Seizures" section of the Zongli Yamen archives contains no record of Dupuis or his activities. Osborne's account is also interesting because he demonstrates how a foreign flag, in this case French, could be and was used unofficially by merchants and arms dealers for their own unauthorized purposes. See p. 204.

36. ZYJLJB, 01-31/10-3. The governor general of the Min Zhe region was responsible for the provinces of Fujian and Zhejiang.

37. This is rule 3 of the supplementary British Treaty signed in Shanghai in 1858. See Wells, *Commercial Guide*, 70.

38. ZYJLJB, 01-31/10-4. ZYJLJB 01-31/10-6 also concerns the smuggling of arms to the Philippines.

7

NEGOTIATED POWER AND
INSTITUTIONAL PLACE

IN 1901, AS PART OF THE BOXER PROTOCOL REFORMS that followed the suppression of the Boxer Rebellion, the Zongli Yamen was transformed into the Ministry of Foreign Affairs (*waiwu bu*).[1] With the transition came a clear statement of the new Ministry's institutional place within the Qing administrative hierarchy. Unlike its predecessor, the new Ministry clearly held an integrative position above that of the Six Boards. In addition, its ministers were to serve only at the Ministry of Foreign Affairs, eliminating the need for concurrent posts.[2] Thus, by decree the Ministry of Foreign affairs had a comprehensive and leading role in foreign affairs. The 1861 Zongli Yamen mandate, by contrast, did not delineate the organization's position as obviously; nor did it grant it integrative powers, although it charged the Yamen with a broad scope of responsibilities. Nonetheless, the Zongli Yamen emerged a powerful and prestigious institution, molding the existing bureaucratic structure to serve its needs. In the process, it successfully carved a position as the head of the new foreign affairs administration. Because the edict creating the Yamen had not clearly positioned it within the Qing structure, Yamen ministers exploited the inherent flexibility within the Qing governmental system to shape and reshape the authority of the new office through policy and practice. Following a developmental path similar to that of the Grand Council, the Zongli Yamen was not an isolated case of institutional reaction and impulse on the part of a panicked Court. Rather, it is a demonstration of the Qing political system reworking itself over the course of a half century in the late nineteenth century, drawing on Manchu and Han precedent and practice alike.

In the case of the Zongli Yamen, the employment of imperial commissioners, the exogenous force of the Opium Wars, the reshaping of the office of daotai and the shaping of the superintendents of trade, and the continued adjustment of Zongli Yamen policies to create a working network of foreign affairs personnel display instances of internal institutional dynamism. By exploring these as a whole, we see how institutions mediated politics in the late Qing and how the impact of these same institutions was, in turn, mediated by the broader political context of the nineteenth century.

The inclusion of the Zongli Yamen and its duties in the 1899 edition of the *Collected Statutes of the Qing Dynasty* speaks to the success of the Yamen ministers in institutionalizing the Foreign Office through practice. The *Statutes* tersely lists its general responsibilities in broad strokes, and like those of the Grand Council, the responsibilities concerned security issues. In descriptions of related offices that came within its purview, we see that arrangements that began informally to make the Zongli Yamen more operational and integrative became more formalized by the end of the century. Significantly, while the superintendents of the southern and northern ports still retained the ability to memorialize urgent matters that needed quick resolution directly to the throne, as outlined in the emperor's 1861 edict, by 1899, the *Statutes* records that they were to report these matters of urgency simultaneously to the Zongli Yamen. Even more importantly, the *Statutes* lists these offices in the section describing the personnel belonging to the Zongli Yamen.[3]

The payment of the Boxer Protocol indemnity burdened the already strapped Qing government, and the Self-Strengthening reform measures were not able to stem the growing discontent with the government in the provinces and save the dynasty from falling in 1911. Although the imperial system gave way to the Republic of China, Qing staying power amid turmoil had proven remarkable. The ability of the late Qing regime to survive serious rebellions and military onslaught by technologically superior foes has long deserved revisiting in a more positive light. Highlighting Qing survival while recognizing its ultimate failure can deepen our understanding of institutional evolution and conceptions of reform and change in China.

Much of the credit for prolonging and regenerating the beleaguered Qing resides with the actions of Court ministers in the mid-nineteenth century. The institutional context within which they acted helped shape their choices. By shifting focus toward the study of organizational and structural effectiveness, I have presented a revisionist view of late Qing reform and administrative history. The staying power of the Qing system and the efforts of Qing officials reveal a state distinguished by flexibility and vitality. The case of the Zongli Yamen illustrates how the Qing system retained and utilized its ability to change and function by drawing on Manchu and Han practices and internal vitality. In fact, the story of the Zongli Yamen demonstrates that the Qing administration and its institutional practice contained and took advantage of dynamism. Recognizing the dynamic features of the Qing system and what made that system viable for nearly three hundred years clarifies how it flourished and maneuvered in accord with its overall political and international context. Such an approach allows for linking the late Qing state with the early Qing state, thereby contributing to bridging the dichotomy in our understanding of the Qing dynasty and rectifying our understanding of the nineteenth century.

As twentieth-century events have shown, Qing dynamism, while remarkable, did not carry the imperial system into the world of nation-states. Nevertheless, from the context of mid-nineteenth-century turmoil, the Zongli Yamen emerged to centralize foreign affairs and lead a broad spectrum of modernization activities. Moreover the Zongli Yamen participated in a complex process of foreign relations that occurred in the provinces, as well as at the state-to-state and ministerial level of the center. The Zongli Yamen's inter-actions with local and provincial officials reflected the multilevel operations of the Qing administration and the many layers of foreign affairs. Together, the various levels of officials developed Qing foreign relations through a process that involved upward and downward and even horizontal flow of information and decisions. The involvement of the various levels of the Qing foreign affairs field administration in decisions and policy formation, in turn, was a manifestation of the negotiated nature of Qing power. By sharing responsibility and decision making with central, provincial and local officials, the Zongli Yamen ministers saw their authority evolve from a group of three specially appointed and extra-bureaucratic imperial commissioners to the institutional head of a regularized foreign affairs field administration.

The goal of the Zongli Yamen was not to control and micromanage all the details of foreign affairs; rather, Yamen ministers strove to determine policy directions and maintain supervisory status of provincial and local involvement in foreign contact. Thus, what has previously been described as failure or weakness on the part of the Zongli Yamen was actually part of a multilevel system under continual negotiation.

Thus, the establishment of the Zongli Yamen in 1861 represented substantial and significant change within the Qing structure. The differences in organization and responsibility between the memorial that proposed and the edict that implemented the Yamen indicate the importance and implications assigned to the debate surrounding the Yamen by contemporary Qing officials. The Yamen's initial position in the Qing hierarchy did not match the terms outlined by Prince Gong, Wenxiang, and Guiliang; however, the Yamen's growth over the next forty years reflected the operation of an alternative, but native, path for growth within the Qing system, namely power accrual through administrative reorganization and shared responsibilities. Constitutional changes, such as the edict in 1861 and the subsequent Yamen reorganization of 1864, were important, but other means existed to maximize inherent flexibility and circumvent rigid institutional limitations at the highest levels of Qing government. As in the case of the Grand Council in the early and middle eighteenth century, concurrent titles, extra-bureaucratic deliberative bodies, and extenuating circumstances allowed the Yamen ministers to accrue power through practice rather than by decree. The daily acts of handling foreign affairs at the central, provincial, and local levels empowered the institution of the Zongli Yamen to a far greater degree than the discursive act of the original organizing memorials and edicts.[4] In other words, the various memorials, memoranda, and edicts provided and reflected the structural context for institutional development, but the Yamen ministers used the tools of the traditional system to navigate their own course toward an operational foreign affairs administration.

The association of Chinese institutional functioning with static tradition has hindered our understanding of the nature of change during the Qing regime. In previous scholarship on the Zongli Yamen, the focus on failure belied the underlying assumption that all systems deemed traditional be abandoned as a prerequisite for modernization. The resultant dichotomy clouded the legacy of the "traditional." This study of the Zongli Yamen shows that examining multilevel administrative functioning and evolution of Qing institutions results in a more vibrant picture of Chinese political history in terms of its internal operations and the manner in which the Qing confronted challenges. Traditional systems, Manchu and Han, could be and were used in innovative ways that allowed for institutional growth and adaptation to challenges. In addition, restoring the internal Chinese operations to the complex field of foreign affairs opens up the voluminous records of the Zongli Yamen and Ministry of Foreign Affairs for reexamination in terms of international history. The instances of institutional dynamism that evolved in the late Qing into the Zongli Yamen, significant in their own right, could also provide a touchstone for comparative studies with more recent Chinese administrative reform efforts that aim to establish greater horizontal and vertical linkages among institutional structures. Additionally, by acknowledging a valid internal dynamic in China, distinct but analogous to the early modern Euro-American experience, we move toward more meaningfully incorporating China on its own footing into world history.

NOTES

1. At the Academia Sinica Institute of Modern History outside Taipei, the Zongli Yamen archives are housed within the Ministry of Foreign Affairs archives. The catalogue for the archives is divided into two volumes: one primarily devoted to Zongli Yamen records and one primarily for the Ministry of Foreign Affairs. See Institute of Modern History, Academia Sinica, *Waijiao dangan mulu huibian: zongli geguo shiwu yamen, 1861–1901; waiwu bu, 1901–1911.* Changing the Zongli Yamen into a full-fledged Ministry of Foreign Affairs was just one of the demands of the Boxer Protocol; others were the destruction of the Dagu forts, the stationing of foreign troops along the approach to Beijing, a permanent legation guard in Beijing, and an indemnity of 450,000,000 taels, which was more than four times the annual revenue of the Qing government. The outcome of the Boxer Rebellion and the terms of the Protocol discredited those who had been opposed to and who had managed to reverse the policies of the "Hundred Days Reform" in 1898. Many of the measures that reformers had called for in 1898 were implemented in the first decade of the twentieth century: the abolition of the examination system, the establishment of new schools with a more Western curriculum, greater administrative and military modernization efforts, greater emphasis on industry, and the gradual transition to a constitutional monarchy. For more on the Boxer Rebellion and the Boxer Protocol, see Esherick, *Origins of the Boxer Uprising;* pages 306–13 cover the settlement following the defeat of the Boxers.

2. See *QWS, juan* 147; and *QSL-GX, juan* 484.6

3. *DQHD, juan* 99–100.

4. Pierre Bourdieu has proposed that the "power of doing" has more to do with structure than with decree. See Pierre Bourdieu in "The Economics of Linguistic Exchange," *Social Science Information,* vol. 16, 1997, 645–68.

APPENDIX A

MEMORIAL PROPOSING THE ZONGLI YAMEN, AUTHORED BY WENXIANG, PRINCE GONG, AND GUILIANG

January 13, 1861:[1]

We observe that the foreigners' overbearing ways first arose in the time of the Jiaqing reign,[2] and continued to worsen with the Treaty of Nanjing. Now that this year the foreigners have entered Beijing, acting against what is right and arrogantly coercing our Court, the crisis of the foreigners has become extreme. Critics, who draw lessons from previous examples of foreign calamities, mainly advocate the use of force, which was the only approach to dealing with foreigners in the past.

However, your servants, in observing the current situation, note that of the various foreigners, the English are overbearing and imperious, the Russians are unpredictable, and the French and Americans secretly follow them. We observe that before the defeat at Dagu, we could use either force or pacification. Since the defeat at Dagu, we can only use pacification and not force.[3] Once foreign troops entered Beijing, we could rely neither on offense or defense. Both strategies, resisting and pacifying, were harmful. Thus, we have to weigh the pros and cons of these two methods in order to act expediently and save ourselves from the present crisis.

After the exchange of the treaty, the foreigners retreated to Tianjin and sailed southward, one after another. Their demands take the treaty as their basis. From this, we can see that the foreigners do not have designs on our lands and people. Thus, with good faith and justice we can befriend them in order to control their nature, while we plan our own recovery. This is slightly different from former times. Your servants in considering an overall strategy see today's opposition to the foreigners as analogous to Shu's handling of Wu. Shu and Wu were enemies. Nonetheless, when Zhuge Liang held power, he sent an envoy to befriend Wu and form an alliance with Wu against the state of Wei.[4] How could he even for a day forget about swallowing the state of Wu! He had to recognize the urgency of the situation and assess the advantages and disadvantages. If he did not suppress the anger in his heart, but lightly put [all of his efforts] into a single test, then his situation would have been worse than that in which the alliance had placed him.

Although today's foreigners cannot be directly compared with Wu and Shu, they are our enemies; thus the situations are still similar. This time, the foreigners' behavior is outrageous and insubordinate. Everyone vigorously shares a common voice of indignation. We, your officials, have a rough understanding of the principles of righteousness: How can we forget the long-term interests of the state? With the Nian raging in the North and the Taipings raging in the South, our military supplies and troops are exhausted. The foreigners have taken advantage of our weakness and the fact that we are tied up [by rebellions.] If we cannot overcome our wrath and treat them as enemies, then we could suffer a sudden disaster. If we forget the harm they can do and make no preparations, then we will bestow sorrow to our sons and grandsons. The ancients had a saying: "Consider peace and friendship for expediency, but consider war and defense as the basic reality." This does not change.

Regarding the current situation, your servants think that the opportunism of the Taiping and the Nian rebels is like a disease of our internal organs. Russia, with her land bordering our own, aims to eat away our land like a silkworm; she is a danger to our arms and elbows [i.e., close at hand]. England's aims are focused on trade. She is violent and acts without regard to human principles. If we do not limit her, we will not be able to stand on our own. She is an affliction of our limbs. Therefore, we must first exterminate the Nian and Taiping rebels; next we should control the Russians, and then control England. Right now all we can do is try to blunt the damage of their actions; we cannot yet act to punish and awe them. If Heaven regrets our misfortune and the rebels are pacified, then through your majesty's wisdom and the exhaustive efforts of your servants, the situation will certainly improve.

If we act on our present plan and follow the treaties and do not allow the foreigners to infringe upon or exceed them even slightly, if on the outside we are trustworthy and friendly while secretly employing the "loose rein," then in a few years, although there may occasionally be foreign demands, [the foreigners] will not be able to do us sudden harm. After carefully examining the whole situation, we propose six regulations for imperial consideration. We request that they be sent to the traveling headquarters so that the high ministers and princes can deliberate on them. If the regulations are approved, then we your officials will manage affairs accordingly. We will memorialize at appropriate times to inform you of other small matters that involve positive and negative changes in the situation.

Vermillion Endorsement:

Let Prince Hui, the princes and ministers in charge of the traveling headquarters, imperial advisors, and ministers of the Grand Council deliberate immediately and memorialize. The memorandum is enclosed.

Six Point Memorandum:

1. In Beijing, we request that a general office be established to be solely responsible for managing the affairs of the various countries. We observe that, hitherto, foreign matters have been reported by memorial by the governors-general and governors of the provinces and collected by the Grand Council. In recent years, military reports have been continuous, and foreign affairs are increasingly complicated. After foreign envoys start residing in Beijing, if no one party is

concentrating on these matters, then their management will be delayed and dawdled upon, and we will not be able to coordinate policy. We request the establishment of an Office for the Management of the Affairs of the Various Foreign Countries (*zongli geguo shiwu yamen*), under the leadership of imperial princes and high ministers. Because the grand councilors draft the imperial edicts, if they do not have a hand in its affairs, we fear there will be discrepancies. Therefore, we request that they serve concurrently in the new office. In addition, we request that the Zongli Yamen be granted an office to facilitate its conduct of business, as well as meetings with foreign officials. We suggest that its staff come from the secretaries serving the Grand Secretariat, the Six Boards, the Lifan Yuan, and the Grand Council, with eight Manchus and eight Chinese being selected and serving in rotation. In order to define responsibilities, the new office will manage all matters in the style of the Grand Council. When military operations stop and foreign affairs simplify, the office will cease functioning. At that time, the Grand Council will once again handle matters as in the old system.

2. In order to facilitate matters, we suggest establishing separate ministerial posts for the open ports of the north and south. We observe that in the early stages of foreign trade during the Daoguang reign, there were only the five trading ports of Guangzhou, Fuzhou, Xiamen, Ningpo, and Shanghai. At that time a single Imperial Commissioner was appointed. Now, with the new treaties, in the north there are the following treaty ports: Niuzhuang in Fengtian, Tianjin in Zhili, Dengzhou in Shandong. In the south there are Canton, Chaozhou and Qiongzhou in Guangdong; Fuzhou, Xiamen, Taiwan-fu (Tainan), and Danshui (Tamsui) in Fujian, and Zhenjiang, Jiujiang, and Hankou along the Yangzi River. The area involved is quite vast, with a distance from north to south stretching seven or eight thousand li. If the imperial commissioner responsible for the original five treaty ports were to administer all of them, not only would he be ineffective, but the foreigners would not agree to such an arrangement.

Furthermore, the port of Tianjin is quite close to Beijing. If there is no minister to administer affairs posted there, we fear that with foreigners conducting trade in Tianjin there could be problems. We recommend that a superintendent of foreign trade residing in Tianjin be appointed to supervise the trade of Niuzhuang, Tianjin, and Dengzhou. Zhili is an important and large area; the governor-general in controlling it cannot solely reside in Tianjin. The financial and judicial commissioners as well each have their own responsibilities and cannot be expected to take on this responsibility. We propose that following the precedent of the Huaiyang Salt Administrative District, the post of the salt commissioner for Changlu be abolished and its responsibilities returned to the Zhili governor-general. The salary for the salt commissioner can then be used for the superintendent of trade. This way, we do not need to create a new office per se, but can use established funds and thus save on expenditures. The former customs revenue will be controlled concurrently by the superintendent of trade, who will report on it separately. Please bestow on the superintendent of trade of the three ports a separate seal, but without the title "Imperial Commissioner." He should be permitted to take several secretaries to assist him. Whenever an important matter arises, he should be permitted to act jointly with the governors-general, governors, and prefects of the three provinces. In this way, matters can be resolved effectively.

The original assignment of imperial commissioner of the five ports was held by the governor-general of Liang Guang. In the ninth year of the Xianfeng reign, it was shifted to the governor-general of Liang Jiang. We observe that currently with the addition of the three inland ports, as well as Chaozhou and Qiongzhou in Guangdong, and Taiwan and Danshui and Fujian, the ports have multiplied and affairs have become more complex. We sincerely fear that this governor-general, Zeng Guofan, if he were to concurrently handle these affairs, would find that no matter how long his whip, it will not reach far enough. In addition, he would not be able to be very familiar with the state of foreign affairs. Therefore, we recommend that the Acting Imperial Commissioner and Governor Xue Huan should remain responsible for managing these affairs. As for the two cities of Tianjin and Shanghai, the officials managing their affairs should follow the practice of the provinces of sending separate reports [to the Zongli Yamen]. In this way these high officials will at all times keep the Zongli Yamen informed and avoid misunderstandings. As for Jilin and Heilongjiang, Russians have in the past crossed the border and occupied our land. Successive military governors have concealed this and not reported it; as a result, we can no longer prevent it from happening. We request that the military governors be instructed to report the border situation exactly as it is [to the Zongli Yamen] and not deviate from the truth in the slightest.

All matters involving foreign affairs should be reported on a monthly basis to the Zongli Yamen for examination. Furthermore, from now on trade in the port of Tianjin will be limited to imports only; no large-scale exports will be allowed. If after a while trade does not flourish, the foreigners will abandon it and leave. We propose that after a time the situation be reexamined to see if we can abolish the post of superintendent of trade and eliminate redundant personnel.

3. For the customs revenue in the newly added ports, we request that separate orders be sent to the provinces that they choose and put in charge upright and honest local officials in the hope of prospering. We observe that the practice regarding duties on foreign goods has been to send the full amount levied to the capital. Customs officials have looked at this as a way to make profit. Embezzlement, fraud, smuggling, and a hundred malpractices arose, creating great obstacles for the collection of customs. Now that twenty percent of customs duties will be deducted, it is especially important to clear accounts as soon as possible in order to avoid complications from developing.

We suggest that responsibility for managing Tianjin customs revenue go to the newly established superintendent of trade for the three ports. For Niuzhuang, responsibility has always been with the Shanhaiguan superintendent of customs. This port's major dutiable good is bean cakes. For eight years, the set regulations have not permitted foreigners to export the cakes.[5] With such a regulation, there will not be many goods, whether imports or exports. Since foreign ships over time will have no profits that they can plan on, they will not be anxious to be there. Therefore, it appears it will not be necessary to establish another office to manage the port. Rather, affairs can still be handled by the Shanhaiguan superintendent of customs. We observe that the majority of revenues managed by this superintendent of customs come from Niuzhuang. The customs collected at Shanhaiguan come after the river is frozen; revenues at Niuzhuang are collected for the most part after the river thaws and before it is frozen. The superintendent should be instructed that from hereon he should reside in Niuzhuang after the second month of each year and return to Shanhaiguan after the river is frozen. In matters involving trade and foreign affairs, the superintendent of customs ought to listen to the superintendent of trade of the three northern ports, in order to avoid misunderstandings. In addition, they ought to follow the regulations of the Customs at Fuzhou and Shanghai and analyze the inland and foreign duties, reporting only the amounts stipulated by treaty; they do not need to confuse calculations by including the duties of the goods on Chinese ships.

As for Dengzhou, there has been illicit foreign trade that has been concealed [from the throne] for many years. Now, with Dengzhou among the newly established treaty ports, we ought to send an official there to concentrate on solely managing the trade. This matter ought to be reported on to the throne by the superintendent of trade in Tianjin in consultation with the governor of Shandong. There is no need to change the situations in the five ports of Yuehai [Canton], Fuzhou, Xiamen, Ningbo, and Shanghai because there have been generals supervising the customs in these places. The newly opened ports of Qiongzhou, Chaozhou, Taiwanfu [Tainan], Danshui, and those along the Yangzi River (Zhenjiang, Jiujiang, and Hankou) should be administered by officials who, after being selected by the governor-generals and governors of the provinces to which the ports belong in consultation with the superintendent of trade in Shanghai, are presented to and appointed by the Court. Foreign affairs in the provinces should be managed by the provincial officials according to the treaties. In addition, revenues from the old and new ports and the number of ships that enter and leave the ports should be reported monthly to the superintendents of trade and imperial commissioners for inspection. The latter should inform the Zongli Yamen and the Board of Revenue on a monthly basis for review.

The newly opened trading ports with Russia of Kulun [Urga], Keshigerer [Kashgar], and Zhangjiakou [Kalgan] and the old ports like Qiaketu [Kiakhta], Taerbahatai [Tarbagatai], and such places, are to be managed by the general of Yili, officials in Kulun, Kashgar, and Zhangjiakou, and the supervisor in Zhangjiakou. Except for Wusuli and Suifenhe which, according to the first article in the Treaty with Russia, are exempt from customs tax, officials in all other ports of trade should carefully manage customs and faithfully report levies. No embezzlement is allowed and the revenue should be ready for appropriation. Formerly it was stipulated that of every one hundred *liang* of silver revenue, 1.2 *liang* of meltage fee was to be charged. Over the eight years, trade articles have been negotiated and the meltage fee reduced. Now that the treaties have been exchanged, the new rules should be applied. As it has been decided to deduct 20 percent of the duties' revenue, a register should be established; then, deficiencies can be investigated to determine how much came from tax revenue. Thus, every year we will levy and collect a certain amount of foreign customs duties, and in all cases procedures will be thoroughly transparent. Since the officials who handle the revenue will not be able to misappropriate funds, not only might they not have enough money to support their families, but also corrupt officials, knowing that there is no way to profit, might make trouble. The latter is especially critical to the overall situation. If no stipulations are made to allocate office expenditure funds, unexpected things might happen. We suggest that the superintendent of trade in Tianjin and the imperial commissioner in Shanghai be ordered to discuss with the governors-general and governors of the treaty port areas transportation expenditures and fees for workers as well as paperwork so that they can examine revenue and ensure that deductions are made and drawbacks avoided.

4. To avoid misunderstandings, we suggest that the military generals and governers-generals and governors of the provinces keep each other informed of their management of foreign affairs in their provinces. We observe that hitherto the Grand Council has not issued copies of letters, edicts, and communications that concern the management of foreign affairs to provincial officials; nor have the provincial officials kept each other informed. Originally this was done to maintain secrecy and prevent information from being divulged. However, now we instruct the officials concerned with foreign trade in the provinces and the imperial commissioners to send regular reports to the Zongli Yamen in the capital. As a result, the military generals, prefect of the imperial prefecture (governor of Beijing), and governors-general should now all keep each other regularly and mutually informed of events in their jurisdictions in order to eliminate misunderstandings. Moreover, when a particular province handles an affair well, other provinces can use its methods as a model. Conversely, when a province does not handle a problem well, other provinces, having knowledge of it, will be able avoid a similar outcome.

In the second month of the ninth year of the Xianfeng reign, the former Governor-general of Liang Jiang He Guiqing sent a memorial to the throne stating:

> Hitherto, matters have been memorialized to the throne secretly, without officials keeping each other informed. Furthermore, there have been no files that an official could check. Even those serving in the same office do not necessarily know the details of each other's affairs. This situation causes misunderstandings and discrepancies and gives rise to abuses of the system. Your servants request

that officials be instructed to mutually inform one another in order to unify practice.

Your servants have found that this memorial reflects the reality of the situation. From now on, the superintendent of trade at Tianjin, the imperial commissioner at Shanghai, and officials in each of the provinces, in addition to reporting to the Zongli Yamen on memorials they send and edicts they receive, should be instructed also to regularly inform each other of the above communications. When an official leaves his post, he should hand over his files to his successor so that the new official can examine them. Thus, the situation will not be obscure to him. However, it is appropriate that such affairs be secret. We should continue to instruct provincial officials to assign reliable men to copy and be familiar with these documents. They should not pass through the hands of clerks. Such precautions are meant to prevent leaks.

5. Your servants request that officials in Guangdong and Shanghai each send two men who can read and speak foreign languages to Beijing to serve as consultants. We observe that in order to engage in negotiations with foreign countries, we need to first understand the natures involved. Currently, their spoken and written languages are unintelligible to us; how can we expect to be able to resolve problems? In the past, it was the custom to establish an office to study a foreign language, as was the case with the Russian Language School. This practice was significant. Now, after the passage of time, we note that [in the case of the Russian School] no one can even understand documents. It seems reasonable we ought to encourage them with rewards. We hear that among the merchants of Shanghai and Guangdong there are those who have specialized in learning the English and French languages. We request that the governors-general and governors of these provinces be instructed to select two such men who are honest and reliable, for a total of four men, to report to Beijing bringing books of each of these countries. In addition, let four or five promising and intelligent boys under the age of thirteen

or fourteen be selected from each of the Eight Banners to study with them. Following the precedent of the Russian School, the men [sent from Shanghai and Canton] should each be given a sufficient salary. After two years, separate them and reward the ones who have become proficient. After all of the bannermen have become proficient in the foreign languages, the practice should stop. We request instructions be issued that the Russian Language School be employed to decide upon satisfactory rules and supervise lessons energetically. For each of the foreign language students who become fluent, we will send a memorial requesting a generous reward to serve as incentive that he not let his abilities deteriorate with the passage of time.

6. In order to have reliable knowledge with which to handle affairs, we request that monthly reports be sent to the Zongli Yamen containing information on the situation of the Chinese and foreign trade at each of the ports, as well as foreign newspapers. We observe that trade is the main basis of the newly established treaties with the foreign countries. Thus, whether trade conditions are peaceful or not is of the utmost importance. Subsequently, to prevent the possibility of news, whether good or bad, of foreign or native trade in either the old or new ports from not reaching the imperial commissioner, we request that each of the military generals, the prefect of the Metropolitan Prefecture, and the governors-general and governors be instructed to report monthly on the situation in the ports. These reports should be memorialized not only to the throne, but also sent to the imperial commissioner and the trade commissioners. They should not be looked upon as a formality, and the information should not be ficti-tious in the slightest. In the handling of foreign affairs, it is all the more important to prepare to know the smallest details, for in such matters, the periphery can move the center. In recent years, we have on occasion made secret inquiries, but these efforts usually resulted only in rumors and not in accurate information. It was difficult to handle matters in this way and get good results. Although foreign newspapers are not necessarily accurate, through careful reading it is possible to obtain the general idea [of events]. The old treaty ports

Guangzhou, Fuzhou, Ningbo, and Shanghai have all had foreign newspapers, all of different names. It can be expected that the newly opened treaty ports will also have foreign newspapers. Thus, we urge that instructions be issued to the Imperial Commissioner and the commissioners of trade and the military generals and the prefect of the Metropolitan Prefecture, and the governors-general and governors of each of the provinces that they send to the Zongli Yamen monthly all foreign newspapers, whether in Chinese or in a foreign language. Through detailed investigation we will have understanding of the situation between China and foreign countries at hand; this is the way to right abuses and correct prejudice.

NOTES

1. This is the date the Xianfeng emperor received the memorial at headquarters of the imperial tour in Rehe. The source for the memorial is *YWSM*-XF 71.17–26.

2. The Jiaqing emperor reigned from 1796 to 1820.

3. When Western forces sailed up the coast in June 1859 in order to ratify the 1858 Treaty of Tianjin, they were repulsed by Chinese troops at the Dagu Forts. The Chinese victory was short-lived, as the following year, the French and British troops returned and occupied Beijing.

4. During the period of the Three Kingdoms, Zhuge Liang (181–234), on behalf of Liu Bei, founder of the Kingdom of Shu, formed a defensive alliance with Sun Quan of the state of Wu to prevent that state from forming an alliance with the state of Wei. For a biography, see Herbert A. Giles, *A Chinese Biographical Dictionary* (Taipei: Cheng Wen Publishing, reprint, 1975), 180–81.

5. The restriction on exporting bean cake from Niuzhuang and Dengzhou was lifted in March 1862. See Williams, *Commercial Guide*, 71.

APPENDIX B

AN EDICT TO THE GRAND SECRETARIAT
FROM THE XIANFENG EMPEROR

January 20, 1861:[1]

Prince Hui and others have submitted a memorial after deliberating on the memorial submitted by Prince Gong Yixin and others concerning the regulations on the management of commerce and restoration of peace. Prince Hui's report states that "Prince Gong and his cohort's discussion of the various articles reflects the reality of the situation. Action should be taken according to their original plan." In Beijing, let there be established the Zongli geguo tongshang shiwu yamen [The Office for the Management of the Commercial Affairs of the Various Countries]. Let Prince Gong, Grand Secretary Guiliang, and Board of Revenue Senior Vice President Wenxiang be despatched immediately to manage it. In addition, let the Board of Rites bestow a seal reading "Office for the Management of the Commercial Affairs of the Various Countries Established by Imperial Order."

Personnel selection must be established. Eight Manchu and eight Chinese are to be chosen from the staffs and secretaries of the Grand Secretariat, the Six Boards, and the Grand Council; sixteen will serve as the set number of secretaries. There is no need [for those working at the Zongli Yamen] to serve concurrently at the Grand Council or to rotate their service.

Let Expectant Board Vice President Chong Hou serve as the superintendent of the three ports and reside in Tianjin. He is to manage the commercial affairs of the three ports of Niuzhuang, Tianjin, and

Dengzhou in cooperation with military governors, governors-general and governors, and governor of Beijing. Moreover, he should be issued a seal reading, "Seal of the Superintendent of Trade for the Three Ports"; the term "Imperial Commissioner" need not be used. Let the commercial affairs of the ports of Guangzhou, Fuzhou, Xiamen, Ningbo, Shanghai, as well as the ports along the Yangzi, and Chaozhou, Qiongzhou, Taiwanfu, and Danshui be handled by Acting Imperial Commissioner and Governor of Jiangsu Xue Huan. Dengzhou and all of the newly established ports, except for Niuzhuang, are to be managed by their respective governors-general and governors in cooperation with officials sent by Chong Hou and Xue Huan. Niuzhuang is to remain under the control of the military commander of Shanhaiguan.

All communications from foreign countries, along with matters concerning trade, must be regularly reported to the throne. Moreover, original communications should be turned over [to the throne] for inspection. Officials should communicate with the Board of Rites, who will, in turn, hand communications over to the Zongli geguo tongshang shiwu yamen. In addition, the respective military governors, governors-general, and governors should keep each other mutually informed.

When an official leaves office, he should hand over his archives to his successor.

As for border affairs in Kirin [Jilin] and Heilongjiang, and Chinese affairs at the border regions, the appropriate military general should report to the throne according to the facts. At the same time, he will also keep the Board of Rites informed. The Board of Rites, in turn, should communicate with the Zongli geguo tongshang shiwu yamen. Even slightly concealing matters will not be permitted.

NOTE

1. *YWSM-XF* 72.1b-2; also printed in *YWYD*, vol. 1, p. 10. J.L. Cranmer-Byng has translated a different edict issued on the same day on the same subject. The edict translated by Cranmer-Byng focuses more on implementation of articles five and six than does the edict above. See Cranmer-Byng, "The Establishment of the Zongli Yamen."

GLOSSARY

Ancha shi	按察使
Anding	安定
Ao haiguan jiandu	奧海關監督
Banli geguo shiwu	辦理各國事務
Baoding	保定
Beile	貝勒
Beiyang dachen	北洋大臣
Bing bu	兵部
Buzheng shi	布政使
Ce	冊
Chang guan	常關
Changzhou fu	常州府
Chaozhou	潮州
Chefoo (Zhifou)	之罘
Chen Da	陳達
Chen Huan	陳歡
Chen Jinshi	陳金式
Cheng Lin	成林
Chong Hou	崇厚
Chongwen Gate	崇文門
Dachen	大臣
Dagu	大沽
Danshui	淡水
Daoguang	道光
Dao	道

Daotai	道臺
Da Qing Huidian	大清會典
Da shi shang zhi xiao shi ze xing	大事上之小事則形
De'an	德安
Deng	等
Dengzhou	登州
Difang jiaoshe	地方交涉
Dong Xun	董恂
Du Shaofang	杜紹芳
Dun Qinwang Yizong	惇親王奕誴
Duolunnuoer	多倫諾介
Fen shou dao	分守道
Fen xun dao	分巡道
Fujian	福建
Fu	府
Fu ju	撫局
Fu yi ju	撫夷局
Fumu guan	父母官
Fuzhou	福州
Gaibu zhidao	該部知道
Gaolianqin	高廉欽
Gexiang jinling	各項禁令
Gong Bu	工部
Gong Qinwang Yixin	恭親王奕訢

Gonghang 公行
Guan dao tai 關道臺
Guanwen 官文
Guiliang 桂良

Hai guan 海關
Haiguan dao 海關道
Haiguan jiandu 海關監督
Han 函
Han Huang De 漢黃德
Hankou 漢口
Hanyang 漢陽
He Guiqing 何桂清
He Weijian 何維鍵
Hengfu 恒福
Heng Qi 恒祺
Hou Deming 侯德明
Hu Bu 戶部
Hu Guang 湖廣
Huangzhou 黃州
Huashana 花沙納
Hubei 湖北
Hui Qinwang
    Mianyu 惠親王綿愉
Huitong siyi guan 會同四譯館

Jiangnan 江南
Jianning 建甯
Jin yun junhuo 禁運軍火
Jinkou 金口
Jinling jibu 禁令緝捕
Jinzhi fan yan 禁止販鹽
Jinzhi yang chuan
    si dao buzhun
    tong shangkou 'an
        禁止洋船私到
        不准通商口岸

Jinzhi yang chuan si
    dao fei tong shangkou
    'an 禁止洋船私
        到非通商口
        岸
Jinzhi yangshang
    li hang chan 禁止洋商
        立行產
Jiujiang 九江
Junji chu 軍機處

Koubei dao 口北道
Koutou 叩頭

Lan Weiwen 藍蔚雯
Lei Qida 雷其達
Leizhou fu 雷州府
Li Bu (Personnel) 吏部
Li Bu (Rites) 禮部
Li Haonian 李鶴年
Li Hanzhang 李瀚章
Li Hongzhang 李鴻章
Liang 兩
Liang Guang 兩廣
Liang Jiang 兩江
Liao Xuanfa 廖選發
Lifan yuan 理蕃院
Lijin 釐金
Lin Zexu 林則徐
Liu Kunyi 劉坤一
Luoding zhou 羅定州

Mao Changxi 毛昶熙
Min Zhe 閩浙
Muyin 穆蔭

Nanjing	南京
Nanyang dachen	南洋大臣
Nanyang tongshang dachen	南洋通商大臣
Ningbo	寧波
Niuzhuang	牛莊
Pingnan	平南
Pingnanrong	平南容
Qianshou	扦手
Qinchai	欽差
Qinchai dachen	欽差大臣
Qiongzhou	瓊州
Qiying	耆英
Rong Lu	榮祿
San kou tongshang dachen	三口通商大臣
Sha sheng yang hang	沙生洋行
Shanghai	上海
Shanghai tongshang dachen	上海通商大臣
Shanhaiguan	山海關
Shantou	汕頭
Shi Siming	石思明
Shuidong	水東
Sushun	肅順
Suzhou	蘇州
Tan Tingxiang	譚廷襄
Tan Zhonglin	譚鐘麟
Tianjin	天津
Tiben	題本
Ting	廳

Tizhi	體制
Tong wen guan	同文館
Tongshang	通商
Tongzhou	通州
Tongzhi (reign)	同治
Tongzhi (subprefect)	通知
Tongzhi zhongxing	同治中興
Waiwu bu	外務部
Wang Wenshao	王文韶
Wei jie	未結
Weishu zhushi	委署主事
Wenxiang	文祥
Wucheng	吳城
Wu kou qinchai dachen	五口欽差大臣
Wu kou tongshang dachen	五口通商大臣
Xiamen	廈門
Xianfeng	咸豐
Xiao dao hui	小刀會
Xian	縣
Xing bu	形部
Xing quan yong	興泉永
Xiyuan	希元
Xu Baoshan	許寶山
Xu Jiyu	徐繼畬
Xuanhua fu	宣化府
Xue Huan	薛煥
Xunfang ju	巡防局
Xunfu	巡撫

Yamen	衙門	Zongli yamen	總理衙門
Yangwu		Zongli geguo	
Yundong	洋務運動	shiwu yamen	總理各國
Yantai	煙臺		事務衙門
Ye Mingchen	葉名琛	Zong shu	總署
Yi jie	已結	Zouzhe	奏摺

Yi Qinwang	
Zaiyuan	怡親王載垣
Yizheng wang	議政王
Yizheng wang	
dachen	議政王
	大臣
Yilibu	伊里布
Ying	營
Yingkou	營口
Yu Kuanwen	裕寬文
Yue haiguan	
Jiandu	奧海關監督

Zeng Guofan	曾國藩
Zhangjiakouting	長家口廳
Zhang Zhidong	張之洞
Zhejiang	浙江
Zheng Qinwang	
Duanhua	鄭親王端華
Zhenjiang	鎮江
Zhifu	知府
Zhili	直隸
Zhixian	知縣
Zhou Fu	周馥
Zhuge Liang	諸葛亮
Zicheng	咨程
Ziqiang yundong	自強運動
Zong	宗
Zongdu	總督

BIBLIOGRAPHY

Western-Language Sources:

Anderson, James. *The Rebel Den of Nùng Trí Cao: Loyalty and Identity along the Sino-Vietnamese Frontier.* Seattle: University of Washington Press, in association with NUS Press, Singapore, 2007.

Antony, Robert J., and Jane Kate Leonard, eds. *Dragons, Tigers, and Dogs: Qing Crisis Management and the Boundaries of State Power in Late Imperial China.* Ithaca, NY: East Asia Program, Cornell University, 2002.

Arrighi, Giovanni, Takeshi Hamashita, and Mark Selden, eds. *The Resurgence of East Asia: 500, 150 and 50 Year Perspectives.* London: Routledge, 2003.

Baark, Erik. *Lightning Wires: The Telegraph and China's Technological Modernization, 1860–1890.* Westport, CT: Greenwood Press, 1997.

Banno, Masataka. *China and the West, 1858–1861: The Origins of the Tsungli Yamen.* Cambridge, MA: Harvard University Press, 1964.

Barlow, Tani. "Colonialism's Career in Postwar China Studies." *positions* 1, no. 1 (Spring 1993): 224–68.

Bartlett, Beatrice S. *Monarchs and Ministers: The Grand Council in Mid-Ch'ing China, 1723–1820.* Berkeley: University of California Press, 1991.

Bastid, Marianne. "Ch'ing-I 清議 and the Self-Strengthening Movement." In *Proceedings of the Conference on the Self-Strengthening Movement in Late Ch'ing China, 1860–1894,* ed. Institute of Modern History, Academia Sinica, vol. 2: 873–93. Taipei: Institute of Modern History, Academia Sinica, 1987.

Beal, Edwin George. *The Origin of Likin, 1853–1864.* Cambridge, MA: Chinese Economic and Political Studies, Harvard University, 1958.

Biggerstaff, Knight. *The Earliest Modern Government Schools in China.* Ithaca: Cornell University Press, 1961.

Biggerstaff, Knight, and Mary Wright. "The Secret Correspondence of 1867–1868: Views of Leading Chinese Statesmen Regarding the Further Opening of China to Western Influence." *Journal of Modern History* 22, no. 2 (June 1950): 122–36.

Bourdieu, Pierre, "The Economics of Linguistic Exchanges." *Social Science Information* 16, no. 6 (1977): 645–68.

Brunnert, H.S., and V.V. Hagelstrom. *Present Day Political Organization of China*. Translated by A. Beltchenko and E.E. Moran. 1912. Reprint, Taipei: Ch'eng Wen, 1978.

Cassel, Pär, "Excavating Extraterritoriality: The 'Judicial Sub-prefect' as a Prototype for the Mixed Court in Shanghai," *Late Imperial China* 24, no. 2 (December 2003): 156–82.

Chan, Wellington K.K. *Merchants, Mandarins, and Modern Enterprise in Late Ch'ing China*. Cambridge, MA: East Asian Research Center, Harvard University, 1977.

Chen Jiang. "Recent Chinese Historiography on the Western Affairs Movement: Yangwu Yundong ca. 1860–1895." *Late Imperial China* 7, no. 1 (1986): 112–27.

Chen Xiafei and Han Rongfang, eds. *Archives of China's Imperial Maritime Customs: Confidential Correspondence between Robert Hart and James Duncan Campbell, 1874–1907*. 4 vols. Beijing: Foreign Language Press, 1990–93.

Chu, Samuel C., and Kwang-Ching Liu, eds. *Li Hung-chang and China's Early Modernization*. Armonk, NY: M.E. Sharpe, 1994.

Ch'ü T'ung-tsu. *Local Government in China under the Ch'ing*. Stanford: Stanford University Press, 1969.

Cohen, Myron L. "Being Chinese: The Peripheralization of Traditional Identity." *Daedalus* 120, no. 2 (1991): 112–34.

Cohen, Paul A. *Discovering History in China: American Historical Writing on the Recent Chinese Past*. New York: Columbia University Press, 1984.

———. "The Post-Mao Reforms in Historical Perspective." *Journal of Asian Studies* 47, no. 3 (August 1988): 519–41

———. "Self-Strengthening in China-Centered Perspective: The Evolution of American Historiography." *Qingji ziqiang yundong yantao hui lunwen ji* 清 季 自 強 運 動 研 討 會 論 文 集 (Proceedings of the conference on the Self-Strengthening Movement in late Qing China, 1860–1894), ed. Institute of Modern History, Academia Sinica, 5–35. Taipei: Institute of Modern History, Academia Sinica, 1988.

Cohen, Paul A., and John E. Schrecker, eds. *Reform in Nineteenth-Century China*. Cambridge, MA: East Asian Research Center, Harvard University, 1976.

Cranmer-Byng, J.L. "The Establishment of the Tsungli Yamen: A Translation of the Memorial and Edict of 1861." *Journal of the Hong Kong Branch of the Royal Asiatic Society* 12 (1972): 41–54.

Cromwell, Valerie, and Zara S. Steiner. "The Foreign Office before 1914: A Study in Resistance." In *Studies in the Growth of Nineteenth-Century Government,* edited by Gillian Sutherland, 167–94. Totowa, NJ: Rowman and Littlefield, 1972.

Crossley, Pamela Kyle. *Orphan Warriors: Three Manchu Generations and the End of the Qing World.* Princeton: Princeton University Press, 1990.

————. *A Translucent Mirror: History and Identity in Qing Imperial Ideology.* Berkeley: University of California Press, 1999.

Elliott, Mark C. *The Manchu Way: The Eight Banners and Ethnic Identity in Late Imperial China.* Stanford, CA: Stanford University Press, 2001.

————. "Whose Empire Shall It Be? Manchu Figurations of Historical Process in the Early Seventeenth Century." In *Time, Temporality, and Imperial Transition: East Asia from Ming to Qing,* edited by Lynn A. Struve, 31–72. Honolulu: Association for Asian Studies and University of Hawai'i Press, 2005.

Elvin, Mark. *The Pattern of the Chinese Past: A Social and Economic Interpretation.* Stanford, CA: Stanford University Press, 1973.

Esherick, Joseph W. "Harvard on China: The Apologetics of Imperialism." *Bulletin of Concerned Asian Scholars* 4, no. 4 (December 1972): 9–16.

————. *The Origins of the Boxer Uprising.* Berkeley: University of California Press, 1987.

Esherick, Joseph, and Mary Backus Rankin, eds. *Chinese Local Elites and Patterns of Dominance.* Berkeley: University of California Press, 1990.

Fairbank, John King. "China's World Order: The Tradition of Chinese Foreign Relations." *Encounter* 27, no. 6 (December 1966): 14–20.

————, ed. *The Chinese World Order: Traditional China's Foreign Relations.* Cambridge, MA: Harvard University Press, 1968.

————. "The Creation of the Treaty System." In *The Cambridge History of China,* vol. 10: *Late Ch'ing, 1800–1911, Part 1,* edited by John King Fairbank. Cambridge: Cambridge University Press, 1978.

————. *The Great Chinese Revolution: 1800–1985.* New York: Harper & Row, 1986.

————. "Patterns behind the Tientsin Massacre." *Harvard Journal of Asiatic Studies* 20, no. 3/4 (1957): 480–511.

————. *Trade and Diplomacy on the China Coast, The Opening of the Treaty Ports, 1842–1854.* Cambridge, MA: Harvard University Press, 1953.

————. *The United States and China.* 4th ed. Cambridge: Harvard University Press, 1979.

Fairbank, John King, and James Peck. "An Exchange." *Bulletin of Concerned Asian Scholars* 2, no. 3 (April–July 1970): 51–70.

Fairbank, John King, and Kwang-ching Liu, eds. *The Cambridge History of China: The Late Ch'ing, 1800–1911, Part 2*, vol. 11. Cambridge: Cambridge University Press, 1980.

Fairbank, John King, and Ssu-yŭ Teng. *Ch'ing Administration; Three Studies by John K. Fairbank and Ssu-yŭ Teng.* Cambridge, MA: Harvard-Yenching Institute Studies, 19, Harvard University Press, 1960.

———. "On the Transmission of Ch'ing Documents." *Harvard Journal of Asiatic Studies* 4, no. 1 (May 1939): 12–46.

———. "On the Ch'ing Tributary System." *Harvard Journal of Asiatic Studies* 6, no. 2 (June 1941): 135–246.

Farquhar, Judith, and James Hevia, "Culture and Postwar American Historiography of China." *positions* 1, no. 2 (1993): 486–525.

Feuerwerker, Albert. *China's Early Industrialization: Sheng Hsuan-huai (1844–1916) and Mandarin Enterprise.* Cambridge, MA: Harvard University Press, 1958.

Folsom, Kenneth E. *Friends, Guests, and Colleagues: The Mu-fu System in the Late Ch'ing Period.* Berkeley: University of California Press, 1968.

Frank, Andre Gunder. *ReOrient: Global Economy in the Asian Age.* Berkeley: University of California Press, 1998.

Giles, Herbert A. *A Chinese Biographical Dictionary.* 1898. Reprint, Taipei: Ch'eng Wen, 1975.

Guy, R. Kent. *The Emperor's Four Treasuries: Scholars and the State in the Late Ch'ien-lung Era.* Cambridge, MA: Council on East Asian Studies, Harvard University, 1987.

———. "Imperial Powers and the Appointment of Provincial Governors in Ch'ing China, 1700–1900." In *Imperial Rulership and Cultural Change in Traditional China*, edited by Frederick P. Brandauer and Chun-chieh Huang, 248–80. Seattle: University of Washington Press, 1994.

Hao, Yen-p'ing. *The Commercial Revolution in Nineteenth-Century China: The Rise of Sino-Western Mercantile Capitalism.* Berkeley: University of California Press, 1986.

———. *The Comprador in Nineteenth Century China: Bridge between East and West.* Cambridge, MA: Harvard University Press, 1970.

Hao, Yen-p'ing, and Erh-min Wang. "Changing Chinese Views of Western Relations, 1840–95." In *The Cambridge History of China*, vol. 11: *Late Ch'ing, 1800–1911, Part 2*, edited by John K. Fairbank and Kwang-Ching Liu, 142–201. Cambridge: Cambridge University Press, 1980.

Hart, Robert. *The I.G. in Peking: Letters of Robert Hart, Chinese Maritime Customs, 1868–1907*. Edited by John King Fairbank, Katherine Frost Bruner, and Elizabeth MacLeod Matheson. Cambridge, MA: Belknap Press of Harvard University Press, 1975.

Hevia, James L. *Cherishing Men from Afar: Qing Guest Ritual and the Macartney Embassy of 1793*. Durham, NC: Duke University Press, 1995.

———. "Sovereignty and Subject: Constituting Relations of Power in Qing Guest Ritual." In *Body, Subject, and Power in China*, edited by Angela Zito and Tani E. Barlow, 181–200. Chicago: University of Chicago Press, 1994.

Hickey, Paul. "Bureaucratic Centralization and Public Finance in Late Qing China, 1900-1911." Ph.D. dissertation, Harvard University, 1990.

Hook, Brian. "Contemporary Perspectives on the Self-Strengthening Movement in Late Ch'ing China." In *Proceedings of the Conference on the Self-Strengthening Movement in Late Ch'ing China, 1860–1894*, ed. Institute of Modern History, Academia Sinica, vol. 2: 1163–84. Taipei: Institute of Modern History, Academia Sinica, 1987.

Horowitz, Richard S. "Central Power and State Making: the Zongli Yamen and Self-Strengthening in China, 1860–1880." Ph.D. dissertation, Harvard University, 1998.

———. "International Law and State Transformation in China, Siam, and the Ottoman Empire during the Nineteenth Century." *Journal of World History* 15, No. 4 (December 2004): 445–86.

———. "State Making Theory and the Study of Modern Chinese History." *Newsletter for Modern Chinese History*. Institute of Modern History, Academia Sinica, No. 19, (March 1995): 84-98.

Hsieh, Pao Chao. *The Government of China (1644–1911)*. Baltimore: The Johns Hopkins Press, 1925.

Hsu, Immanuel C.Y. *China's Entrance into the Family of Nations: the Diplomatic Phase, 1858–1860*. Cambridge, MA: Harvard University Press, 1960.

———. "Late Ch'ing Foreign Relations, 1866–1905." In *The Cambridge History of China*. Vol. 11: *The Late Ch'ing, 1800–1911, Part 2*, edited by John K. Fairbank and Kwang-Ching Liu, 70–141. Cambridge: Cambridge University Press, 1980.

———. *The Rise of Modern China*. 2nd edition. New York: Oxford University Press, 1975.

Hu, Sheng. *Imperialism and Chinese Politics*. Beijing: Foreign Languages Press, 1981.

Hucker, Charles O. *A Dictionary of Official Titles in Imperial China.* Stanford, CA: Stanford University Press, 1985.

Hummel, Arthur W., ed. *Eminent Chinese of the Ch'ing Period (1644–1912),* 2 vols. Washington, DC: U.S. Government Printing Office, 1943–1944.

Immergut, Ellen M. "The Theoretical Core of the New Institutionalism," *Politics and Society* 26, no. 1 (March 1998): 5–34.

Kennedy, Thomas L. "Self-Strengthening: An Analysis Based on Some Recent Writings." *Ch'ing-shih wen-t'i* 3.1 (November 1974): 3–35.

Keohane, Robert O., and Lisa L. Martin. "The Promise of Institutionalist Theory." *International Security* 20, no. 1 (Summer 1995): 39–51.

Kim, K.H. *Japanese Perspectives of China's Early Modernization: A Bibliographic Survey.* Ann Arbor: University of Michigan Center for Chinese Studies, 1974.

Kuhn, Philip. "Ideas behind China's Modern State." *Harvard Journal of Asiatic Studies* 55, no. 2 (December 1995): 295–337.

———. *Rebellion and Its Enemies in Late Imperial China: Militarization and Social Structure, 1796–1864.* Cambridge, MA: Harvard University Press, 1970.

———. *Soulstealers: The Chinese Sorcery Scare of 1768.* Cambridge, MA; Harvard University Press, 1990.

Lazich, Michael C. "American Missionaries and the Opium Trade in Nineteenth-Century China." *Journal of World History* 17, no. 2 (June 2006): 197–223.

Legge, James, trans. *Li Chi: Book of Rites, An Encyclopedia of Ancient Ceremonial Usages, Religious Creeds, and Social Institutions.* Edited with introduction and study guide by Ch'u Chai and Winberg Chai. New Hyde Park, NY: University Books, 1967.

Leung, Philip Yuen-sang. "Crisis Management in Late Qing China: Changing Roles of the Expectant Officials." *Hong Kong Journal of Modern Chinese History.* No. 1 (2003): 95–112.

———. *The Shanghai Taotai: Linkage Man in a Changing Society, 1843–90.* Honolulu: University of Hawaii Press, 1990.

———. "The Shanghai-Tientsin Connection: Li Hung-chang's Political Control over Shanghai." In *Li Hung-chang and China's Early Modernization,* edited by Samuel C. Chu and Kwang-Ching Liu. Armonk, NY: M.E. Sharpe, 1994.

Levenson, Joseph. *Confucian China and Its Modern Fate: A Trilogy.* Berkeley: University of California Press, 1968.

Li, Yi. *Chinese Bureaucratic Culture and Its Influence on the 19th-century Steamship Operation, 1864–1885: The Bureau for Recruiting Merchants.* Lewiston, NY: E. Mellen Press, 2001.

Liao, Kuang-sheng. *Antiforeignism and Modernization in China, 1860–1980.* Hong Kong: The Chinese University Press, 1986.

Lieberthal, Kenneth, and Michel Oksenberg. *Policy Making in China: Leaders, Structures, and Processes.* Princeton, NJ: Princeton University Press, 1988.

Liu, Kwang-Ching. "Li Hung-chang in Chihli: The Emergence of a Policy, 1870–1875." In *Li Hung-chang and China's Early Modernization,* edited by Samuel C. Chu and Kwang-Ching Liu, 49-75. Armonk, NY: M.E. Sharpe, 1994.

———. "Nineteenth-century China: The Disintegration of the Old Order and the Impact of the West." In *China in Crisis,* vol. 1, *China's Heritage and the Communist Political System, Book 1,* edited by Ping-ti Ho and Tang Tsou, 93–178. Chicago: University of Chicago Press, 1968.

———. "Politics, Intellectual Outlook and Reform: the T'ung-wen Kuan Controversy of 1867." In *Reform in Nineteenth-century China,* edited by Paul A. Cohen and John E. Schrecker. Cambridge, MA: East Asian Research Center, Harvard University, 1976.

Liu, Lydia H. *The Clash of Empires: The Invention of China in Modern World Making.* Cambridge, MA: Harvard University Press, 2004.

Mancall, Mark. *China at the Center: 300 Years of Foreign Policy.* New York: The Free Press, 1984.

Mann, Susan. *Local Merchants and the Chinese Bureaucracy, 1750–1950.* Stanford, CA: Stanford University Press, 1987.

Martin, W.A.P. *A Cycle of Cathay or China, South and North, with Personal Reminiscences, 3rd edition. 1900.* Reprint, Taipei: Ch'eng Wen, 1966.

Mayers, William Frederick. *The Chinese Government: A Manual of Chinese Titles, categorically arranged and explained, with an appendix.* 3rd edition, 1897. Reprint, Taipei: Ch'eng Wen, 1970.

Meng, S.M. *The Tsungli Yamen: Its Organization and Functions.* Cambridge, MA: East Asian Research Center, Harvard University, 1962.

Mesny, William. *Mesny's Chinese Miscellany: A Test Book of Notes on China and the Chinese,* vol. 1. Shanghai: China Gazette Office, 1896.

Metzger, Thomas. *The Internal Organization of the Ch'ing Bureaucracy: Legal, Normative, and Communication Aspects.* Cambridge, MA: Harvard University Press, 1973.

Morse, Hosea Ballou. *The International Relations of the Chinese Empire*. 3 vols. 1910–1918. Reprint, Taipei: Ch'eng-wen, 1978.

———. *The Trade and Administration of the Chinese Empire*. 1907. Reprint, Taipei: Ch'eng-wen, 1975.

Moulder, Frances. *Japan, China, and the Modern World Economy: Toward a Reinterpretation of East Asian Development ca. 1600 to ca. 1918*. Cambridge: Cambridge University Press, 1977.

Najita, Tetsuo. "Conceptual Consciousness in the Meiji Ishin." In *Meiji Ishin: Restoration and Revolution*, edited by Nagai Michio and Miguel Urrutia, 83–102. Tokyo: United Nations University, 1985.

O'Neill, Patricia. "Missed Opportunities: Late Eighteenth Century Chinese Relations with England and the Netherlands." Ph.D. dissertation, University of Washington, 1995.

Osborne, Milton. *River Road to China: The Search for the Source of the Mekong, 1866–73*. 1st American edition, New York: Atlantic Monthly Press, 1996.

Parker, Jason H. "The Rise and Decline of I-Hsin, Prince Kung, 1858–1865: A Study of the Interaction of Politics and Ideology in Late Imperial China." Ph.D. dissertation, Princeton University, 1979.

Peck, James. "The Roots of Rhetoric: The Professional Ideology of America's China Watchers." *Bulletin of Concerned Asian Scholars*, 2, no.1 (October 1969): 59–69.

Pelissier, Roger. *The Awakening of China, 1793–1949*. Martin Keiffer, ed. and trans. London: Secker & Warburg, 1967.

Perdue, Peter C. *China Marches West: The Qing Conquest of Central Eurasia*. Cambridge, MA: Belknap Press of Harvard University Press, 2005.

Perry, Elizabeth J. *Rebels and Revolutionaries in North China, 1845–1945*. Stanford, CA: Stanford University Press, 1981.

Playfair, G.M.H. *The Cities and Towns of China: A Geographical Dictionary*. 2nd edition. 1910. Reprint, Taipei: Ch'eng-wen, 1978.

Polachek, James M. *The Inner Opium War*. Cambridge, MA: Council on East Asian Studies, Harvard University Press, 1992.

Pomeranz, Kenneth. "Beyond the East-West Binary: Resituating Development Paths in the Eighteenth-Century World." *Journal of Asian Studies* 61, no. 2 (May 2002): 539–90.

———. *The Great Divergence: China, Europe, and the Making of the Modern World Economy*. Princeton, NJ: Princeton University Press, 2000.

Pong, David. *Shen Pao-chen and China's Modernization in the Nineteenth Century*. New York: Cambridge University Press, 1994.

————. "The Vocabulary of Change: Reformist Ideas of the 1860s and 1870s." In *Ideal and Reality: Social and Political Change in Modern China, 1860–1949*, edited by David Pong and Edmund S.K. Fung. Lanham, MD: University Press of America, 1985.

Rankin, Mary Backus. "Social and Political Change in Nineteenth-Century China." In *Historical Perspectives on Contemporary Asia*, edited by Merle Goldman and Andrew Gordon, 42–84. Cambridge, MA: Harvard University Press, 2000.

Rawski, Evelyn S. *The Last Emperors: A Social History of Qing Imperial Institutions*. Berkeley: University of California Press, 1998.

Reed, Bradly Ward. *Talons and Teeth: County Clerks and Runners in the Qing Dynasty*. Stanford, CA: Stanford University Press, 2000.

Remer, C. F. *The Foreign Trade of China*. 1928. Reprint, Taipei: Ch'eng Wen, 1967.

Rhoads, Edward. *Manchus and Han: Ethnic Relations and Political Power in Late Qing and Early Republican China, 1861–1928*. Seattle: University of Washington Press, 2000.

Rockhill, William Woodville. "Diplomatic Missions to the Court of China: The Kotow Question II." *The American Historical Review* 2, no. 4 (July 1897): 627–43.

Rossabi, Morris. *China and Inner Asia: from 1368 to the Present*. New York: Pica Books, 1975.

Rossabi, Morris, ed. *China Among Equals: The Middle Kingdom and Its Neighbors, 10th–14th Centuries*. Berkeley: University of California Press, 1983.

Rowe, William T. *Hankow: Commerce and Society in a Chinese City, 1796–1889*. Stanford, CA: Stanford University Press, 1984.

Scully, Eileen P. *Bargaining with the State from Afar: American Citizenship in Treaty Port China, 1844–1942*. New York: Columbia University Press, 2001.

Skinner, G. William, ed. *The City in Late Imperial China*. Stanford, CA: Stanford University Press, 1977.

————. "Marketing and Social Structure in Rural China: Part I." *Journal of Asian Studies* 24, no. 1 (1964): 3–43.

Smith, Richard J. "Chinese Military Institutions in the Mid-Nineteenth Century, 1850–1860." *Journal of Asian History* 8, no. 2 (1974): 122–61.

Spector, Stanley. *Li Hung-chang and the Huai Army: A Study in Nineteenth Century Regionalism*. Seattle: University of Washington Press, 1964.

Struve, Lynn A., ed. *The Qing Formation in World Historical Time*. Cambridge, MA: Harvard University Asia Center, Harvard University Press, 2004.

————, ed. *Time, Temporality, and Imperial Transition: East Asia from Ming to Qing.* Honolulu: Association for Asian Studies and University of Hawaii Press, 2005.

Sturdevant, Sandra, "Imperialism, Sovereignty, and Self-strengthening: A Reassessment of the 1870's." In *Reform in Nineteenth-Century China*, edited by Paul A. Cohen and John E. Schrecker. Cambridge, MA: East Asian Research Center, Harvard University, 1976.

Swisher, Earl. *Early Sino-American Relations, 1841–1912: The Collected Articles of Earl Swisher, edited by Kenneth W. Rea.* Boulder, CO: Westview Press, 1977.

Tai, En-Sai. *Treaty Ports in China (A Study in Diplomacy).* 1918. Reprint, Arlington, VA: University Publications of America, Inc., 1976.

Teng, Ssu-yü, and John K. Fairbank. *China's Response to the West: a documentary survey, 1839–1923.* Cambridge, MA: Harvard University Press, 1954.

Teng, Tony Yung-Yuan. "Prince Kung and the Survival of the Ch'ing Rule, 1858–1898." Ph.D. dissertation, University of Wisconsin, 1972.

Thelen, Kathleen, and Sven Steinmo. "Historical Institutionalism in Comparative Politics." In *Structuring Politics: Historical Institutionalism in Comparative Analysis*, edited by Sven Steinmo, Kathleen Thelen, and Frank Longstreth, 1–32. Cambridge: Cambridge University Press, 1992.

Tilly, Charles, "Reflections on the History of European State-making." In *The Formation of National States in Western Europe*, edited by Charles Tilly. Princeton: Princeton University Press, 1975.

Ting, Reuben Tse-min. "The Establishment of the Tsungli Yamen and the Dispatch of the First Chinese Mission to Foreign Powers," M.A. thesis. University of Washington, 1949.

Tsai, Shih-shan. "Ch'ing Diplomacy: Structure and Functioning." *Asian Profile* 4, no. 1 (February 1976).

Wakeman, Jr., Frederic. *Strangers at the Gate: Social Disorder in South China, 1839–1861.* Berkeley, CA: University of California Press, 1966.

Wang, Fei-Ling. *Institutions and Institutional Change in China: Premodernity and Modernization.* NY: St. Martin's Press, 1998.

Wang, Tseng-tsai. "The Audience Question: Foreign Representatives and the Emperor of China, 1858–1873." *Historical Journal* 14, no. 3 (Sept. 1971): 617–26.

————. *Tradition and Change in China's Management of Foreign Affairs: Sino-British relations, 1793–1877.* Taipei: China Committee for Publication Aid and Prize Awards under the auspices of Soochow University, 1972.

Watt, John R. *The District Magistrate in Late Imperial China.* NewYork: Columbia University Press, 1972.

———. "The Yamen and Urban Administration." In *The City in Late Imperial China,* edited by G. William Skinner, 353–90. Stanford: Stanford University Press, 1977.

Williams, S. Wells. *The Chinese Commercial Guide, containing Treaties, Tariffs, Regulations, Tables, Etc., Useful in the Trade to China and Eastern Asia; with an Appendix of Sailing Directions for those Seas and Coasts.* Fifth edition. 1863. Reprint, Taipei: Ch'eng Wen, 1966.

———. *The Middle Kingdom: A Survey of the Geography, Government, Literature, Social Life, Arts, and History of the Chinese Empire and its Inhabitants.* Revised 1883 edition. Reprint, Taipei: Ch'eng-wen, 1965.

Wills, John E., *Embassies and Illusions: Dutch and Portuguese Envoys to K'ang-hsi, 1666–1687.* Cambridge, MA: Council on East Asian Studies, Harvard University, 1984.

———. "Tribute, Defensiveness, and Dependency: Uses and Limits of Some Basic Ideas about Mid-Ch'ing Foreign Relations." *American Neptune* 48, no. 4 (Fall 1988): 225–29.

Wong, J.Y. "The 'Arrow' Incident: A Reappraisal." *Modern Asian Studies* 8, no. 3 (1974): 373–89.

———. "Harry Parkes and the 'Arrow' War in China." *Modern Asian Studies* 9, no. 3 (1975): 303–20.

———. *Yeh Ming-ch'en: Viceroy of Liang Kuang 1852–8.* Cambridge: Cambridge University Press, 1976.

Wong, R. Bin. *China Transformed: Historical Change and the Limits of the European Experience.* Ithaca, NY: Cornell University Press, 1997.

———. "Great Expectations: The 'Public Sphere' and the Search for Modern Times in Chinese History." *Studies in Chinese History* 3 (October 1993): 7–49.

Wood, Frances. *No Dogs and Not Many Chinese: Treaty Port Life in China, 1843–1943.* London: John Murray Publishers, 2000.

Wright, Mary Clabaugh. *The Last Stand of Chinese Conservatism; The T'ung-chih Restoration, 1862–1874.* Stanford: Stanford University Press, 1957.

———. "The Modernization of China's System of Foreign Relations." In *Imperial China: The Decline of the Last Dynasty and the Origins of Modern China, the 18th and 19th Centuries,* edited by Franz Schurmann and Orville Schell, 206–35. New York: Random House, 1967.

Wright, Stanley F. *Hart and the Chinese Customs.* Belfast: published for the Queen's University by W. Mullan, 1950.

————. *The Origin and Development of the Chinese Customs Service, 1843–1911. An Historical Outline.* Shanghai: 1936.

Wu, Silas H.L. *Communication and Imperial Control in China: Evolution of the Palace Memorial System, 1693–1735.* Cambridge, MA: Harvard University Press, 1970.

————. "The Memorial Systems of the Ch'ing Dynasty (1644–1911)." *Harvard Journal of Asiatic Studies* 27 (1967): 7–75.

Zelin, Madeleine. *The Magistrate's Tael, Rationalizing Fiscal Reform in Eighteenth Century Ch'ing China.* Berkeley: University of California Press, 1984.

Zheng, Yongnian. *Discovering Chinese Nationalism in China: Modernization, Identity, and International Relations.* Cambridge: Cambridge University Press, 1999.

Zito, Angela. *Of Body and Brush: Grand Sacrifice as Text/Performance in Eighteenth-Century China.* Chicago: University of Chicago Press, 1997.

Zito, Angela, and Tani Barlow, eds. *Body, Subject and Power in China.* Chicago: University of Chicago Press, 1994.

Chinese Secondary Sources:

Bao Zunpeng, Li Dingyi, and Wu Xiangxiang 包 遵 彭 ; 李 定 一 ; 吳 相 湘 , eds. *Zhongguo jin dai shi lun cong* 中 國 近 代 史 論 叢 . 10 vols. Taibei: Zheng zhong shu ju, 1956–1959.

Chen Gonglu 陳 恭 祿. "Siguo Tianjin tiaoyue chengli zhi jingguo" 四 國 天 津 條 約 成 立 之 經 過 (The Four Powers and the establishment of the Tianjin Treaty). In *Zhongguo jin dai shi lun cong* 中 國 近 代 史 論 叢 , vol. 3., edited by Bao Zunpeng, Li Dingyi, and Wu Xiangxiang 包 遵 彭 ; 李 定一 ; 吳 相 湘. Taibei: Zheng zhong shu ju, 1956.

Chen Siqi, 陳 思 齊. "Zongli Yamen sheli beijing ji qi jiaose zhi yanjiu" 總 理 衙 門 設 立 背 景 及 其 角 色 之 研 究 (A Study of the background of the establishment of the Zongli Yamen and its role). M.A. thesis. Zhengzhi University, Taiwan, 1985.

Chen Wenjin 陳 文 進. "Qingdai zhi zongli yamen ji qi jingfei" 清 代 之 總 理 衙 門 及 其 經 費 (The Qing Zongli Yamen and its expenses). *Zhongguo jindai jingjishi yanjiu jikan* 中 國 近 代 經 濟 史 研 究 集 刊 1 , no. 1 (November 1932).

Chen Xiyu 陳希育. "Qingdai Fujian de waimao gangkou" 清代福建的外貿港口 (The foreign trade ports in Fujian in the Qing dynasty). *Zhongguo Shehui jingji shi yanjii* 中國社會經濟史研究 4 (1988).

Duan Changguo 段昌國. "Gong Xin Wang Yixin yu Xian Tong zhi waijiao yu zhengzhi jiufen, 1858–1864" 恭親王奕訢與咸同之外交與政治糾紛自 1858 年至 1864 年 (Prince Gong and disputes of foreign policy and government during the Xianfeng and Tongzhi reigns, 1858–1864). M.A. thesis. National Taiwan University, 1973.

Fu Zongmao 傅宗懋. *Qingdai dufu zhidu* 清代督撫制度 (The governor and governor-general system of the Qing dynasty). Taibei: National Zhengzhi University, 1963.

Jindai Lishi Suo, Zhongyang Yanjiu Yuan 近代歷史所中央研究院 (Institute of Modern History, Academia Sinica). *Liu shi nian lai de Zhongguo jindaishi yanjiu* 六十年來的中國近代史研究 (Studies of modern Chinese history: A bibliographical review, 1928–1988), 2 vols. Taibei: Institute of Modern History, Academia Sinica, 1989.

———, *Qingji ziqiang yundong yantaohui lunwen ji* 清季自強運動研討會論文集 (Proceedings of the conference on the Self-Strengthening Movement in late Qing China, 1860–1894), 2 vols. Sponsored by Institute of Modern History, Academia Sinica. Taibei: Institute of Modern History, Academia Sinica, 1987.

———, *Waijiao dangan mulu huibian: zongli geguo shiwu yamen, 1861–1901; waiwu bu, 1901–1911* 外交檔案目錄彙編：總理各國事務衙門，1861–1901；外務部，1901–1911 (Collection of the catalogues for documents of modern China's foreign affairs). 2 vols. Taibei: Institute of Modern History, Academia Sinica, 1991.

Li Guoqi 李國祁. *Zhongguo xiandaihua de quyu yanjiu: Min Zhe Tai diqu, 1860–1916* 中國現代化的區域研究：閩浙臺地區, 1860–1916 (Modernization in China, 1860–1916: A regional study of social, political, and economic change in Fujian, Zhejiang, and Taiwan). Taibei: Institute of Modern History, Academia Sinica, 1985.

Li Hongzhang 李鴻章. *Li Wenzhong gong peng liao han gao* 李文忠公朋僚函稿 (Letters of Li Hongzhang). Shanghai: Shanghai guji chubanshe, 1995–1999.

Li Yi 李毅. "Dao Xian nianjiande Zhongwai jiaoshe" 道咸年間的中外交涉 (Negotiations between China and the West during the Daoguang and Xianfeng Reigns). *Huanan shifan daxue xuebao, shehui kexueban* (Journal of South China Normal University, Social Science Edition), no. 2 (1986): 72–77.

————. "Zai ping Ye Mingchen de buzhan buhe bushou" 再 評 葉 名 琛 的 不 戰 不 和 不 守 (A reconsideration of Ye Mingchen's policy of not warring, not embracing peace, and not defending). *Guangzhou yanjiu*, no. 1 (1987): 51–54.

Li Zhigang 黎 志 剛. "Ziqiang yundong" 自 強 運 動. In *Liushi nian lai de Zhongguo jindai shi yanjiu* 六 十 年 來 的 中 國 近 代 史 研 究, vol. 2. Taibei: Institute of Modern History, Academia Sinica, 1989.

Liu Guanghua 劉 光 華, "Wan Qing Zongli Yamen zuzhi ji diwei zhi yanjiu" 晚 清 總 理 衙 門 組 織 及 地 位 之 研 究 (A study of the Late Qing Zongli Yamen's organization and position). M.A. thesis. Zhengzhi University, Taiwan, 1973.

————. "Zhong Fa zhanzheng yiqian Zongli Yamen dui wai zhengce zhi yanjiu" 中 法 戰 爭 以 前 總 理 衙 門 對 外 政 策 之 研 究 (A study of the Zongli Yamen and foreign policy before the Sino-French War). Ph.D. dissertation. Zhengzhi University, Taiwan, 1981.

Liu Xinxian 劉 心 顯, "Zhongguo waijiao zhidu de yange" 中 國 外 交 制 度 的 沿 革 (The Evolution of China's System of Foreign Affairs). In *Zhongguo jindaishi luncong* 中 國 近 代 史 論 叢, Series II, vol. 5, edited by Bao Zunpeng, Li Dingyi, and Wu Xiangxiang 包 遵 彭 , 李 定 一 吳 相 湘. Taibei: Zheng zhong shu ju, 1956.

Liu Zhicheng 劉 芝 城. "Qingchao zongli geguo shiwu yamen" 清 朝 總 理 各 國 事 務 衙 門 (The Qing Zongli Yamen). *Qinghua zhoukan* 清 華 周 刊, 41, nos. 11, 12 (1934).

Liu Ziyang 劉 子 揚. *Qingdai difang guanzhi kao* 清 代 地 方 官 制 考 (A study of Qing dynasty local government). Beijing: Zijincheng Press, 1994.

Luo Bingmian 羅 炳 綿. "Zongli yamen yu Manzu benwei zhengce" 總 理 衙 門 與 滿 族 本 位 政 策 (The Zongli Yamen and basic Manchu policy). In *Qingji ziqiang yundong yantanhui lunwen ji* (Proceedings of the Conference on the Self-Strengthening Movement in late Qing China, 1860–1894). Taibei: Institute of Modern History, Academia Sinica, 1987.

Luo Yudong 羅 玉 東. *Zhongguo lijin shi* 中 國 釐 金 史 (A history of China's lijin), 2 vols. Shanghai: Commercial Press, 1936.

Qian Shifu 錢 實 甫, ed. *Qingdai zhiguan nianbiao* 清 代 職 官 年 表 (Table of Qing dynasty officials), 4 vols. Beijing: Zhonghua Shuju, 1980.

Qiu Zuming 丘 祖 銘. "Zhongguo waijiao jiguan zhi yange" 中 國 外 交 機 關 之 沿 革 (The evolution of China's foreign policy organizations). *Waijiao pinglun* 外 交 評 論 4, no. 5 (May 1935).

Su Jing 蘇 精. *Qingji Tongwenguan ji qi shisheng* 清季同文館及其師生 (The Qing dynasty's Tong Wen Guan and its teachers and students). Taibei: Su Jing, 1985.

Su Yunfeng 蘇雲峰, *Zhongguo xiandaihua de quyu yanjiu—Hubei sheng, 1860–1916* 中國現代化的區域研究：湖北省 1860–1916 (Modernization in China, 1860–1916: A regional study of social, political and economic change in Hubei). 2ⁿᵈ edition. Taibei: Institute of Modern History, Academia Sinica, 1987.

Sun Yutang 孫毓堂. *Zhong Ri jiawu zhanzheng qian waiguo ziben zai Zhongguo jingying de jindai gongye* 中日甲午戰爭前外國資本在中國經營的近代工業 (Foreign investment in China's modern industries before the Sino-Japanese War). Shanghai: Shanghai renmin chuban she, 1955.

Tian Tao 田濤, ed. *Qing chao tiaoyue quanji* 清朝條約全集 (A complete collection of the treaties of the Qing dynasty), 3 vols. Harbin: Heilongjiang People's Press, 1999.

Wang Ermin 王爾敏 and Chen Shanwei 陳善偉, eds., *Qingmo yiding zhongwai shangyue jiaoshe* 清末議定中外商約交涉, 2 vols. Taibei: Zhongwen Daxue Chuban she, 1993.

Wang Ermin 王爾敏. "Rujia chuantong yu jindai Zhong Xi sichao zhi huitong" 儒家傳統與近代中西思潮之彙通 (The Confucian tradition and the understanding of Western ideas in modern times). *Xinya xueshu jikan* (New Asia Quarterly) 2 (1979): 163–78.

Wang Mingcan 王明燦, "Yixin dui xifang de renshi" 奕訢對西方的認識 (Yixin's knowledge of the West), M.A. thesis. Dong Hai University, Taizhong, Taiwan, 1993.

Wang Zengcai (Wang Tseng-tsai) 王曾才. "Zhongguo dui xifang waijiao zhidu de fanying" 中國對西方外交制度的反應 (China's reaction to the Western diplomatic system). In *Qingji waijiao shi lun ji* 清季外交史論集 (A collection of essays on Late Qing diplomatic history). Wang Zengcai (Wang Tseng-tsai), ed. Taibei: Commercial Press, 1978.

———, "Ziqiang yundong shiqi Zhongguo waijiao zhidu de fazhan" 自強運動時期中國外交制度的發展 (China's foreign affairs system during the Self-Strengthening Movement). In *Qingji ziqiang yundong yantaohui lunwen ji* (Proceedings of the conference on the Self-Strengthening Movement in late Qing China, 1860–1894), compiled by The Institute of Modern History, Taibei: The Institute of Modern History, Academia Sinica 1987.

Wei Xiumei 魏秀梅, ed., *Qingji zhiguanbiao, fu renwu lu* 清季職官表: 附人物錄 (Offices and personnel in the Late Qing Period: Metropolitan officials and high officials in provinces and dependencies, 1796–1911). Taibei: Institute of Modern History, Academia Sinica, 1977.

Wu Fuhuan 吳福環. *Qingji Zongli Yamen yanjiu* 清季總理衙門研究 (A study of the Qing Zongli Yamen). Taibei: Wen Jin Press, 1995.

Wu Jiyuan 吳吉遠. *Qingdai difang zhengfu de sifa zhineng yanjiu* 清代地方政府的司法職能研 (Research on the judicial function of local authorities in the Qing dynasty). Beijing: Zhongguo Shehui Kexue Chubanshe, 1998.

Xiao Yishan 蕭一山. *Qingdai houqi zhi shehui yu jingji* 清代後期之社會與經濟 (Late Qing society and economy), vol. 4. *Qingdai tong shi* 清代通史 (A general history of the Qing period), 5 vols., Shanghai: The Commercial Press, 1927–1928.

Zhang Zhongfu 張忠紱. "Qingting banli waijiao zhi jiguan yu shouxu" 清廷辦理外交之機關與手續 (The Qing Court's organizations and procedures for handling foreign affairs). In *Zhongguo jindaishi luncong* 中國近代史論叢, vol. 3. Bao Zunpeng, Li Dingyi, and Wu Xiangxiang 包遵彭, 李定一吳相湘, eds. Taibei: Zhengzhong Shuju, 1956.

———. "Yapian zhan qian Qingting banli waijiao zhi jiguan yu shouxu" 鴉片戰前清廷辦理外交之機關與手續 (The Pre-Opium War Qing foreign policy organizations and methods). *Waijiao Yuebao* 外交月報 (Foreign affairs monthly), 2, no. 2 (February 1933).

———. "Zi yapian zhanzheng zhi Ying Fa lianjun qi zhong Qingting banli waijiao zhi jiguan yu shouxu" 自鴉片戰爭之英法聯軍期中清廷辦理外交之機關與手續 (The Qing dynasty's foreign policy organizations and methods in the period from the Opium War to the British and French allied forces occupation)." *Waijiao Yuebao* 外交月報 (Foreign affairs monthly) 2, no. 5 (May 1933).

———. "Zongli geguo shiwu yamen zhi yuanqi" 總理各國事務衙門之緣起 (The origins of the Zongli Yamen). *Waijiao yuebao* 外交月報 (Foreign affairs monthly) 3, no. 7 (July 1933).

Zhou Ziya 周子亞. "Wo guo waijiao jigou yange kao" 我國外交機構沿革考 (A study of the evolution of China's diplomatic institutions). In *Zhongguo jindaishi luncong* 中國近代史論叢, vol. 3. Bao Zunpeng, Li Dingyi, and Wu Xiangxiang 包遵彭, 李定一吳相湘, eds., Taibei: Zhengzhong Shuju, 1956.

Zhao Zhongfu 趙 中 孚. ed. *Weng Tonghe Riji Paiyinben* 翁 同 龢 日 記 排 印 本 (A typeset edition of the Diary of Weng Tonghe with Index), 6 vols. Taibei: Chinese Materials and Research Aids Service Center, 1970.

Zhongguo yeshi jicheng 中 國 野 史 集 成: 先 秦 清 末. vol. 50. Chengdu: Sichuan bashu shushe 四 川 巴 蜀 書 社, 1993.

Published Documents:

DQHD—*Qing hui dian* 清 會 典 (Collected Statutes of the Qing Dynasty). Guangxu edition. Reprint. Beijing: Zhonghua Shuju, 1991.

DQLS—*Da Qing lichao shilu Dezong chao* 大 清 歷 朝 實 錄 德 宗 朝 (Veritable records of the successive reigns of the Ch'ing dynasty, Dezong [Guangxu]) reign). Compiled by Da Manzhou diguo guowuyuan. Tokyo: Okura Shuppan Kabushiki Kaisha, 1937–1938.

DYZZ—*Dierci yapian zhanzheng* 第 二 次 鴉 片 戰 爭 (Collected documents of the Second Opium War), edited by Qi Sihe 齐 思 和, et al. Shanghai: Shanghai renmin chubanshe, 1978–1979.

GCDX—*Guangxu chao donghua xulu* 光 緒 朝 東 華 續 錄 (The Donghua Records, continued: Guangxu period), compiled by Zhu Shoupeng 朱 壽 朋. Shanghai: 1909.

GZD—*Gongzhong dang: Guangxu chao* 宮中檔光緒朝奏摺 (Secret Palace Memorials of the Guangxu period), edited by the National Palace Musuem, Taibei: National Palace Musuem, 1973–1975.

JZWZJ—*Jindai Zhongguo waijiaoshi ziliao jiyao* 近 代 中 國 外 交 史 資 料 輯 要 (*A sourcebook of imperial documents relating to the modern diplomatic history of China*). Compiled by Jiang Tingfu (Tsiang T'ing-fu) 蔣 廷 黻. 1931– 34, Reprint, Taibei: Taiwan Commercial Press, 1958–1959.

QGF—*Qingting zhi gaige yu fandong* 清 廷 之 改 革 與 反 動, parts 1, 2 (Qing Court reform and reactionism). Vol. 7 of *Geming yuanliu yu geming yundong* 革 命 源 流 與 革 命 運 動 (Revolutionary origins and the revolutionary movement). Zhonghua Minguo kaiguo wushi nian wenxian bian wei yuanhui 中 華 民 國 開 國 五 十 年 文 獻 編 案 員 會 comp. Taibei: Zhengzhong Shuju, 1963–1965.

QSG—*Qing Shi Gao* 清 史 稿 (Draft history of the Qing dynasty). Beijing: Zhonghua shu ju, 1994.

QSL—*Da Qing lichao shilu* 大 清 歷 朝 實 錄 (Veritable Records of the Qing Dynasty). 60 vols. Beijing: Zhonghua Shuju, 1985–1987.

QSLZ—*Qing shi lie zhuan* 清 史 列 傳. Beijing: Zhonghua shu ju, 1987.

QXWT--Qingchao xu wenxian tongkao 清 續 文 獻 通 考 (A supplement of the Qing Classified Historical Documents). Compiled by Liu Jinzao 劉 錦 藻. 1935. Reprint, Taibei: Xinxing shu ju, 1963.

QWS—Qingji waijiao shiliao 清 季 外 交 史 料 (Historical materials concerning foreign relations of the late Qing). 218 *juan.* Compiled by Wang Yanwei 王 彥 威. Beijing: Waijiao shiliao bian zuan chu, 1932–1935.

YWSM—Chou ban yiwu shimo 籌 辦 夷 務 始 末 (The complete management of foreign affairs) 1929–1931. Reprint, Taibei: Wenhai chuban she, 1970–1971.

> *YWSM-DG*—80 *juan* for the Daoguang reign
> *YWSM-TZ*—100 *juan* for the Tongzhi reign
> *YWSM-XF*—80 *juan* for the Xianfeng reign
> *YWYD—Yangwu Yundong* 洋 務 運 動 (The Westernization

movement). Edited by the Chinese Historical Society. Shanghai: Renmin chubanshe, 1961.

Archives:

JJC—Junjichu 軍 機 處 (Grand Council) archives at Number One Historical Archives, Beijing

ZYQD—Zongli Geguo Shiwu Yamen Qing Dang 總 理 各 國 事 務 衙 門 清 檔 (The Qing dynasty Archives of the Office for Managing Foreign Affairs). Institute of Modern History, Academia Sinica, Taipei, Taiwan.

ZYJLJB—Jinling jibu 禁令缉捕 (Documents concerning the prohibitions and arrests).

ZYDFJS—Difang jiaoshe 地方交涉(Documents concerning conduct of foreign relations on a local level).

INDEX

Amherst Mission, 37, 64n10
Anderson, James A., 63n5
appellate decision-making
power, 69n57
Arrow Incident (1856), 44,
67n29

Banner system, 73
Banno Masataka, 8, 28n14, 50,
53, 67nn30–31, 68n47
Barlow, Tani, 26n8
Bartlett, Beatrice, 9–10, 16,
30n19–20, 54, 69n48, 98n21,
99n31, 155n41
Bastid, Marianne, 27n13
Beal, Edwin George, 96n12
Board of Colonial Affairs, 36
Board of Rites, 34, 37, 81, 86,
87, 89, 105, 135
The Book of Rites, 41
Bourdieu, Pierre, 182n4
Boxer Protocol, 177–78,
182n1
Bruce, Sir Frederick, 49
Bulletin of Concerned Asian
Scholars, 29n16
Bureau of Defense, ad hoc,
50–51

Canton, 110
Canton commissioner system,
42–43
Cassel, Pär, 73, 95–96n9
Catholicism, animosity toward,
118–119
Chang Lin, 125
Chen Da, 147
Chen Jiang, 24n3, 126n1
Chen Jinshi, 168, 169

Chen Siqi, 28n15
Chen Wenjin, 29n15
Cheng Lin, 119
Cherishing Men from Afar (Hevia),
36–37
China
Euro-American imperial assaults
on, 1–5, 12
See also People's Republic of China
China, scholarship literature,
3–10, 12–19, 181
bureaucratic rationalization
perspective, 17–18
China-centered approach, 8–10
Chinese scholarship, 8
global context perspective, 12–15
historical institutionalism, 18–19
impact-response approach, 3–4
imperialist perspective, 29n16
institutional approach, 8
Manchu leadership focus, 15–16
modernization framework,
Western-centric, 4–7, 25–26nn5–9
personality scholars, 7
China Marches West (Perdue), 16
China's Response to the West
(Fairbank), 4
China Transformed (Wong), 13
Chong Hou, 116, 117, 118, 119, 123,
125, 129n31, 130n35, 131n52, 195
Chu, Samuel C., 131n45
Cohen, Paul A., 9, 24–25n3, 27n13,
29n16
cohong system, 37–38, 64n11
Collected Statutes of the Qing Dynasty
distinction between tributary and
Western states, 37, 63–64n9
Grand Council responsibilities, 79
Grand Secretariat responsibilities,
79

CORNELL EAST ASIA SERIES

Order online: www.einaudi.cornell.edu/eastasia/publications
or contact Cornell University Press Services, P.O. Box 6525, 750 Cascadilla Street, Ithaca, NY 14851, USA. Tel toll-free: 1-800-666-2211; Fax: 1-800-688-2877; E-mail: orderbook@cupserv.org or ceas@cornell.edu

www.ingramcontent.com/pod-product-compliance
Lightning Source LLC
Chambersburg PA
CBHW070400270326
41926CB00014B/2629